# DANCERS AND CHOREOGRAPHERS

## A SELECTED
## BIBLIOGRAPHY

Cyril W. Beaumont, Ballet Historian, Critic and Publisher.
London, 1964

# DANCERS AND CHOREOGRAPHERS

## A SELECTED BIBLIOGRAPHY

## LESLIE GETZ

*A Dance Research Foundation Book*

ASPHODEL PRESS
MOYER BELL
Wakefield, Rhode Island & London
MCMXCV

Published by Moyer Bell

First Edition

**LIBRARY OF CONGRESS CATALOGING-IN-PUBLICATION DATA**

Getz, Leslie.
  Dancers and choreographers : a selected bibliography / Leslie Getz. — 1st ed.
    p.     cm.
  Includes index.
    1. Ballet dancers—Bibliography.
  2. Dancers—Bibliography.
  3. Choreographers—Bibliography.   4. Ballet dancing—Bibliography.   5. Modern dance—Bibliography.   6. Choreography—Bibliography.
  I. Title.
  Z7514.D2G48   1995
  [GV1785]
  016.7928—dc20
  ISBN 1-55921-108-3, cloth
  ISBN 1-55921-109-1, paper          94-12129
                                         CIP

Copyeditor and Index author: Barbara Palfy
Life Dates: Leland Windreich

Printed in the United States of America
Distributed in North America by Publishers Group West, P. O. Box 8843, Emeryville CA 94662, 800-788- 3123 (in California 510-658-3453) and in Europe by Gazelle Book Services Ltd., Falcon House, Queen Square, Lancaster LA1 1RN England 524-68765.

In Memory

**Cyril W. Beaumont**

1891-1976

A Great Historian

A Wise Counselor

# Contents

# List of Illustrations

# ATTENTION

To understand the scope of specific parameters of this work it is ESSENTIAL to read the *Introduction* first. This will both facilitate and maximize the use of the document.

# INTRODUCTION

This bibliography is a compilation of English-language materials about dancers and choreographers. Its focus is exclusively ballet and modern dance. It covers the full range of twentieth-century dance book literature as well as all the academic/scholarly periodicals in the field from the United States, Great Britain, Canada, and Australia. With the exception of a handful of items, all the material has been published in the twentieth century. However, the entire span of the history of the ballet is covered. Modern dance, of course, is a form that was only given birth at the turn of the century.

The popular/commercial magazines, such as *Dance Magazine* (U.S.), *Dancing Times* (U.K.), *Dance International* (Canada), and *Dance Australia* (Australia), are used only in the case of special birthday or anniversary issues, memorial numbers, or to cull out series of articles that could be considered of monograph length. I have chosen to concentrate on the academic/scholarly journals as these are the specialist periodicals that reflect a consistent depth of research and analysis. In addition, they have been produced in far fewer number than the popular/commercial magazines and are frequently difficult to locate even in major urban areas. On the other hand, the full spectrum of book literature about dancers and choreographers is represented.

To avoid repetition and to conserve space I employ a system of key listings for those books from which I cite four or more sections or chapters and for all the academic/scholarly periodicals. There are seventy-nine key books, mostly collections of interviews, brief biographies, and artistic statements. Each is indicated by the first three letters (in capitals) of the author's or editor's name, followed by the page numbers of the entry on a specific artist. In cases where an author/editor has produced more than one such compilation or where there are several authors/editors whose last name begins with the same three letters, the abbreviation is augmented by a number, dictated by the alphabetical listing of their books under the code. In many cases the only entry about an artist is a key-book listing. Otherwise, key-book listings are always found at the foot of an entry, after the books and/or periodical articles about the artist. There are seventeen key periodicals. These are represented by reductions of their titles to abbreviations (e.g., *Ballet Review* is *BR*, *Dance Research* is *DR*, *York Dance Review* is *YDR*, etc.). The titles of all other cited periodicals are spelled out in full. The main text of the bibliography is augmented by a list of standard reference works, many of which will guide readers to the periodical literature about dancers and choreographers not covered in this volume.

In any work of this length and complexity anomalies are bound to crop up and decisions about content must be made and then adhered to for consistency. Here are a few such cases that need to be mentioned. I include several works about well-known dance teachers—many formerly dancers, some not—whose teaching has shaped generations of dancers. One of the most remarkable teachers was Louis Horst, a musician, who had an enormous influence on the formative years of American modern dance. I also list works on four teaching/performing entities which cannot be overlooked: Bennington School of Dance, Judson Dance Theater, Pilobolus, and Grand Union. Lastly, though there are many excellent and very informative book reviews, I decided at the outset that these would not be appropriate to this work. The purpose of this bibliography is to guide people to materials, not to analyses of them.

There is material here for the specialist scholar, the interested audience member, the young student, and the fan. It is my hope that librarians, in particular, as regular recipients of requests for guidance to specific subject materials, will find this a useful work.

—Leslie Getz
New York City

# ACKNOWLEDGMENTS

Compiling a book-length bibliography is a difficult and complex undertaking, requiring the pursuit of myriad details and of absolute precision of execution. These features are compounded in the dance field by a literature that is still quite limited, frequently scarce, and far-flung. I have not hesitated to call on expert advice and the response has been, without exception, very gratifying.

This book would not exist without the friendship and forbearance of Don McDonagh. He commissioned the work on behalf of Dance Research Foundation, put his computer at my disposal for its production, and offered much practical advice and encouragement all the way along the very bumpy road of its compilation.

Barbara Palfy, a brilliant bibliographer with a radar eye for form and detail, was my copy editor. In working with me on this project, she led me by the hand through the art of bibliography. The knowledge and skills I have acquired from her in the process I will use and cherish the rest of my life.

What good is a manuscript without a publisher? And in this case, a manuscript would not even have been produced without a commission firmly in hand. Enter Patrick O'Connor, a man who likes to make good things happen, and who can best be described as "godfather" to this project. It was he who introduced me to Don McDonagh, and then, when the manuscript was completed, found a publisher for it.

Robert Greskovic read the first draft of the manuscript and made many valuable suggestions, one of which altered my whole concept of the project and caused me to retrace my steps and add material I had previously excluded. In the process the text expanded by at least fifty percent. He also loaned rare periodicals from his private collection for use as illustrations.

Leland Windreich also saw the first draft of the manuscript and observed that its alphabetical order made it "all over the map" in terms of period. He suggested I add the life dates of the artists. I saw at once the good sense of this suggestion and asked him if he would undertake the task. He agreed and produced the dates with great accuracy and dispatch. Working with resources available to him in Vancouver, British Columbia, he found all but approximately 145 artist's life dates. These I searched for at the Dance Collection at Lincoln Center, and even there many could not be found. Locating the rest was an arduous job involving scores of telephone calls. I thank the following individuals/institutions for their help in the process: Lawrence and Miriam Adams (Dance Collection Danse, Toronto), Peter Bassett (Senior Librarian, Laban Centre, London), George Dorris, Robert Greskovic, George Jackson, Erica Lake (former Librarian, Dance Notation Bureau), Barbara Palfy, Ivan Sygoda (Pentacle), The New York Family History Center of the Church of Jesus Christ Latter Day Saints, and the United States History, Local History and Genealogy Division of The New York Public Library.

Several people made excellent suggestions or provided specific help on the bibliography: Mary Bopp allowed me to draw liberally from her splendid book *Research in Dance: A Guide to Resources* (New York & Toronto: G.K. Hall & Co., 1993) for the list Resources for Dance Research (pp. 257–262). Mary Ellen Dick gave me office support and expert computer assistance for the project when I was in California. George Dorris suggested I employ a system of key books and key periodicals to save time and space and to avoid repetition. It was then Cher de la Mere (Reference Librarian, Art and Music Department, Main Library at Civic Center, San Francisco Public Library) who put a superb example of key listings in my hands that acted as my guide for the preparation of the document. John Gingrich proofread portions of the manuscript, always effectively, under tight time constraints. The late Harriet Nicewonger came up with the idea of adding running heads to the text, which makes it far easier to use. At the point when I had to organize and alphabetize all my notes for typing, my cousin, Carla Nowell, let me usurp and litter the floor of her spacious living room for three days.

I am indebted to the following individuals for answering specific research questions and/or loaning material: Judith Blumert, Mary Cargill, Ivan de Gonzalez, George Dorris, Robert Greskovic, Baird Hastings, George Jackson, Joann Kealiinohomoku, David Leonard, Serge Leslie, Mary Ann O'Brian Malkin, Don McDonagh, Erik Näslund, Judith Otten, Mara Peets, Patricia A. Rowe, Marcia B. Siegel, and Otis Stuart.

For advice on several of the Canadian entries, I am grateful to Lawrence and Miriam Adams (Dance Collection Danse, Toronto), James E. Neufeld, and Annette Wengle (Senior Collections Librarian, Arts Department, Metropolitan Toronto Reference Library).

David Vaughan (Archivist, Cunningham Foundation) was unfailingly helpful in answering my questions about material on Merce Cunningham, and put his own excellent bibliography on the great choreographer at my disposal. He, too, provided material for illustrations from his private collection.

The Dance Collection, The New York Public Library for the Performing Arts, is a mecca for anyone engaged in long-term, serious dance research. It was a privilege and luxury to use this unique resource for much of my work on the document. I want to thank the professional staff for their guidance in the use of the collection, and I am particularly grateful to all the pages who brought out many hundreds of books and periodicals at my request. The document was also enhanced by runs of periodicals found at the Billy Rose Theatre Collection, The New York Public Library for the Performing Arts, and at the Dance Notation Bureau.

I am indebted to Lincoln Kirstein, Jeanne T. Newlin (Curator, Harvard Theatre Collection), and Madeleine M. Nichols (Curator, Dance Collection, The New York Public Library for the Performing Arts) for providing letters of support at a critical time in the search for financial assistance for this project.

Special thanks to The Harkness Foundations for Dance for their generous grant to assist with the editorial expenses of the project. This timely support has made it possible for *Dancers and Choreographers: A Selected Bibliography* to be published much sooner than would otherwise have been possible.

# METHOD OF ASCRIBING
# LIFE DATES

Dates for dancers and choreographers listed were derived primarily from the first and the second revised edition of Koegler's *Concise Oxford Dictionary of Ballet*. Other sources for information include several of the titles listed in this bibliography under "Dictionaries," *The Encyclopedia of Theatre Dance in Canada*, obituaries in *Dance Magazine* and other journals, and in some instances the bibliographic sources themselves for each name. Approximate birth dates within a decade were provided when estimates could be made from known career information.

The *Dictionary Catalog of the Dance Collection of The New York Public Library* and its annual supplements, *Bibliographic Guide to Dance*, were useful for settling conflicts in dates and for establishing the authorized name-form for some subjects. In that this service closely follows policies for name entries advocated by the U.S. Library of Congress, dates for artists with distinctive names are no longer essential when not easily ascertained from standard biographical sources.

Approximate dates of birth, death, or career periods are indicated as follows:

| | |
|---|---|
| ca. 1929– | approximate date of birth |
| 1755-ca. 1802 | approximate date of death |
| b. 1910 | only birth date known |
| d. 1955 | only death date known |
| 18– | born in the 19th century |
| fl. 1770-1789 | flourished in period cited |
| 190?– | born between 1900 and 1909 |
| 1789-184? | died between 1840 and 1849 |

# KEY BOOKS:

## Mostly Interviews,
## Brief Biographies,
## Artistic Statements

**ARM**    Armitage, Merle. *Dance Memoranda*. Edited by Edwin Corle. New York: Duell, Sloan & Pearce, 1946.

**ATK**    Atkinson, Margaret F., and May Hillman. *Dancers of the Ballet: Biographies*. New York: Knopf, 1955.

**AUS/1**    Austin, Richard. *The Art of the Dancer*. London: Barrie & Jenkins, 1982.

**AUS/2**    ———. *The Ballerina*. London: Vision, 1974.

**BAN**    Banes, Sally. *Terpsichore in Sneakers: Post-Modern Dance*. Boston: Houghton Mifflin, 1980.

**BEL**    Belknap, S. Yancey. *Ballet Close-Ups*. New York: Kamin Publishers, 1941.

**BLA**    Bland, Alexander, and John Percival. *Men Dancing: Performers and Performances*. New York: Macmillan, 1984.

**BRO**    Brown, Jean Morrison, ed. *The Vision of Modern Dance*. Princeton, N.J.: Princeton Book Company, Publishers, 1979.

**CAF**    Caffin, Caroline, and Charles H. Caffin. *Dancing and Dancers of Today: The Modern Revival of Dancing as an Art*. New York: Dodd, Mead & Company, 1912; reprint New York: Da Capo Press, 1978.

**CLA**      Clarke, Mary. *Six Great Dancers*. London: Hamish Hamilton, 1957.

**COE**      Coe, Robert. *Dance in America*. New York: Dutton, 1985.

**COH/1**    Cohen, Selma Jeanne, ed. "The Male Image." *Dance Perspectives* 40 (Winter 1969).

**COH/2**    ——, ed. *The Modern Dance: Seven Statements of Belief*. Middletown, Conn.: Wesleyan University Press, 1966.

**CRO**      Crowle, Pigeon. *Enter the Ballerina*. London: Faber & Faber, 1955.

**DAV**      Davidson, Gladys. *Ballet Biographies*. rev. ed. London: Werner Laurie, 1954.

**DEM/1**    Demidov, Alexander. *The Russian Ballet: Past and Present*. Translated by Guy Daniels. Prepared by The Novosti Press Agency Publishing House, Moscow. Garden City, N.Y.: Doubleday, 1977.

**DEM/2**    de Mille, Agnes. *Dance to the Piper*. Boston: Little, Brown and Company, 1952.

**DEM/3**    ——. *Portrait Gallery*. Boston: Houghton Mifflin, 1990.

**DRU**      Drury, Maxine. *To Dance, To Dream*. Racine, Wis.: Western Publishing Company, 1965.

**FOS**      Foster, Susan Leigh. *Reading Dancing: Bodies and Subjects in Contemporary American Dance*. Berkeley, Los Angeles, London: University of California Press, 1986.

**FOW**      Fowler, Carol. *Dance*. Contributions of Women. Minneapolis, Minn.: Dillon Press, 1981.

**FRA**      Franks, A.H. *Twentieth Century Ballet*. New York: Pitman, 1954.

**GAL**      Gale, Joseph. *Behind Barres: The Mystique of Masterly Teaching*. New York: Dance Horizons, 1980.

**GIB**      Gibbon, Monk. *"The Tales of Hoffmann": A Study of the Film*. London: Saturn Press, 1951; reprint New York & London: Garland Publishing, 1977.

**GRE/1**      Greskovic, Robert. "The Grigorovich Factor and the Bolshoi." *Ballet Review* 5, no. 2 (1975-1976).

**GRE/2**      ———. "New York City Ballet: A Year and Its Dancers." *Ballet Review* 7, no. 4 (1978-1979).

**GRE/3**      ———. "Some Artists of the New York City Ballet." *Ballet Review* 4, no. 4 (1973).

**GRU/1**      Gruen, John. *People Who Dance: 22 Dancers Tell Their Own Stories*. Princeton, N.J.: Princeton Book Company, Publishers, 1988.

**GRU/2**      ———. *The Private World of Ballet*. New York: Viking, 1975.

**GUE**      Guest, Ivor. *Adventures of a Ballet Historian: An Unfinished Memoir*. New York: Dance Horizons, 1982.

**HAL**      Hall, Fernau. *An Anatomy of Ballet*. London: Andrew Melrose, 1953. Published simultaneously in the United States as *World Dance* by A.A. Wyn, New York.

**HAS/1**  Haskell, Arnold. *Balletomania: Then and Now*. New York: Knopf, 1977.

**HAS/2**  Hastings, Baird. *Choreographer and Composer*. Boston: Twayne Publishers, 1983. [On cover: Choreographer and Composer: Theatrical Dance and Music in Western Culture].

**HOD**  Hodgson, Moira, text, with photography by Thomas Victor. *Quintet: Five American Dance Companies*. New York: Morrow, 1976.

**HUR**  Hurok, S. *S. Hurok Presents: A Memoir of the Dance World*. New York: Hermitage House, 1953. British edition appeared under the title *S. Hurok Presents . . . The World of Ballet*. London: Robert Hale, 1955. Variant pagination and different plates. Key symbol refers only to American edition.

**JOR**  Jordan, Stephanie. *Striding Out: Aspects of Contemporary and New Dance in Britain*. London: Dance Books, 1992.

**KON**  Koner, Pauline. *Solitary Song*. Durham, N.C. & London: Duke University Press, 1989.

**KRE**  Kreemer, Connie. *Further Steps: Fifteen Choreographers on Modern Dance*. New York: Harper & Row, 1987.

**LIV**  Livet, Anne, ed. *Contemporary Dance*. New York: Abbeville Press, 1978.

**LLO**  Lloyd, Margaret. *The Borzoi Book of Modern Dance*. New York: Knopf, 1949.

**LYL**  Lyle, Cynthia. *Dancers on Dancing*. New York & London: Drake Publishers, 1977.

**MAG**  Magriel, Paul, ed. *Chronicles of the American Dance*. New York: Henry Holt, 1948.

**MAR**    Martin, John. *America Dancing: The Background and Personalities of the Modern Dance.* New York: Dodge Publishing, 1936.

**MAS**    Mason, Francis. *I Remember Balanchine: Recollections of the Ballet Master by Those Who Knew Him.* New York: Doubleday, 1991.

**MAY/1**    Maynard, Olga. *The American Ballet.* Philadelphia: Macrae Smith, 1959.

**MAY/2**    ———. *American Modern Dancers: The Pioneers.* Boston: Little Brown & Company, 1965.

**MAZ**    Mazo, Joseph H. *Prime Movers: The Makers of Modern Dance in America.* New York: William Morrow, 1977.

**MCC**    McConnell, Jane T. *Famous Ballet Dancers.* New York: Thomas Y. Crowell Company, 1955.

**MCD**    McDonagh, Don. *The Rise and Fall and Rise of Modern Dance.* New York: Outerbridge & Dienstfrey, 1970.

**MIG**    Migel, Parmenia. *The Ballerinas: From the Court of Louis XIV to Pavlova.* New York: Macmillan, 1972.

**MON** Montague, Sarah. *The Ballerina: Famous Dancers and Rising Stars of Our Time*. New York: Universe Books, 1980.

**MOO/1** Moore, Lillian. *Artists of the Dance*. New York: Thomas Y. Crowell, 1938.

**MOO/2** ———. *Echoes of American Ballet*. Edited by Ivor Guest. New York: Dance Horizons, 1976.

**MUI** Muir, Jane. *Famous Dancers*. Famous Biographies for Young People. New York: Dodd, Mead & Company, 1956.

**NEW/1** Newman, Barbara. *Striking a Balance: Dancers Talk About Dancing*. Boston: Houghton Mifflin, 1982.

**NEW/2** Newman, Barbara. *Striking a Balance: Dancers Talk About Dancing*. Rev. ed. New York: Limelight Editions, 1992.

**NOB** Noble, Peter, ed. *British Ballet*. London: Skelton Robinson, [1949].

**PAG** Page, Ruth. *Class: Notes on Dance Classes Around the World, 1915-1980*. Edited and Additional Notes by Andrew M. Wentink. Princeton, N.J.: Princeton Book Company, Publishers, 1984.

**PAL** Palmer, Winthrop. *Theatrical Dancing in America: The Development of the Ballet from 1900*. New York: Bernard Ackerman, 1945.

**PET** Petitjean, Pierre, photography, with text by Holly Brubach. *Ten Dancers: On Stage, Backstage, at Home, and On the Road*. New York: William Morrow, 1982.

**PRE** Prevots, Naima. *Dancing in the Sun: Hollywood Choreographers, 1915-1937*. Ann Arbor, Mich. & London: UMI Research Press, 1987.

**ROG**    Rogosin, Elinor. *The Dance Makers: Conversations with American Choreographers.* New York: Walker & Company, 1980.

**ROS**    Roslavleva, Natalia. *Era of the Russian Ballet.* New York: Dutton, 1966; reprint New York: Da Capo Press, 1979.

**SCH/1**  Schlundt, Christena L. *Dance in the Musical Theatre: Jerome Robbins and His Peers, 1934–1965.* New York & London: Garland Publishing, 1989. A joint publication with The New York Public Library. Error on cover: read 1934 for 1943.

**SCH/2**  Scholl, Tim. *From Petipa to Balanchine: Classical Revival and the Modernization of Ballet.* London & New York: Routledge, 1994.

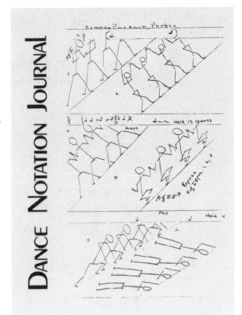

**SID**    Sidimus, Joysanne. *Exchanges: Life After Dance.* Toronto: Press of Terpsichore, 1987.

**SIE**    Siegel, Marcia B., ed. "Dancer's Notes." *Dance Perspectives* 38 (Summer 1969).

**SLO**    Slonimsky, Juri. *The Soviet Ballet.* New York Philosophical Library, 1947.

**SMA**    Smakov, Gennady. *The Great Russian Dancers.* New York: Knopf, 1984.

**SOR/1**  Sorell, Walter, ed. *The Dance Has Many Faces.* Cleveland & New York: World Publishing, 1951.

**SOR/2** Sorell, Walter, ed. *The Dance Has Many Faces.* 2d ed., rev. New York & London: Columbia University Press, 1966.

**SWI/1** Swift, Mary Grace. *Belles & Beaux on Their Toes: Dancing Stars in Young America.* Washington, D.C.: University Press of America, 1980.

**SWI/2** Swinson, Cyril, ed. *Dancers and Critics.* London: Adam & Charles Black, 1950.

**SWI/3** Switzer, Ellen. *Dancers! Horizons in American Dance.* New York: Atheneum, 1982.

**TER** Terry, Walter. *The Dance in America.* rev. ed. New York: Harper & Row, 1971; reprint New York: Da Capo Press, 1981.

**TRA** Tracy, Robert, with Sharon DeLano. *Balanchine's Ballerinas: Conversations with the Muses.* New York: Simon & Schuster, 1983.

**VAN** Van Vechten, Carl. *The Dance Writings of Carl Van Vechten.* Edited, and with an Introduction by Paul Padgette. New York: Dance Horizons, c. 1974.

**WIL** Wiley, Roland John. *A Century of Russian Ballet: Documents and Accounts, 1810-1910.* Oxford: Clarendon Press, 1990. [On cover: A Century of Russian Ballet: Documents and Eyewitness Accounts, 1810-1910].

**ZHD** Zhdanov, Leonid, photography, with texts compiled by Noi Avaliani. *Bolshoi's Young Dancers.* Translated from the Russian by Natalie Ward. Moscow: Progress Publishers, c. 1975.

# KEY PERIODICALS

**BR**     *Ballet Review* (1965– )

**C&D**     *Choreography and Dance* (1988– )

**CBY**     *Current Biography Yearbook*, formerly *Current Biography: Who's News and Why* (1940– )

**DC**     *Dance Chronicle* (1977– )

**DI**     *Dance Index* (1942-1948)

**DN**     *Dance Now* (1992– )

**DNJ**     *Dance Notation Journal* (1983-1989)

**DP**     *Dance Perspectives* (1959-1976)

**DR**     *Dance Research* (1983– )

**DRA**     *Dance Research Annual* (1967-1989)

**DRJ**     *Dance Research Journal* (1969– )

**DS**     *Dance Scope* (1965-1981)

**PAJ**     *Performing Arts Journal* (1976– )

**SDH**     *Studies in Dance History* (1989– )

**TDR**     *The Drama Review*, formerly *Tulane Drama Review* (1955–)

**W&P**     *Women & Performance* (1983– )

**YDR**     *York Dance Review* (1973-1978)

# DANCERS AND CHOREOGRAPHERS:

## A Selected Bibliography

**Adams, Carolyn** (1943– )
Adams, Carolyn. "Lifeline to Taylor." *BR* 13, no. 4 (Winter 1986): 18-20.

**Adams, Diana** (1926-1993)
    "Adams, Diana." *CBY 1954*: 7-9.
    Russell, Francia, Edward Gorey, and Francis Mason. "Recollecting Diana Adams." *BR* 21, no. 3 (Fall 1993): 18-27.
    ATK: 2-6. MAS: 347-353. TRA: 120-127.

**Adams, Lawrence** (1936– ) and **Miriam** (1944– )
    Chitty, Elizabeth. "Fifteen is an Amoeba." *YDR* Issue #4 (Spring 1975): 38-40. Article appended by a Chronology of Works, compiled by Jennifer Mascall (pp. 40-42).
    SID: 27-37.

**Agadati, Baruch** (1895-1976)
    Manor, Giora, ed. *Agadati: The Pioneer of Modern Dance in Israel*. Tel-Aviv: Sifrial Poalim & The Dance Library of Israel, 1986. Bilingual: Hebrew/English.

**Ailey, Alvin** (1931-1989)
    "Ailey, Alvin (Jr.)." *CBY 1968*: 12-14.
    Ailey, Alvin, with A. Peter Bailey. *Revelations: The Autobiography of Alvin Ailey*. New York: Carol Publishing Group, 1995.
    Latham, Jacqueline Quinn Moore. "A Biographical Study of the Lives and Contributions of Two Selected Contemporary Black

**Ailey, Alvin** *(continued)*

Male Dance Artists—Arthur Mitchell and Alvin Ailey—in the Idioms of Ballet and Modern Dance, Respectively." Unpublished dissertation, Texas Woman's University, 1973. Ann Arbor, Mich.: University Microfilms International, 1974. Order No. 74-22,241. DAI 35-04A, p. 2143.

Lewis-Ferguson, Julinda. *Alvin Ailey, Jr.: A Life in Dance.* New York: Walker and Company, 1994.

Mazo, Joseph H. *The Alvin Ailey American Dance Theater.* New York: William Morrow, 1978.

Moore, William. "Alvin Ailey (1931-1989)." *BR* 17, no. 4 (Winter 1990): 12-17.

Pinkney, Andrea Davis, text, with illustrations by Brian Pinkney. *Alvin Ailey.* New York: Hyperion Books for Children, 1993.

GRU/2: 417-423. HOD: 48-83. MAZ: 243-256. ROG: 102-117. VAN: 42-45.

**Åkesson, Birgit** (1908– )
HAL: 220-226.

**Akimov, Boris** (1946– )
ZHD: 256-271.

**Albertieri, Luigi** (1860-1930)
PAG: 35-39.

**Alexeyeva, Lyudmila** (1890-1964)
René, Natalia. "Lyudmila Alexeyeva 1890-1964." *DS* 1, no. 2 (Spring 1965): 22.

**Algeranoff, Harcourt** (1903-1967)
DAV: 1-2.

**Algeranova, Claudie** (1924– )
DAV: 3-4.

**Allan, Maud** (1873-1956)
Allan, Maud. *My Life and Dancing.* London: Everett & Co., [1908]. Cherniavsky, Felix. *Did She Dance: Maud Allan in Performance.*

**Allard, Maud** *(continued)*

Toronto: Dance Collection Danse, 1992. Published on four floppy diskettes (text equivalent to a book-length manuscript), MS DOS 5 ¼″ or 3.5″, will operate on most IBM Personal Computers or compatibles and also the Macintosh. This publication also incorporates a "reprint" of Maud Allan's *My Life and Dancing*, originally published by Everett & Co., London, [1908].

——. "Maud Allan." Part 1: "The Early Years, 1873-1903"; Part 2: "First Steps to a Dancing Career, 1904-1907"; Part 3: "Two Years of Triumph, 1908-1909"; Part 4: "The Years of Touring, 1910-1915"; and Part 5: "The Years of Decline." *DC* 6, no. 1 (1983): 1-36; *DC* 6, no. 3 (1983): 189-227; *DC* 7, no. 2 (1984): 119-158; *DC* 8, nos. 1&2 (1985): 1-50; and *DC* 9, no. 2 (1986): 177-236.

——. "Maud Allan's Tour of India, the Far East, and Australia." In *Society of Dance History Scholars Proceedings*, pp. 74-79. Ninth Annual Conference, City College, City University of New York, 14-17 February 1986.

——. *The Salome Dancer: The Life and Times of Maud Allan*. Toronto: McClelland & Stewart, 1991.

McDearmon, Lacy. "Maud Allan: The Public Record." *DC* 2, no. 2 (1978): 85-105.

Weigand, Elizabeth. "Maud Allan and J.T. Grein." In *Society of Dance History Scholars Proceedings*, pp. 233-238. Sixth Annual Conference, The Ohio State University, 11-13 February 1983.

——. *"The Rugmaker's Daughter*, Maud Allan's 1915 Silent Film." *DC* 9, no. 2 (1986): 237-251.

CAF: 73-81. MAG: 221-223. VAN: 29-32.


**Allard, Marie** (1742-1802)

MIG: 50-58.


**Alonso, Alicia** (1921– )

"Alonso, Alicia." *CBY 1955*: 15-17.

"Alonso, Alicia." *CBY 1977*: 17-20.

Alonso, Alicia. "Performing Giselle." In *American Ballet Theatre*, pp. 333-342, by Charles Payne. New York: Knopf, 1978.

Arnold, Sandra Martín. *Alicia Alonso: First Lady of the Ballet*. New York: Walker and Company, 1993.

**Alonso, Alicia** *(continued)*

Gamez, Tana de. *Alicia Alonso: At Home and Abroad.* New York: Citadel Press, 1971.

Siegel, Beatrice. *Alicia Alonso: The Story of a Ballerina.* New York & London: Frederick Warne, 1979.

Simon, Pedro. *Alicia Alonso [and] Vladimir Vasiliev: "Giselle."* Translated by Susana Medea Benjamin. Havana: Editorial Arte y Literatura, 1981. Bilingual: Spanish/English.

Terry, Walter, text, with photography by Steven Caras. *Alicia and her Ballet Nacional de Cuba: An Illustrated Biography of Alicia Alonso.* Garden City, N.Y.: Anchor Books, 1981.

ATK: 7-11. DAV: 4-6. DEM/3: 70-91. MON: 34-35. NEW/1: 60-71.

**Alston, Richard** (1948– )

Jordan, Stephanie. "Interviews with Richard Alston and Nigel Osborne." *C&D* 1, pt. 4 (1992): 57-72.

Kane, Angela. "Richard Alston: Twenty-one Years of Choreography." *DR* 7, no. 2 (Autumn 1989): 16-54.

Robertson, Allen. "Full Circle." *DN* 4, no. 1 (spring 1995): 18-23.

JOR: 105-130; 219-227.

**Ananiashvili, Nina** (1964– )

Kaplan, Larry. "A Conversation with Nina Ananiashvili." *BR* 19, no. 3 (Fall 1991): 49-56.

NEW/2: 398-426.

**Anastos, Peter** (1948– )

Croce, Arlene. "The Tiresias Factor." *The New Yorker* 66, no. 15 (May 28, 1990): 41-44, 46-48, 50, 52-55, 58-64.

Remine, Shields. "Peter Anastos on the Silver Screen." *BR* 20, no. 4 (Winter 1992): 32-45.

Spiegelman, Willard. "Anastos on Tchikaboumskaya, *Cinderella,* and Baryshnikov." *BR* 12, no. 1 (Spring 1984): 43-54.

**Andersen, Ib** (1954– )

"Andersen, Ib." *CBY 1984*: 9-12.

Cunningham, Kitty. "A Conversation with Ib Andersen." *BR* 9, no. 3 (Fall 1981): 28-40.

**Angiolini, Gaspero** (1731-1803)

Carones, Laura. "Noverre and Angiolini: Polemical Letters." *DR* 5, no. 1 (Spring 1987): 42-54.

**Ari, Carina** (1897-1970)

Näslund, Erik. "Carina Ari." *DR* 7, no. 2 (Autumn 1989): 70-80.

**Armitage, Karole** (1954– )

Greskovic, Robert. "Armitagean Physics, or The Shoes of the Ballerina." *BR* 13, no. 2 (Summer 1985): 73-89.

Schjeldahl, Peter. *Karole Armitage and David Salle: 3 Years of The Ballet Stage*. ArT RANDOM 19. Kyoto: Kyoto Shoin International, 1989.

Stuart, Otis. "The Neoclassical Phrasing of the Now Karole Armitage." *BR* 15, no. 4 (Winter 1988): 54-58.

**Aroldingen, Karin von** (see **von Aroldingen, Karin**)

**Aronson, Fannie** (1904?-1991)

Michigan Dance Association. *Dance Education in Michigan, Recollections of Three Pioneers: Grace Ryan, Ruth Murray & Fanny Aronson*. East Lansing: Michigan Dance Association, c. 1979.

**Arpino, Gerald** (1928– )

"Arpino, Gerald (Peter)." *CBY 1970*: 17-19.

Maynard, Olga. "Arpino and the Berkeley Ballets." *Dance Magazine* 47, no. 9 (September 1973): 47-61. A Dance Magazine Portfolio.

GRU/2: 385-389.

**Ashley, Merrill** (1950– )

"Ashley, Merrill." *CBY 1981*: 4-7.

Ashley, Merrill. *Dancing for Balanchine*. New York: Dutton, 1984.

Kaplan, Larry. "A Conversation with Merrill Ashley." *BR* 17, no. 1 (Spring 1989): 79-90.

——. "Merrill Ashley and Balanchine's *Ballade*." *BR* 10, no. 4 (Winter 1983): 21-28.

GRE/2: 9-23. GRE/3: 24-25. MAS: 571-576. MON: 94-95.

NEW/1: 380-393. TRA: 176-181.

**Ashton, Frederick** (1904-1988)

Acocella, Joan. "Ashton's *Romeo*: A Wise Virgin." *BR* 13, no. 3 (Fall 1985): 60-67.

"Ashton, Frederick." *CBY 1951*: 19-21.

Ashton, Frederick. "My Garden at Chandos." *BR* 11, no. 2 (Summer 1983): 27-29.

Barnes, Clive. "Frederick Ashton and His Ballets." *DP* 9 (Winter 1961).

Beaumont, Cyril W. "Frederick Ashton: English Choreographer." In *Souvenirs de Ballet*, pp. 6-12. Edited by Duncan Melvin. London: Mayfair Publications, 1949.

Brinson, Peter. "The Elevation of Sir Fred." *YDR* Issue #6 (Spring 1977): 3-5.

Croce, Arlene. "Waltzing Mice." *BR* 3, no. 6 (1971): 72-75.

*Dance Now* 3, no. 3 (Autumn 1994). A special issue celebrating the life and work of Frederick Ashton. Articles: David Vaughan. "Frederick Ashton and His Ballets: A Final Chapter" (pp. 2-13). An update to the author's magnificent biography *Frederick Ashton and His Ballets* (New York: Knopf, 1977). Katherine Healy. "Recollections of Ashton's Juliet" (pp. 14-19, 21-23). Els Grelinger. "Ashton at Work" (pp. 24-25). Ann Nugent. "For Freddy, Yes for Freddy . . ." (pp. 26-33). Alexandra Tomalonis with Henning Kronstam. "Dancing for Ashton" (pp. 34-44). This is an abridged version of an article that first appeared in *DanceView* 11, no. 4 (Summer 1994). Kathrine Sorley Walker. "Ashton Ballets: Post-Mortem Performance" (pp. 45-51). Cormac Rigby. "Wordless as the Flight of Birds" (pp. 53-61).

*Dance Theatre Journal* 2, no. 3 (Autumn 1984). A special issue celebrating Frederick Ashton at eighty. Articles: Alastair Macaulay. "Ashton at Eighty" (pp. 2-7). Richard Alston. "Appropriate Steps" (pp. 8-9). Robert Greskovic. "Thoughts on Classicism and Ashton" (pp. 10-12). Richard Glasstone. "Ashton, Cecchetti and the English School" (pp. 13-14).

*DanceView* 12, no. 3 (Spring 1995). Three articles consider the Ashton heritage today: David Vaughan. "Celebrating Ashton" (pp. 2-6). Mary Cargill. "Can This Choreographer Be Saved?" (pp. 7-10). Alastair Macaulay. "Gender, Sexuality, Community" (pp. 11-16).

**Ashton, Frederick** *(continued)*

Dickson, Elizabeth, text, with photography by Derry Moore. "Architectural Digest Visits: Sir Frederick Ashton." *Architectural Digest* 34, no. 3 (April 1977): 90-97.

Dominic, Zoë, photography, with text by John Selwyn Gilbert. *Frederick Ashton: A Choreographer and His Ballets.* London: George G. Harrap & Company, 1971.

Doob, Penelope B.R. "A Conversation with Sir Frederick Ashton." *YDR* Issue #7 (Spring 1978): 16-25.

Farjeon, Annabel. "Choreographers: Dancing for de Valois and Ashton." *DC* 17, no. 2 (1994): 195-206.

Godden, Rumer. *The Tale of the Tales: The Beatrix Potter Ballet.* London: Frederick Warne, 1971.

Harvey, Cynthia, with David Vaughan. "Working with Ashton." *BR* 17, no. 3 (Fall 1989): 33-37.

"Homage to Ashton." In *The Ballet Annual 1961: A Record and Year Book of the Ballet.* Edited by Arnold L. Haskell and Mary Clarke. Fifteenth Issue. New York: Macmillan, 1960. Articles: Arnold L. Haskell. "The Quality of Frederick Ashton" (pp. 43-45). Marie Rambert. "Ashton's Early Days" (pp. 45-46, 49). Margot Fonteyn. "A Choreographer of Genius" (pp. 49-50). Michael Somes. "Working with Frederick Ashton" (pp. 50, 53-54). George Balanchine. "A Tribute to Frederick Ashton in Letter Form" (p. 55). Vera Volkova. "Frederick Ashton in Denmark" (pp. 56 & 59).

Hunt, Marilyn. "Intimate Tragedy." *BR* 13, no. 3 (Fall 1985): 68-72.

Jordan, Stephanie. "Ashton and *The Sleeping Beauty*." *DN* 2, no. 2 (Summer 1993): 43-49.

———. "Ashton's Musicality: Some Preliminary Observations." *Dance Theatre Journal* 11, no. 1 (Winter 1993-1994): 16-19.

**Ashton, Frederick** *(continued)*

"Looking at Ballet: Ashton and Balanchine, 1926-1936." *SDH* 3, no. 2 (Fall 1992). Compiled by Jane B. Roberts and David Vaughan. Edited by David Vaughan and John V. Chapman. Papers from the eponymous conference held at Russell Sage College, Troy, New York, July 13-14, 1991. Introductory texts and articles related to Ashton: Jane B. Roberts. Foreword and Acknowledgments (p. v). David Vaughan. Preface (pp. vii-x). David Vaughan. *"Le Baiser de la Fée*: Nijinska, Ashton, Balanchine" (pp. 1-8). Alastair Macaulay. "Ashton's Classicism and *Les Rendezvous"* (pp. 9-14). Jane B. Roberts. "Masked, Mysterious Ballets of Ashton and Balanchine, 1926-1936" (pp. 21-39). Jane Pritchard. " 'The Nostalgic World of Fantasy': Some Neoromantic Elements in Works by Ashton and Balanchine" (pp. 39-44). Works by Frederick Ashton and George Balanchine, 1926-1936 (pp. 53-56).

Macaulay, Alastair. "Performing Pigeons." *BR* 8, no. 1 (1980): 84-95.

———. *Some Views and Reviews of Ashton's Choreography.* Collected Writings, No. 1. Guildford, Surrey: National Resource Centre for Dance, 1987.

McDonagh, Don. "Au Revoir?" *BR* 3, no. 4 (1970): 14-19.

Rigby, Cormac. "A Ballet of Perfect Englishness." *DN* 1, no. 4 (Winter 1992-1993): 22-27.

Tomalonis, Alexandra. "Dancing for Ashton and Balanchine: Talking with Henning Kronstam." *DanceView* 11, no. 4 (Summer 1994): 24-55.

Vaughan, David. "Frederick Ashton." *Dance Magazine* 48, no. 5 (May 1974): 43-58. A Dance Magazine Portfolio.

———. "Frederick Ashton: A Last Look Back." *BR* 16, no. 2 (Summer 1988): 60-61.

———. *Frederick Ashton and His Ballets.* New York: Knopf, 1977.

———. "Frederick Ashton and *Rhapsody.*" *BR* 8, nos. 2&3 (1980): 272-283.

———. "Reading About Ashton." *BR* 4, no. 2 (1972): 45-60.

Zoete, Beryl de. "Frederick Ashton: Background of a Choreographer." In her *The Thunder and the Freshness*, pp. 34-42. London: Neville Spearman; New York: Theatre Arts Books, 1963.

———. "Three British Choreographers." In her *The Thunder and the Freshness*, pp. 43-55. London: Neville Spearman; New York: Theatre Arts Books, 1963. Portion on Ashton, pp. 51-55.

**Ashton, Frederick** *(continued)*
DAV: 6-12. FRA: 93-111. GIB: 85-87. HAL: 185-199. HAS/2: 161-166. HUR: 268-272. SOR/1: 247-250.

**Asylmuratova, Altinay** (1961– )
Greskovic, Robert. "Altinaï Assylmouratova." *BR* 11, no. 2 (Summer 1983): 80-82.

**Augusta, Mme** (see **Fuchs, Caroline Augusta Josephine Thérèse**)

**Babilée, Jean** (1923– )
Goldschmidt, Hubert. "A Conversation with Jean Babilée." *BR* 22, no. 2 (Summer 1994): 24-47.
Stoop, Norma McLain. "The Charismatic Career of Jean Babilée." *Dance Magazine* 53, no. 7 (July 1979): 64-77.
ATK: 12-15. BLA: 128-131. DAV: 12-16. SWI/2: 22-26.

**Baccelli, Giovanna**
(fl. 1774-1788; d. 1801; née **Zanerini**)
Guest, Ivor. "The Italian Lady of Knole." In *The Ballet Annual 1957: A Record and Year Book of the Ballet*, pp. 78-85. Edited by Arnold L. Haskell. Eleventh Issue. New York: Macmillan, 1956.

**Balanchine, George** (1904-1983)
Anderson, Jack. *The One and Only: The Ballet Russe de Monte Carlo*. New York: Dance Horizons, 1981.
——. *"The One and Only: The Ballet Russe de Monte Carlo*—The

**Balanchine, George** *(continued)*
    Balanchine Years." *BR* 8, no. 4 (1980): 311-352. An extract from
    Anderson's book *The One and Only*. New York: Dance Horizons,
    1981.

Ashley, Merrill. "Class with Balanchine." *BR* 12, no. 3 (Fall 1984):
    7-19. An extract from Merrill Ashley's *Dancing for Balanchine*.
    New York: Dutton, 1984.

Au, Susan. "*Apollo*: The Transformation of a Myth." *DRA XIV* (1983):
    50-63.

"Balanchine." *DNJ* 6 (Winter/Spring 1988-89). Contents: Muriel
    Topaz. "The Balanchine Project: A Brief History" (pp. 1-2). Dawn
    Lille Horwitz. "Victoria Simon on Balanchine and Notation" (pp.
    3-5). Virginia Doris. "A Notator's View" (pp. 6-13). Nancy
    Reynolds. "An Introduction to the Ballets: *Prodigal Son, Ser-
    enade, Concerto Barocco, The Four Temperaments, La Françaix,
    Scotch Symphony, Western Symphony, Agon, Stars and Stripes,
    Donizetti Variations, Raymonda Variations, A Midsummer Night's
    Dream, Bugaku, Tarantella, Rubies, Valse Fantaisie*, and *Cortège
    Hongrois*," with notation examples (pp. 15-74). Nancy Reynolds.
    Selected Bibliography: Balanchine Repertory and Technique
    Since 1974 (p. 75). Balanchine Labanotation Project, 1984-88: A
    Summary of Notated Scores (p. 76).

"Balanchine, George." *CBY 1942*: 48-50.

"Balanchine, George." *CBY 1954*: 62-64.

Balanchine, George. *Balanchine's Complete Stories of the Great
    Ballets*. Edited by Francis Mason. Garden City, N.Y.: Doubleday,
    1954. Rev. and enl. ed. Garden City, N.Y.: Doubleday, 1977.
    Co-authored with Francis Mason.

——. *Balanchine's New Complete Stories of the Great Ballets*. Edited
    by Francis Mason. Garden City, N.Y.: Doubleday, 1968.

——. *By George Balanchine*. New York: San Marco Press, 1984.

——. "The Dance Element in Stravinsky's Music." *BR* 10, no. 2
    (Summer 1982): 14-18. This essay first appeared in *Dance Index*
    4, nos. 10-12 (1947), and is included in *Stravinsky in the Theatre*,
    ed. by Minna Lederman, New York: Pellegrini & Cudahy, 1949;
    reprint New York: Da Capo Press, 1975.

——. "How I Became a Dancer and Choreographer." In *Bal-
    anchine's Complete Stories of the Great Ballets*, pp. 485-497.
    Edited by Francis Mason. Garden City, N.Y.: Doubleday, 1954.

**Balanchine, George** *(continued)*

———. "Notes and Comments on Dancers, Dancing, and Choreography." In *Balanchine's Complete Stories of the Great Ballets*, pp. 521-532. Edited by Francis Mason. Garden City, N.Y.: Doubleday, 1954.

———, and Bernard Taper. "Television and Ballet." In *The Eighth Art: Twenty-Three Views of Television Today*, pp. 117-123. New York, Chicago, San Francisco: Holt, Rinehart and Winston, c. 1962.

———, and Francis Mason. *101 Stories of the Great Ballets*. Garden City, N.Y.: Doubleday, 1975.

"Balanchine as Teacher." *BR* 19, no. 4 (Winter 1991): 61-97. The transcript of a symposium, moderated by Francis Mason, with Leda Anchutina, Merrill Ashley, Toni Bentley, Todd Bolender, Mary Day, Daniel Duell, Joseph Duell, Jillana, Lincoln Kirstein, Robert Lindgren, W. McNeil Lowry, Paul Mejia, Arthur Mitchell, Kent Stowell, John Taras, Richard Thomas, Edward Villella, Barbara Weisberger, and Patricia Wilde. Introduced with a short essay by Lincoln Kirstein, "The Contribution, Moral and Physical, of Balanchine's Instruction and Repertory."

"Balanchine: New Approaches." *C&D* 3, pt. 3 (1993). Eleni Bookis Hofmeister, Issue Editor. Contents: Eleni Bookis Hofmeister. Introduction (p. 1). Roger Copeland. "Backlash Against Balanchine" (pp. 3-11). Eleni Bookis Hofmeister. "Balanchine and Humphrey: Comparing *Serenade* and *Passacaglia*" (pp. 13-30). Deborah Gans. "The Architecture of Balanchine" (pp. 31-47). Hubert Doris. "Some Thoughts on Balanchine and the Waltz" (pp. 49-56). Sally Banes. "Balanchine and Black Dance" (pp. 59-77). Notes on Contributors (pp. 79-80). Index (pp. 81-83).

"Balanchine's *Nutcracker*." *BR* 16, no. 3 (Fall 1988): 82-99. The transcript of a discussion, edited and adapted for publication, heard at a symposium held by the New York City Ballet Guild at State Theater, 15 December 1986. Participants: Peter Boal, Selma Jeanne Cohen, Judith Fugate, Zippora Karz, Dominick Nervi, Shaun O'Brien, Joan Marie Ruane, and Violette Verdy.

*Ballet Review* 21, no. 1 (Spring 1993). A special issue marking the tenth anniversary of Balanchine's death. Feature articles: Fleming Rutledge. "An Analogue of Man and Woman" (pp. 18-21). Mary Stewart Hammond. "Cosmetics" (pp. 22-23). Robert Garis. "The Balanchine Enterprise" (pp. 24-44). Garson Kanin. "Balanchine

**Balanchine, George** *(continued)*

> in Hollywood" (pp. 45-49). Otis Stuart. "The Phoenix and the Lyre" (pp. 50-56). Nancy Lassalle and Madeleine M. Nichols, curators, and Susan Au, comp. "Balanchine: An Exhibition at Lincoln Center" (pp. 57-87). Alexandra Danilova, Tamara Geva, Erick Hawkins, Morton Gould, Richard Buckle, Maria Tallchief, Clive Barnes, Francis Mason, Nancy Reynolds, Don McDonagh, Leslie Copeland, Merrill Ashley, Don Daniels, Leslie Getz, Maitland McDonagh, Robert Greskovic, Marvin Hoshino. "Balanchine: First Impressions" (pp. 88-95). Leslie Getz. "Balanchine: A Selected Bibliography" (pp. 96-99).

Bentley, Toni. "Balanchine and the Kirov." *BR* 14, no. 3 (Fall 1986): 38-43.

Boultenhouse, Charles. "New York, 1952: *Metamorphoses*." *BR* 23, no. 1 (Spring 1995): 29-31.

Buckle, Richard, in collaboration with John Taras. *George Balanchine: Ballet Master*. New York: Random House, 1988.

*Choreography by George Balanchine: A Catalogue of Works*. Project directors: Leslie George Katz, Nancy Lassalle and Harvey Simmonds. New York: Eakins Press Foundation, 1983; trade edition New York: Viking, 1984.

Chujoy, Anatole. *The New York City Ballet*. New York: Knopf, 1953; reprint, with a new Preface by Edward Villella, New York: Da Capo Press, 1981.

Cluzel, Magdeleine E. "Balanchine and the New York City Ballet." In her *Glimpses of the Theatre and Dance*, pp. 58-62. Translated from the French by Lily and Baird Hastings. New York: Kamin Publishers, 1953.

Cohen, Selma Jeanne. "The Prodigal Son." *C&D* 2, no. 3 (1992): 49-56. An article which considers the parable of the Prodigal Son as it has inspired choreographers from Pierre Gardel (in 1812) to the present. Places Balanchine's masterpiece on this theme in historical context.

Crisp, Clement. "Balanchine's Operas." *BR* 16, no. 3 (Fall 1988): 43-44.

Croce, Arlene. *Afterimages*. New York: Knopf, 1977.

——. "The Balanchine Show." *The New Yorker* 69, no. 16 (June 7, 1993): 99-103.

**Balanchine, George** *(continued)*

——. *Going to the Dance.* New York: Knopf, 1982.

——. *"Serenade:* In the Beginning." In *Allegro*, pp. 23-26, 61, 63, 65. Edited by Thomas W. Schoff. Published in conjunction with the School of American Ballet's 1993 Workshop Performance Benefit, held at the Juilliard Theater, New York City, June 7, 1993.

——. *Sight Lines.* New York: Knopf, 1987.

——. "The Spelling of *Agon.*" *The New Yorker* 69, no. 21 (July 12, 1993): 84-92.

Daly, Ann. "The Balanchine Woman: Of Hummingbirds and Channel Swimmers." *TDR* 31, no. 1/T-113 (Spring 1987): 8-21.

*Dance Index* 4, nos. 2-3 (February-March 1945). Contents: George Balanchine. "Notes on Choreography" (pp. 20-31). Agnes de Mille. "Balanchine's Choreography (1930)" (pp. 32-35). Edwin Denby. "A Note on Balanchine's Present Style" (pp. 36-38). Ballets, Musicals, and Motion Pictures with Choreography by George Balanchine (pp. 39-40).

*Dance Magazine* 57, no. 7 (July 1983). A special memorial issue celebrating the art of George Balanchine. Feature articles: "Edwin Denby on Balanchine" (pp. 44-45). Lili Cockerille Livingston. "Inside Interview with Mr. B" (pp. 46-51). Joan Ross Acocella. "A Balanchine Chronology" (pp. 52-55). B.H. Haggin. "Reflections on Balanchine" (pp. 56-61). "Danilova on Balanchine" (pp. 62-63). "Toumanova on Balanchine" (p. 64). John Gruen. "Balanchine Remembered" (pp. 65-75). "Peter Martins on Balanchine" (pp. 76-77). "Kaleidoscope: A Gallery of Balanchine-and-Family Photographs" (pp. 78-83). Burton Taylor. "Dancing Balanchine" (pp. 84-89). Glenn Loney. "Balanchine on Broadway" (pp. 90-93). Marian Horosko. "See the Music, Hear the Dance" (pp. 94-97).

Daniels, Don. "Academy: The New World of *Serenade.*" *BR* 5, no. 1 (1975-1976): 1-12.

Garis, Robert. "Balanchine Institutionalized." *Salmagundi* No. 50-51 (Fall 1980-Winter 1981): 234-241.

——. "Beginnings, Balanchine." *Raritan: A Quarterly Review* 2, no. 4 (Spring 1983): 47-69.

——. "The Dancer and the Dance, Balanchine: Change, Revival, Survival." *Raritan: A Quarterly Review* 5, no. 2 (Fall 1985): 1-34.

**Balanchine, George** *(continued)*

——. *Following Balanchine.* New Haven, Conn. & London: Yale University Press, 1995.

*George Balanchine: A Reference Guide, 1987.* Nancy Lassalle, Project Director. Jane Emerson, Editor. New York: Ballet Society, 1987.

Goldner, Nancy, and Lincoln Kirstein, text, with photography by Richard Benson. *Coppélia: New York City Ballet.* New York: Eakins Press Foundation, 1974.

Graff, Ellen. "*The Four Temperaments* and *Orpheus*: Models of a Modern Classical Tradition." *BR* 13, no. 3 (Fall 1985): 54-59.

Gurewitsch, Matthew. "On Original Instruments: Reflections on the Balanchine Legacy." *BR* 14, no. 4 (Winter 1987): 72-76.

DANCE NOTATION JOURNAL
Volume 6            Winter/Spring 1988–89

**B**ALANCHINE

Haggin, B.H. *Discovering Balanchine.* New York: Horizon Press, 1981.

Holy Fathers' of the Seven Oecumenical Councils Russian Orthodox Church. *The George Balanchine Memorial Cross.* Text by Arlene Croce (reprinted from *The New Yorker* 67, no. 19, July 1, 1991, p. 6) and Abbot Adrian. New York: Holy Fathers' of the Seven Oecumenical Councils Russian Orthodox Church in association with The Eakins Press Foundation, 1992.

Jackson, George. [Balanchine Style]. Part 1: "George By George (Personal Reflections on the Evolution of Balanchine Style)"; Part 2: "Requirements for a Book About Balanchine: The Dancing"; and Part 3: "Requirements for a Book About Balanchine: The Handwriting." *Washington DanceView* 8, no. 2 (Winter 1988): 9-10; *Washington DanceView* 8, no. 3 (Spring 1989): 8-9; and *Washington DanceView* 8, no. 4 (Summer-Autumn 1989): 8-10.

**Balanchine, George** *(continued)*

Jordan, Stephanie. "*Agon*: A Musical/Choreographic Analysis." *DRJ* 25, no. 2 (Fall 1993): 1-12.

———. "*Ballet Imperial*." *DN* 2, no. 4 (Winter 1993-1994): 28-37.

———. "Music Puts a Time Corset on the Dance." *DC* 16, no. 3 (1993): 295-321.

Kahn, Marion Clare, comp., and Susan Au, ed. "Balanchine: A Selected Bibliography." Part One and Part Two. *BR* 11, no. 2 (Summer 1983): 9-11 and *BR* 11, no. 3 (Fall 1983): 97-99.

Kirstein, Lincoln, "Balanchine and the Waltz." In *Vienna Waltzes*, pp. [7-10]. Comp. and ed. by Nancy Lassalle. New York: New York City Ballet, 1977. An ancillary article in this publication, which places Balanchine's *Vienna Waltzes* in historical context, is George Jackson's "Viennese Waltzes" (pp. [2-6]).

———, text, with photography by Martha Swope and George Platt Lynes. *The New York City Ballet*. New York: Knopf, 1973.

———. *Portrait of Mr. B*. New York: A Ballet Society Book/Viking, 1984. A volume of photographs with an introductory essay, "A Ballet Master's Belief," by Lincoln Kirstein.

———. "The Position of Balanchine." *Salmagundi* No. 33-34 (Spring-Summer 1976): 211-215.

———. *Thirty Years: Lincoln Kirstein's "The New York City Ballet."* New York: Knopf, 1978. Expanded to include the years 1973-1978, in celebration of the company's thirtieth anniversary.

———, ed. *Union Jack: The New York City Ballet*. Photographs by Martha Swope and Richard Benson. New York: Eakins Press Foundation, 1977.

Klass, Roseanne. "Finding *The Figure in the Carpet*." *BR* 14, no. 1 (Spring 1986): 38-52.

Kolnik, Paul, and Costas, photography, with a brief introductory text by Francis Mason. "Dinner with Balanchine." *BR* 21, no. 3 (Fall 1993): 65-73. A pictorial overview of the grand finale of New York City Ballet's Balanchine Celebration.

Kotlowitz, Robert. "Mr. Balanchine Builds a Ballet." *Harper's Magazine* 219, no. 1313 (October 1959): 67-73. An inside look at the creation of *Native Dancers*.

Krokover, Rosalyn, and Harold C. Schonberg. "Ballet in America: One-man Show?" *Harper's Magazine* 229, no. 1372 (September 1964): 92-96.

**Balanchine, George** *(continued)*

Levin, David Michael. "Balanchine's Formalism." *Salmagundi* No. 33-34 (Spring-Summer 1976): 216-236.

Lobenthal, Joel. "*Symphonie Concertante* Revived." *BR* 11, no. 2 (Summer 1983): 12-21.

"Looking at Ballet: Ashton and Balanchine, 1926-1936." *SDH* 3, no. 2 (Fall 1992). Compiled by Jane B. Roberts and David Vaughan. Edited by David Vaughan and John V. Chapman. Papers from the eponymous conference held at Russell Sage College, Troy, New York, July 13-14, 1991. Introductory texts and articles related to Balanchine: Jane B. Roberts. Foreword and Acknowledgments (p. v). David Vaughan. Preface (pp. vii-x). David Vaughan. "*Le Baiser de la Fée*: Nijinska, Ashton, Balanchine" (pp. 1-8). Robert Greskovic. "*Le Fils Prodigue*: A Ballet Old and New" (pp. 15-20). Jane B. Roberts. "Masked, Mysterious Ballets of Ashton and Balanchine, 1926-1936" (pp. 21-30). Constance Valis-Hill. "Visions of the Marvelous: George Balanchine's *Luna Park, or The Freaks*" (pp. 31-37). Jane Pritchard. "'The Nostalgic World of Fantasy': Some Neoromantic Elements in Works by Ashton and Balanchine" (pp. 39-44). Bruce Fleming. "Balanchine's *Serenade* as a Modernist Work" (pp. 45-51). Works by Frederick Ashton and George Balanchine, 1926-1936 (pp. 53-56).

Lowry, W. McNeil. "Conversations with Balanchine." *The New Yorker* 59, no. 30 (September 12, 1983): 52-54, 57, 60, 63-64, 66, 68, 71-78, 81-82, 87-88.

——. "Conversations with Kirstein." Part One and Part Two. *The New Yorker* 62, no. 43 (December 15, 1986): 44-48, 51-52, 56-57,

**Balanchine, George** *(continued)*

59-62, 71-74, 76-80. *The New Yorker* 62, no. 44 (December 22, 1986): 37-40, 43-44, 48-56, 58-63.

Maiorano, Robert, and Valerie Brooks. *Balanchine's "Mozartiana": The Making of a Masterpiece.* New York: Freundlich Books, 1985.

Mason, Francis. *I Remember Balanchine: Recollections of the Ballet Master by Those Who Knew Him.* New York: Doubleday, 1991.

Maynard, Olga. "Balanchine and Stravinsky: The Glorious Undertaking." *Dance Magazine* 46, no. 6 (June 1972): 43-58. A Dance Magazine Portfolio.

McDonagh, Don. *George Balanchine.* Boston: Twayne Publishers, 1983.

Meyerowitz, Joel, text and photography. *George Balanchine's "The Nutcracker."* Boston & New York: Little, Brown and Company, 1993.

Miller, Raphael Francis. "The Contributions of Selected Broadway Musical Theatre Choreographers: Connolly, Rasch, Balanchine, Holm, and Alton." Unpublished dissertation, University of Oregon, 1984. Ann Arbor, Mich.: University Microfilms International, 1984. Order No. 842,2855. DAI 45-07A, p. 1922.

Milstein, Nathan. "My Friend George Balanchine." Parts One and Two. *BR* 18, no. 3 (Fall 1990): 23-34 and *BR* 18, no. 4 (Winter 1990-1991): 82-90. Reprinted from *From Russia to the West: The Musical Memoirs and Reminiscences of Nathan Milstein* by Nathan Milstein and Solomon Volkov. Translated by Antonina W. Bouis. New York: Henry Holt, 1990.

The Museum of Broadcasting. *A Celebration of George Balanchine: The Television Work.* Catalogue of the eponymous exhibition, September 21-November 15, 1984. New York: The Museum of Broadcasting, 1984.

Newman, Barbara. "Returning for Balanchine." *BR* 21, no. 4 (Winter 1993): 74-81.

Pierpont, Claudia Roth. "Balanchine's Romanticism." *BR* 12, no. 2 (Summer 1984): 6-17.

Reynolds, Nancy. "Documenting Mr. B." *Dancing Times* 72 [i.e. 73], no. 873 (June 1983): 704-709. Nancy Reynolds, who was director of research for *Choreography by George Balanchine: A Catalogue of Works*, gives an account of the way in which the work was accomplished.

**Balanchine, George** *(continued)*

——. "The Red Curtain: Balanchine's Critical Reception in the Soviet Union." In *Society of Dance History Scholars Proceedings*, pp. 47-57. Fifteenth Annual Conference, University of California, Riverside, 14-15 February 1992.

——. *Repertory in Review: 40 Years of the New York City Ballet*. Introduction by Lincoln Kirstein. New York: Dial Press, 1977.

Ricco, Edward. "The Sitwells at the Ballet: IV. *The Triumph of Neptune*." *BR* 6, no. 1 (1977-1978): 80-90.

Rose, Brian. *Televising the Performing Arts: Interviews with Merrill Brockway, Kirk Browning, and Roger Englander*. Contributions to the Study of Music and Dance, No. 29. Westport, Conn. & London: Greenwood Press, 1992. In the Merrill Brockway section see: Working with George Balanchine (pp. 45-55).

Scholl, Tim. "Balanchine's 'Blessed Vision.'" *BR* 19, no. 2 (Summer 1991): 28-29.

Selleck, Nancy. "*Barocco* Turns 50." *BR* 19, no. 1 (Spring 1991): 88-96.

Shearer, Moira. *Balletmaster: A Dancer's View of George Balanchine*. London: Sidgwick & Jackson, 1986.

Siegel, Marcia B. "Fable in a Lucite Landscape." *BR* 19, no. 3 (Fall 1991): 71-74.

Slonimsky, Yuri. "Balanchine: The Early Years." Translated by John Andrews. *BR* 5, no. 3 (1975-1976): 1-64.

Souritz, Elizabeth. "The Young Balanchine in Russia." *BR* 18, no. 2 (Summer 1990): 66-71.

"Staging Balanchine's Ballets: A Symposium." *BR* 11, no. 3 (Fall 1983): 81-96. The edited transcript of a symposium, chaired by Nancy Reynolds, heard 19 June 1982 at the Dance Critics Association conference "Reconstruction and Revival: Which Dance Is This Anyway?" at the Milford Plaza Hotel, New York.

Switzer, Ellen. *The Nutcracker: A Story & A Ballet*. Photographs by Steven Caras and Costas. New York: Atheneum, 1985.

Swope, Martha, photography. *"A Midsummer Night's Dream": The Story of the New York City Ballet's Production*. Introduction by Lincoln Kirstein. Edited by Nancy Lassalle. New York: Dodd, Mead & Company, 1977.

Taper, Bernard. *Balanchine*. New York: Harper & Row, 1963;

B

**Balanchine, George** *(continued)*

reprint, with an additional chapter, "At Seventy," New York: Macmillan, 1974; reprint with two additional chapters, "An Appetite for Renewal" and "The Last Year," New York: Times Books, 1984. Another edition of Taper's biography is in preparation, which will have chapters examining the Balanchine legacy a decade after his death.

Terry, Walter. "The Choreography of George Balanchine." In *The Ballet Annual 1951: A Record and Year Book of the Ballet*, pp. 56-63. Edited by Arnold L. Haskell. Fifth Issue. London: Adam & Charles Black, n.d.

Tomalonis, Alexandra. "Dancing for Ashton and Balanchine: Talking with Henning Kronstam." *DanceView* 11, no. 4 (Summer 1994): 24-55.

Turnbaugh, Douglas. "A New Look at Balanchineballet." In *The Dance Experience: Readings in Dance Appreciation*, pp. 310-317. Edited by Myron Howard Nadel and Constance Nadel Miller. New York: Praeger, 1970. Article preceded by an abstract/analysis of its contents: "Leadership or Control?" (p. 309). This article first appeared, with notes to the text (not included in the Nadel volume), in *Dance Scope* 1, no. 2 (Spring 1965): 28-34.

Vaughan, David. "Balanchine Ballerinas: 1925-1933." *Dance Magazine* 53, no. 1 (January 1979): 63-[78]. A Dance Magazine Portfolio.

———. "Balanchine: Lost and Found." *BR* 16, no. 3 (Fall 1988): 45-46.

Volkov, Solomon. *Balanchine's Tchaikovsky: Interviews with George Balanchine*. Translated by Antonina W. Bouis. New York: Simon & Schuster, 1985.

Wilkins, Darrell. "*The Four Temperaments*: An Interpretation." *BR* 21, no. 2 (Summer 1993): 81-87.

Youskevitch, Igor. "George Balanchine As I Knew Him." In *Society of Dance History Scholars Proceedings*, pp. 212-215. Eleventh Annual Conference, North Carolina School of the Arts, 12-14 February 1988.

COE: 35-73. DAV: 16-22. FOS: 14-23; 41-57. FRA: 44-57. GRU/2: 278-286. HAL: 162-176. HAS/1: 95-98; 105-110. HAS/2: 122-160. MCC: 107-116. MOO/1: 239-253. SCH/1: see Index of Choreographers, p. 135. SCH/2: 79-104. SOR/1: 31-40.

**Bales, William** (1910-1990)
LLO: 186-192.

**Ballard, Michael** (1942-1991)
Cunningham, Kitty, with Michael Ballard. *Conversations with a Dancer*. New York: St. Martin's Press, 1980.

**B**

**Ballon, Claude** (1676-1739; known as **Jean Balon**)
Astier, Régine. "Claude Ballon, Dancing Master to Louis XIV: A Biography." In *Society of Dance History Scholars Proceedings*, p. 170. Ninth Annual Conference, City College, City University of New York, 14-17 February 1986.

**Bannon, Kathleen** (194?– )
SID: 39-46.

**Barbarina, La** (see **Campanini, Barbara**)

**Baronova, Irina** (1919– )
Sorley Walker, Kathrine. "Irina Baronova: A Life in Ballet." *DN* 4, no. 1 (Spring 1995): 9-15, 17.
DAV: 22-25. MOO/1: 232-235.

**Barr, Margaret** (1904–1991)
von Sturmer, Caryll. *Margaret Barr: Epic Individual*. Sydney: L. von Sturmer, 1993.

**Baryshnikov, Mikhail** (1948– )
Alovert, Nina. *Baryshnikov in Russia*. Translated by Irene Huntoon. New York: Holt, Rinehart and Winston, 1984.
Aria, Barbara. *Misha: The Mikhail Baryshnikov Story*. New York: St. Martin's Press, 1989.
Barnes, Patricia, text, with photography by Louis Péres. *Mikhail Baryshnikov*. Dance Horizons Spotlight Series. Brooklyn, N.Y.: Dance Horizons, 1975.
"Baryshnikov, Mikhail (Nikolayevich)." *CBY 1975*: 26-28.
Baryshnikov, Mikhail, text, with photography by Martha Swope. *Baryshnikov at Work: Mikhail Baryshnikov Discusses His Roles.*

**Baryshnikov, Mikhail** *(continued)*

Edited and introduced by Charles Engell France. New York: Knopf, 1976.

——, Introduction and Commentaries. *Baryshnikov in Color*. Edited by Charles Engell France. With photography by Martha Swope and others. New York: Abrams, 1980.

Croce, Arlene. "Le Mystère Baryshnikov." *Vogue* (The Paris/ French-Language Edition, Décembre/Janvier 1986-87): 216-221; reprinted in Arlene Croce's *Sight Lines*, pp. 329-334. New York: Knopf, 1987.

Fraser, John. *Private View: Inside Baryshnikov's American Ballet Theatre*. New York: Bantam Books, 1988.

Garis, Robert. "Some Baryshnikov Questions." *BR* 10, no. 2 (Summer 1982): 7-13.

LeMond, Alan. *Bravo Baryshnikov!* New York: Grosset & Dunlap, 1978.

Shearer, Sybil. "About Baryshnikov." *BR* 14, no. 1 (Spring 1986): 72-74.

Smakov, Gennady. *Baryshnikov: From Russia to the West*. New York: Farrar Straus & Giroux, 1981.

Swope, Martha. *Baryshnikov on Broadway*. New York: Harmony Books, 1980.

BLA: 164-169. GRE/2: 63-72. GRU/2: 216-220. SMA: 238-252. SWI/3: 202-211.

**Bauman, Art** (1939-1993)

MCD: 283-295.

**Bausch, Pina** (1940– )

"Bausch, Pina." *CBY 1986*: 31-35.

Birringer, Johannes. "Pina Bausch: Dancing Across Borders." Chapter 6 in his *Theatre, Theory, Postmodernism*. Drama and Performance Studies. Bloomington & Indianapolis: Indiana University Press, 1991; reprinted from *TDR* 30, no. 2/T-110 (Summer 1986): 85-97.

Goldberg, Marianne. "Artifice and Authenticity: Gender Scenarios in Pina Bausch's Dance Theatre." *W&P* 4, no. 2/Issue #8 (1989): 104-117.

**Bausch, Pina** *(continued)*

Hoghe, Raimund. "The Theatre of Pina Bausch." *TDR* 24, no. 1/T-85 (March 1980): 63-74.

Kaplan, Larry. "Pina Bausch: Dancing Around the Issue." *BR* 15, no. 1 (Spring 1987): 74-77.

Kozel, Susan. "Bausch and Phenomenology." *DN* 2, no. 4 (Winter 1993-1994): 49-55.

Nugent, Ann. "*The Green Table* and *Café Müller.*" *DN* 1, no. 3 (Autumn 1992): 34-41.

Sanchez-Colberg, Ana. "'You put your left foot in, then you shake it all about . . .': Excursions and Incursions into Feminism and Bausch's Tanztheater." In *Dance, Gender and Culture*, pp. 151-163. Edited by Helen Thomas. New York: St. Martin's Press, 1993.

Servos, Norbert. *Pina Bausch Wuppertal Dance Theater: Or the Art of Training a Goldfish—Excursions into Dance.* Translated by Patricia Stadié. Cologne: Ballett-Bühnen Verlag, 1984.

Wehle, Philippa. "Pina Bausch's Tanztheater—A Place of Difficult Encounter." *W&P* 1, no. 2 (Winter 1984): 25-36.


**Beauchamps, Pierre** (1689-1761)

Astier, Régine. "Pierre Beauchamps and the Ballets de Collège." *DC* 6, no. 2 (1983): 138-163.

Kunzle, Régine. "Pierre Beauchamp: The Illustrious Unknown Choreographer." Parts One and Two. *DS* 8, no. 2 (Spring/Summer 1974): 32-42 and *DS* 9, no. 1 (Fall/Winter 1974-75): 30-45.

HAS/2: 30-44.


**Beaugrand, Léontine** (1842-1925)

Beaumont, Cyril W. "Léontine Beaugrand." In his *Three French Dancers of the 19th Century*, pp. 29-35. Essays on Dancing and Dancers, No. 9. London: C.W. Beaumont, 1935.


**Becket, Marta** (1924– )

Becket, Marta. *Death Valley Junction: The Story of the Amargosa Opera House.* Las Vegas: Nevada Publications, c. 1979.

———. *A Theatrical Portrait: Before the Amargosa Opera House* [Death Valley Junction, Nev.: the author, c. 1984].

Wilkens, Jan. "Playing All the Parts: The Exceptional Marta Becket." *Dance Teacher Now* 15, no. 9 (November/December 1993): 116-122, 124.

### Bedells, Phyllis (1893-1985)

Bedells, Phyllis. *My Dancing Days*. London: Phoenix House, 1954.

Genné, Beth. "Openly English: Phyllis Bedells and the Birth of British Ballet." *DC* 18, no. 3 (1995): 437-451.

### Béjart, Maurice (1927– )

"Béjart, Maurice." *CBY 1971*: 30-33.

*Béjart: Dancing the 20th Century*. Antwerp, Belgium: Mercatorfonds N.V., 1978. Bilingual: German/English.

Stengele, Roger, text, with photography by Robert Kayaert. *Who's Béjart*. Brussels: J. Verbeeck, n.d.

GRU/2: 181-186.

### Belair, Alida (1944– )

Belair, Alida. *Out of Step: A Dancer Reflects*. Melbourne: Melbourne University Press, 1993.

### Belcher, Ernest (1883-1973)

Prevots, Naima. "Ernest Belcher and American Dance." *DC* 10, no. 2 (1987): 170-222.

———. "Ernest Belcher: Early Visionary of American Ballet." In *Society of Dance History Scholars Proceedings*, pp. 171-181. Ninth Annual Conference, City College, City University of New York, 14-17 February 1986.

PRE: 53-113.

### Ben-David, Ehud (1939-1977)

Manor, Giora. *Ehud Ben-David: Israeli Dancer 1939-1977*. Tel-Aviv: The Israel Dance Society, 1978.

### Benesh, Rudolf (1916-1975) and Joan (1920– )

"Benesh, Rudolf (Frank) and Joan (Dorothy)." *CBY 1957*: 48-50.

Benesh, Rudolf and Joan. *An Introduction to Benesh Dance Notation*. London: A. & C. Black, 1956.

———. *Reading Dance: The Birth of Choreology*. London: Souvenir Press (Educational & Academic), 1977.

Causley, Marguerite. *An Introduction to Benesh Movement Notation: Its General Principles and its Use in Physical Education*. London: Max Parrish, 1967.

**Benesh, Rudolf** *(continued)*

Hall, Fernau. "Benesh Notation and Choreology." *DS* 3, no. 1 (Fall 1966): 30-37.

**Bennett, Tracy** (1951-1992)

GRE/3: 25-26.

**Bennington** (**Bennington School of the Dance** 1934-1939; the last year at Mills College as **Bennington School of the Arts** 1940-1941)

Belitt, Ben. "Words for Dancers, Perhaps: An Interview/Memoir on The Bennington School of the Dance." *BR* 8, nos. 2&3 (1980): 200-243.

Kriegsman, Sali Ann. *Modern Dance in America: The Bennington Years.* Boston: G.K. Hall & Co., 1981.

Martin, John, text, with photography by Thomas Bouchard. "Days of Divine Indiscipline." *DP* 12 (Autumn 1961).

Siegel, Marcia B. "A Conversation with Hanya Holm." *BR* 9, no. 1 (Spring 1981): 5-30.

SVETLANA BERIOSOVA

WITH FORTY-SIX ILLUSTRATIONS

**Bentley, Toni** (1958– )

Bentley, Toni. *Winter Season: A Dancer's Journal.* New York: Random House, 1982.

**Bergsma, Deanne** (1941– )

GRU/2: 142-146. NEW/1: 286-294.

**Beriosova, Svetlana** (1932– )

"Beriosova, Svetlana." *CBY 1960*: 30-32.

Franks, A.H. *Svetlana Beriosova: A Biography.* London: Burke, 1958; reprint New York: Da Capo Press, 1978.

**Beriosova, Svetlana** *(continued*

Swinson, Cyril. *Svetlana Beriosova*. Dancers of To-Day, No. 9. New York: Macmillan, 1956.

CRO: 151-172. DAV: 25-27. MON: 54-55.

**Berk, Fred** (1911-1980)

Ingber, Judith Brin. "Fred Berk: The Metamorphosis of a European Dancer, 1939-1949." *DC* 7, no. 1 (1984): 1-32.

――――. "Stage for Dancers: A Dance Series Organized by Fred Berk, New York, 1950-53." In *Society of Dance History Scholars Proceedings*, pp. 178-188. Eighth Annual Conference, University of New Mexico, 15-17 February 1985.

――――. *Victory Dances: The Story of Fred Berk, a Modern Day Jewish Dancing Master*. Tel-Aviv: Israel Dance Library, 1985.

――――. "The Vienna Years 1927-1939." *DRJ* 13, no. 2 (Spring 1981): 25-31.

**Bessmertnova, Natalia** (1941– )

Atlas, Helen V., text, with photography by Mira. *Natalia Bessmertnova*. Dance Horizons Spotlight Series. Brooklyn, N.Y.: Dance Horizons, 1975.

"Bessmertnova, Natalya." *CBY 1988*: 56-59.

DEM/1: 184-191. GRE/1: 20-22. SMA: 158-163. ZHD: 142-185.

**Bettis, Valerie** (1920-1982)

Amer, Rita F. "*The Desperate Heart*: A Dance of Images." *DNJ* 4, no. 1 (Spring 1986): 31-35.

"Bettis, Valerie (Elizabeth)." *CBY 1953*: 65-67.

Simpson, Herbert M. "Valerie Bettis: Looking Back." *Dance Magazine* 51, no. 2 (February 1977): 51-66. A Dance Magazine Portfolio.

LLO: 253-264. SCH/1: see Index of Choreographers, p. 135.

**Bigottini, Emilie** (1784-1858)

MIG: 93-111.

**Bilderback, Carolyn** (192?– )

Bilderback, Carolyn. *Gatherings from a Dancer's Journal*. Weston, Conn.: Magic Circle Press, 1992.

**Bintley, David** (1957– )
   Bintley, David. *"Sylvia."* *DN* 2, no. 2 (Summer 1993): 4-7, 9.
   Rigby, Cormac. *"Tombeaux."* *DN* 2, no. 1 (Spring 1993): 49-53.

**Bissell, Patrick** (1957-1988)
   Greskovic, Robert. "A Portrait of the Artist as a Young Dancer." *BR*
      8, nos. 2 & 3 (1980): 284-294.
   GRU/1: 1-16.

**Blair, David** (1932-1976)
   "Blair, David." *CBY 1961*: 57-59.

**Blangy, Hermine** (ca. 1820-ca. 1865)
   SWI/1: 273-282.

**Blasis, Carlo** (1797-1878)
   Blasis, Carlo. *An Elementary Treatise Upon the Theory and Practice
      of the Art of Dancing.* Translated with a Biographical Sketch and
      Foreword by Mary Stewart Evans. New York: Dover Publications,
      1968. An unabridged and revised edition of the third (1954)
      edition published by Kamin Dance Publishers.
   Souritz, Elizabeth. "Carlo Blasis in Russia (1861–1864)." *SDH* 4,
      no. 2 (Fall 1993).
   MOO/1: 147-154.

**Blum, Anthony** (1936– )
   GRE/3: 17-18. GRU/2: 325-331.

**Bodenwieser, Gertrud** (1890-1959)
   Bodenwieser, Gertrud. *The New Dance.* [Vaucluse, Australia, printed
      by Rondo Studios for M. Cuckson, 196-?].
   Denton, Meg Abbie, and Genevieve Shaw. "Gertrud Bodenwieser:
      *The Demon Machine.*" *DNJ* 4, no. 1 (Spring 1986): 21-29.
   Forster, Marianne. "Reconstructing European Modern Dance: Boden-
      wieser, Chladek, Leeder, Kreutzberg, Hoyer." In *Proceedings of the
      Conference "Dance Reconstructed: Modern Dance Art Past, Present,
      Future,"* pp. 137-149. Rutgers University, New Brunswick, New
      Jersey, October 16 and 17, 1992.

**Bodenwieser, Gertrud** *(continued)*

Grayburn, Patricia, ed. *Gertrud Bodenwieser: A Celebratory Monograph on the 100th Anniversary of her Birth.* Guildford, Surrey: University of Surrey, 1990.

MacTavish, Shona Dunlop. *An Ecstasy of Purpose: The Life and Art of Gertrud Bodenwieser.* Dunedin, N.Z.: Published by Shona Dunlop MacTavish, Les Humphrey and Associates, 1987.

**Bogatyrev, Alexander** (1949– )

ZHD: 292-299.

**Bogdanova, Nadezhda** (1836-1897)

WIL: 185-213.

**Bolender, Todd** (1914– )

Hastings, Baird. "Todd Bolender." *Chrysalis* 3, nos. 5-6 (1950): 11-15. Issue title: "Three Choreographers."

MAS: 177-181.

**Bolm, Adolph** (1884-1951)

Beaumont, Cyril. "Adolf Bolm." In *The Ballet Annual 1952: A Record and Year Book of the Ballet*, pp. 54-55. Edited by Arnold L. Haskell. Sixth Issue. New York: Macmillan, n.d.

Dougherty, John. "Perspective on Adolph Bolm." Parts One; Two; and Three. *Dance Magazine* 37, no. 1 (January 1963): 44-50; *Dance Magazine* 37, no. 2 (February 1963): 44-47, 58-59; and *Dance Magazine* 37, no. 3 (March 1963): 50-53.

BEL: 12-19. PAG: 12-23. PRE: 153-172.

**Bonfanti, Maria** (1847-1921)

Barker, Barbara. "Maria Bonfanti." Part 4 in her *Ballet or Ballyhoo: The American Careers of Maria Bonfanti, Rita Sangalli, and Giuseppina Morlacchi*, pp. 169-227. New York: Dance Horizons, 1984.

**Bonnefous, Jean-Pierre** (1943– )

GRE/3: 8-10. GRU/2: 349-352. NEW/1: 328-344.

**Booth, Laurie** (1954– )

Booth, Laurie. "The Making of *River Run.*" In *Parallel Structures: Art, Dance, Music*, pp. 60-61. Guest edited by Clare Farrow. Art & Design Profile No. 33. London: Academy Editions, 1993.

Briginshaw, Valerie. "Approaches to New Dance: An Analysis of Two Works." An analysis of Laurie Booth's *Manipulatin' Motion (Pictures)* (1981) in Chapter 9 of *Dance Analysis: Theory and Practice*, pp. 170-178. Edited by Janet Adshead. London: Dance Books, 1988.

**Boris, Ruthanna** (1918– )

ATK: 16-18. MAS: 159-162. TRA: 64-69.

**Börlin, Jean** (1893-1930)

Baer, Nancy Van Norman, ed. *Paris Modern: The Swedish Ballet, 1920-1925.* San Francisco: The Fine Arts Museums of San Francisco, 1995. The catalogue of the eponymous exhibition held at The Museum at the Fashion Institute of Technology, New York City, October 10, 1995-January 13, 1996; McNay Art Museum, San Antonio, Texas, February 12, 1996-May 19, 1996; and California Palace of the Legion of Honor, San Francisco, June 15, 1996-September 9, 1996.

Banes, Sally. "An Introduction to the Ballets Suédois." *BR* 7, nos. 2&3 (1978-1979): 28-59.

Häger, Bengt. *Ballets Suédois (The Swedish Ballet).* New York: Abrams, 1990.

HAL: 135-138.

**Borovansky, Edouard** (1902-1959)

Salter, Frank. *Borovansky: The Man Who Made Australian Ballet.* Sydney: Wildcate Press, 1980.

**Bortoluzzi, Paolo** (1938-1993)

GRU/2: 202-206.

**Bournonville, Antoine** (1760-1843)

Bournonville, Antoine. "Antoine Bournonville's Diaries from 1792." Parts One and Two. Edited and translated from the original

**Bournonville, Antoine** *(continued)*

French to Danish by Julius Clausen. Translated from the Danish to English by Leslie Getz. *BR* 2, no. 6 (1969): 3-21 and *BR* 3, no. 1 (1969): 56-70.

Lawson, William James. "Antoine Bournonville." In *Stern's Performing Arts Directory 1992*, p. D-7. Edited by William James Lawson. New York: Robert D. Stern/Dance Magazine, 1991.

**Bournonville, August** (1805-1879)

Aschengreen, Erik. "August Bournonville: A Ballet-Poet Among Poets." Translated by Patricia N. McAndrew. *DRA IX* (1978): 3-21.

——. "The Beautiful Danger: Facets of the Romantic Ballet." *DP* 58 (Summer 1974). "August Bournonville and the Romantic Ballet in Denmark," pp. 33-50.

——. "Bournonville Style and Tradition." *DR* 4, no. 1 (Spring 1986): 45-62.

——. "Bournonville: Yesterday, Today, and Tomorrow." Translated by Henry Godfrey. *DC* 3, no. 2 (1979): 102-151.

Bournonville, August. "The Ballet Poems of August Bournonville: The Complete Scenarios." Translated by Patricia McAndrew. Parts One, Two, Three, Four, Five, Six, Six [i.e., Seven], Eight, Nine, Ten, Appendix One, and Appendix Two. *DC* 3, no. 2 (1979): 165-219; *DC* 3, no. 3 (1979-80): 285-324; *DC* 3, no. 4 (1979-80): 435-475; *DC* 4, no. 1 (1981): 46-75; *DC* 4, no. 2 (1981): 155-193; *DC* 4, no. 3 (1981): 297-322; *DC* 4, no. 4 (1981): 402-451; *DC* 5, no. 1 (1982): 50-97; *DC* 5, no. 2 (1982): 213-230; *DC* 5, no. 3 (1982-83): 320-348; *DC* 5, no. 4 (1982-83): 438-460; and *DC* 6, no. 1 (1983): 52-78.

——. *My Theatre Life*. Translated from the Danish by Patricia N. McAndrew. Middletown, Conn.: Wesleyan University Press, 1979.

**Bournonville, August** *(continued)*

——. "The Tenth of May, 1826." Translated by Henry Godfrey. *DC* 3, no. 2 (1979): 97-101.

*Bournonville Ballet Technique: Fifty Enchaînements.* Selected and Reconstructed by Vivi Flindt and Knud Arne Jürgensen. London: Dance Books, 1992. Appendix I: Complete Transcription of Hans Beck's Skole Pas (1893). Appendix II: The Bournonville School 1893-1979: A Survey of the Music and Choreographic Sources. A video, also titled *Bournonville Ballet Technique: Fifty Enchaînements*, was issued in conjunction with this book in the U.S. in VHS format and in England in VHS (PAL) format. Running time 44 minutes. Color. Produced by Jacob Mydtskov. Features Rose Gad and Johan Kobborg of the Royal Danish Ballet, with music played by pianist Julian Thurber.

*Bournonville Ballet Technique: Piano Scores.* Compiled and arranged by Knud Arne Jürgensen. London: Dance Books, 1992.

"The Bournonville Centenary 1879-1979." *Dance Magazine* 53, no. 11 (November 1979). A five-part Dance Magazine Portfolio. August Bournonville, translated by Henry Godfrey. "The Choreographic Musings of August Bournonville from *The Danish Ballet*, 1876" (pp. 67-71). Iris M. Fanger. "The Royal Danish Ballet's Kirsten Ralov: Keeping the Bournonville Tradition" (pp. 71-77). Selma Jeanne Cohen. "Bournonville and the Question of Preservation" (pp. 77-78). David Vaughan. "Books on Bournonville: His Life [*My Theatre Life*]" (pp. 79-80). Rose Anne Thom. "Books on Bournonville: His Technique [*The Bournonville Technique*, Kirsten Ralov, Editor]" (p. 80).

*The Bournonville School.* Kirsten Ralov, ed. 4 Parts. The Dance Program, Vol. 12. New York & Basel: Audience Arts/A Division of Marcel Dekker, 1979. Part 1: "The Daily Classes: Technique, Exercises, Combinations." Text by Kirsten Ralov. Foreword by Walter Terry. Edited by Sandra Caverly. Part 2: "Music." Arranged by Harald Agersnap. Recorded by Poul Gnatt. Part 3: "Benesh Notation." Recorded by Sandra Caverly, as demonstrated by Kirsten Ralov. Part 4: "Labanotation." Recorded by Ann Hutchinson Guest, as demonstrated by Kirsten Ralov.

Bruhn, Erik, and Lillian Moore. *Bournonville and Ballet Technique: Studies and Comments on August Bournonville's "études choréographiques."* London: Adam & Charles Black; New York: Macmillan, 1961.

**Bournonville, August** *(continued)*

Christensen, Charlotte, Bjarne Jørnaes, and Ole Nørlyng. *Billedhuggeren og Balletmesteren: Om Thorvaldsen og Bournonvilles Kunst* [Sculptor and Balletmaster: About Thorvaldsen and Bournonville's Art]. Copenhagen: Thorvaldsens Museum, 1992. With English translation by Gaye Kynoch of the three major essays.

"A Chronology of Bournonville's Stage Works: Ballets and Divertissements, Individual Dances, and Stagings of Operas and Plays." Patricia McAndrew, comp. *DC* 3, no. 2 (1979): 167-178.

Cunningham, Kitty. "Watching Bournonville." *BR* 4, no. 6 (1974): 24-31.

Guest, Ann Hutchinson, ed. *"The Flower Festival in Genzano": Pas de Deux*. Language of Dance Series, No. 1. New York: Gordon and Breach, 1987.

Hallar, Marianne, and Alette Scavenius, eds. *Bournonvilleana*. Translated by Gaye Kynoch. Copenhagen: The Royal Theatre in coöperation with Rhodos, 1992. There is also a Danish-language edition of this work.

Haslam, Henley. "Notes on *Konservatoriet*: How to Perform Bournonville." *BR* 2, no. 6 (1969): 21-24.

Horosko, Marian. "Bournonville's Joys—Briefly." *BR* 16, no. 3 (Fall 1988): 62-66.

Jürgensen, Knud Arne, comp. *The Bournonville Ballets: A Photographic Record 1844-1933*. London: Dance Books, 1987. Includes extensive annotations to the photographs by Knud Arne Jürgensen.

———. "Is the *Flower Festival Pas de Deux* by Bournonville and Paulli?" *DR* 12, no. 2 (Autumn 1994): 66-113.

———. "New Light on Bournonville." *DC* 4, no. 3 (1981): 264-278.

LaPointe, Janice Deane McCaleb. "Birth of a Ballet: Bournonville's *A Folk Tale*, 1854." Unpublished dissertation, Texas Woman's University, 1980. Ann Arbor, Mich.: University Microfilms International, 1981. Order No. 811,0522. DAI 41-12A, p. 4888.

———. "Creative Integration: A Selective Study of August Bournonville and His Musical Collaborators." *DRA XVI* (1987): 87-97.

McAndrew, Patricia. "Bournonville: Citizen and Artist." *DC* 3, no. 2 (1979): 152-164.

Moore, Lillian. *Bournonville's London Spring*. New York: New York Public Library, 1965.

**Bournonville, August** *(continued)*

Mørk, Ebbe, ed. *Salut for Bournonville: i 100-året for hans dod* [Salute to Bournonville on the 100th Anniversary of his Death]. Copenhagen: Statens Museum for Kunst, [1979]. Bilingual: Danish/English.

Nørlyng, Ole, and Henning Urup, eds. *Bournonville: Tradition - Rekonstruktion*. Copenhagen: Reitzels Forlag, 1989. Many of the articles in this book are given in English summary.

Sayers, Lesley-Anne. "Bournonville Our Contemporary." *DN* 1, no. 4 (Winter 1992-1993): 58-63.

Smuin, Michael. "On Reading Bournonville." *DS* 14, no. 2 (Winter 1980): 7-13.

Terry, Walter. *The King's Ballet Master: A Biography of Denmark's August Bournonville*. New York: Dodd, Mead & Company, 1979.

*Theatre Research Studies II*. Copenhagen: The Institute for Theatre Research, The University of Copenhagn, 1972. [On cover: *Teatervidenskabelige Studier II*]. A collection of six articles on different aspects of Bournonville's work.

Waren, Florence. "Petipa and Bournonville: Ballet Seminar at Varna." *PAJ* 2, no. 3 (Winter 1978): 85-93.

HAS/2: 90-96.

**Bowman, Patricia** (1908– )

Gruen, John. "Patricia Bowman." *Dance Magazine* 50, no. 10 (October 1976): 47-62. A Dance Magazine Portfolio.

Ware, Walter. "Patricia Bowman." In his *Ballet Is Magic: A Triple Monograph*, pp. 37-52. New York: IHRA Publishing Company, 1936.

BEL: 20-23. GRU/1: 145-157.

**Boyarchikov, Nikolai** (1935– )

McDonagh, Don, and Catherine Edmunds. "A Conversation with Nikolai Boyarchikov." *BR* 20, no. 4 (Winter 1992): 58-63.

Skliarevskaia, Inna. "Introducing Nikolai Boyarchikov." *BR* 20, no. 4 (Winter 1992): 52-57.

**Boyce, Johanna** (1954– )

Boyce, Johanna. "Three Dances." *DS* 14, no. 4 (December 1980): 47-50. The three dances are *Tracings*, *Ghost Dance*, and *Pass*.

Martin, Carol. "Johanna Boyce: An Interview." *DS* 14, no. 4 (December 1980): 35-46.

**Bozzacchi, Giuseppina** (1853-1870)

Guest, Ivor. *The Ballet of the Second Empire 1858-1870*. London: Adam & Charles Black, 1953.

**Brae, June** (1917– )

DAV: 28-29.

**Brangwen** (see **Vernon, Barbara**)

**Bravo, Guillermina** (1920– )

Dallal, Alberto. "Death in the Work of Guillermina Bravo." In *Society of Dance History Scholars Proceedings*, pp. 29-36. Seventh Annual Conference, Goucher College, Towson, Maryland, 17-19 February 1984.

**Brenaa, Hans** (1910-1988)

Schønberg, Bent. *Hans Brenaa: Danish Ballet Master*. Translated by Joan Tate. Edited by Jeff Groman. London: Dance Books, 1990.

**Briansky, Oleg** (1929– )

Newberry, Joyce A. "The Briansky School." *DS* 14, no. 2 (Winter 1980): 48-53.

**Brown, Ronald** (1954– )

SWI/3: 180-184.

**Brown, Trisha** (1936– )

Brown, Trisha, and Douglas Dunn. "Dialogue: On Dance." *PAJ* 1, no. 2 (Fall 1976): 76-83.

———. "Three Pieces." *TDR* 19, no. 1/T-65 (March 1975): 26-32. The three pieces are *Roof*, *Primary Accumulation*, and *Drift*.

Goldberg, Marianne. "Trisha Brown: All of the Person's Person Arriving." *TDR* 30, no. 1/T-109 (Spring 1986): 149-170.

Sears, David. "A Trisha Brown - Robert Rauschenberg Collage." *BR* 10, no. 3 (Fall 1982): 47-51.

Sommer, Sally. "Equipment Dances: Trisha Brown." *TDR* 16, no. 3/T-55 (September 1972): 135-141.

———. "Trisha Brown Making Dances." *DS* 11, no. 2 (Spring/Summer 1977): 7-18.

**Brown, Trisha** *(continued)*

Sulzman, Mona. "Choice/Form in Trisha Brown's *Locus*: A View from Inside the Cube." *DC* 2, no. 2 (1978): 117-130.

"Trisha Brown: An Informal Performance." In *Breakthroughs: Avant-Garde Artists in Europe and America, 1950-1990*, pp. 246-251. Wexner Center for the Arts, The Ohio State University, [Columbus]. New York: Rizzoli, 1991.

Vail, June. "Moving Bodies, Moving Souls: Trisha Brown Company in Stockholm, 1989." In *Society of Dance History Scholars Proceedings*, pp. 187-199. Fifteenth Annual Conference, University of California, Riverside, 14-15 February 1992.

Wynne, Peter. *Judson Dance: An Annotated Bibliography of the Judson Dance Theater and of Five Major Choreographers— Trisha Brown, Lucinda Childs, Deborah Hay, Steve Paxton, and Yvonne Rainer.* Englewood, N.J.: author, May 1978. BAN: 76-95. BRO: 162-171. LIV: 42-57.

**Brown, Vida** (1922– )
MAS: 367-369.

**Bruce, Christopher** (1945– )

Kane, Angela. "Christopher Bruce's Choreography: Inroads or Re-tracing Old Steps?" *Dancing Times* 82, no. 973 (October 1991): 44-47, 49, 51, 53. A Dance Study Supplement.

Nugent, Ann. "Waiting with Certainty." *DN* 2, no. 3 (Autumn 1993): 18-21.

**Bruhn, Erik** (1928-1986)

Bivona, Elena. "Bruhn: Star Trip." *BR* 2, no. 3 (September-October 1968): 15-22.

"Bruhn, Erik (Belton Evers)." *CBY 1959*: 51-53.

**Bruhn, Erik** *(continued)*

Bruhn, Erik. "Restaging the Classics." In *American Ballet Theatre*, pp. 317-332, by Charles Payne. New York: Knopf, 1978.

——, text, with photography by Fred Fehl. "Beyond Technique." *DP* 36 (Winter 1968).

——, and Lillian Moore. *Bournonville and Ballet Technique: Studies and Comments on August Bournonville's "études chorégraphiques."* London: Adam & Charles Black; New York: Macmillan, 1961.

Gruen, John. *Erik Bruhn: Danseur Noble*. New York: Viking, 1979.

BLA: 132-136. GRU/1: 121-124. GRU/2: 268-277.

**Brusock, James** (ca. 1938– )

SID: 47-54.

**Buckeridge, Dorothy** (1922– )

Nesbitt, Dorothy Buckeridge. *Scrapbook of a Dancer*. Wrightsville Beach, N.C.: the author, 1988.

**Bujones, Fernando** (1955– )

"Bujones, Fernando." *CBY 1976*: 64-67.

Bujones, Fernando. *Fernando Bujones*. Rio de Janeiro: Imprinta Gráfica e Editora, 1984. Bilingual: Spanish/English.

PET: 178-197.

**Butcher, Rosemary** (1947– )

Butcher, Rosemary. "What Is Dance?" *DN* 1, no. 2 (Summer 1992): 18-19, 21.

JOR: 160-181; 231-232.

**Butler, John** (1918-1993)

"Butler, John." *CBY 1955*: 87-88.

Carlsen, Peter, text, with photography by Richard Champion. "The Collectors: John Butler in New York." *Architectural Digest* 34, no. 4 (May/June 1977): 74-79.

Victor, Thomas. *The Making of a Dance: Mikhail Baryshnikov and Carla Fracci in "Medea."* Choreographed by John Butler. New York: Holt, Rinehart and Winston, c. 1976.

SCH/1: see Index of Choreographers, p. 135.

**Caccialanza, Gisella** (1914– )

Cecchetti, Enrico. "Letters from the Maestro: Enrico Cecchetti to Gisella Caccialanza." Translated by Gisella Caccialanza. Edited by Sally Bailey. *DP* 45 (Spring 1971).

**Caffinière, Alexandre de la** (1971– )

Kanter, Katharine. "A Higher Degree of Freedom." *DN* 2, no. 3 (Autumn 1993): 62-67.

**Calegari, Maria** (1957– )

SWI/3: 159-162.

**Callaghan, Domini** (1923– )

DAV: 29-31.

**Camargo, Marie** (1710-1770)

Beaumont, Cyril. "La Camargo." In his *Three French Dancers of the 18th Century*, pp. 9-17. Essays on Dancing and Dancers, No. 6. London: C.W. Beaumont, 1934.

Montagu-Nathan, M. *Mlle Camargo*. Artists of the Dance. London: British-Continental Press, 1932.

Vince, Stanley W.E. "Camargo in London, 1750-1754." *Theatre Notebook* 12, no. 4 (Summer 1958): 117-126.

MIG: 31-38. MOO/1: 21-29.

**Campanini, Barbara** (1721-1799; known as **La Barbarina**)

MIG: 39-45.

**Campbell, Marian Van Tuyl** (see **Van Tuyl, Marian**)

**Camryn, Walter** (1903-1984)
PAG: 60-63.

**Caras, Stephen** (1950– )
GRE/3: 27.

**Carlson, Carolyn** (1943– )
Turnbull, Ann Veronica. "Carolyn Carlson's Years at Il Teatro La Fenice, Venice, Italy, 1980-84: A Unique Experiment on the Italian Dance Scene." In *Society of Dance History Scholars Proceedings*, pp. 85-114. Fifteenth Annual Conference, University of California, Riverside, 14-15 February 1992.

**Caron, Leslie** (1931– )
"Caron, Leslie." *CBY 1954*: 157-158.
ATK: 19-22. MCC: 95-106.

**Caroso, Fabritio** (b. ca. 1553; orig. **F.C. de Sermoneta**)
Gelernter, Judith. "Mannerist Aesthetics in the Court Dance of Fabritio Caroso." In *Society of Dance History Scholars Proceedings*, pp. 129-139. Seventeenth Annual Conference, Brigham Young University, Provo, Utah, 10-13 February 1994.

**Carter, Jack** (1923– )
Jackson, Frank, text, with photography by Paul Wilson. "Jack Carter." In his *They Make Tomorrow's Ballet: A Study of the Work of Jack Carter, Michael Charnley, John Cranko*, pp. 1-8. London: Meridian Books, 1953.

**Carter, William** (1936-1988)
Tobias, Tobi. "Bill Carter: An Interview." *Dance Magazine* 49, no. 5 (May 1975): 43-58. A Dance Magazine Portfolio.

**Castelli, Victor** (1952– )
GRE/3: 24.

## Cecchetti, Enrico (1850-1928)

Beaumont, Cyril. *Enrico Cecchetti: His Legacy to the Dance*. London: Cecchetti Society Branch of the Imperial Society of Teachers of Dancing, n.d.

——. *Enrico Cecchetti: A Memoir*. London: C.W. Beaumont, 1929.

——. *A Primer of Classical Ballet for Children* (Cecchetti Method). Rev. ed. London: C.W. Beaumont, 1971.

——. *A Second Primer of Classical Ballet for Children* (Cecchetti Method). Rev. and enl. ed. London: C.W. Beaumont, 1973.

——. *A Third Primer of Classical Ballet for Children* (Cecchetti Method). With ten dances variously arranged by Eleanor Banks, Margaret Craske, Margaret Saul, Peggy van Praagh & Laura Wilson. Rev. ed. London: C.W. Beaumont, 1971.

——, and Stanislas Idzikowski. *A Manual of the Theory and Practice of Classical Theatrical Dancing* (Classical Ballet) (Cecchetti Method). Preface by Maestro Cav. Enrico Cecchetti. Rev. ed. by Cyril W. Beaumont. London: C.W. Beaumont, 1947.

Cecchetti, Enrico. "Letters from the Maestro: Enrico Cecchetti to Gisella Caccialanza." Translated by Gisella Caccialanza. Edited by Sally Bailey. *DP* 45 (Spring 1971).

Celli, Vincenzo. "Enrico Cecchetti." *DI* 5, no. 7 (July 1946).

Craske, Margaret, and Derra de Moroda. *The Theory and Practice of Advanced Allegro in Classical Ballet* (Cecchetti Method). Edited and with a Preface by Cyril Beaumont. Rev. ed. London: C.W. Beaumont, 1971.

——, and Cyril W. Beaumont. *The Theory and Practice of Allegro in Classical Ballet* (Cecchetti Method). London: C.W. Beaumont, 1968.

Imperial Society of Teachers of Dancing, Cecchetti Society Branch. *The Cecchetti Society*. London: The Dancing Times, June 1959 (A *Dancing Times* Supplement).

Poesio, Giannandrea. "Enrico Cecchetti: The Influence of Tradition." Chapter 8 in *Dance History: An Introduction*, pp. 117-131. Edited by Janet Adshead-Lansdale and June Layson. 2d ed., rev. and updated. London & New York: Routledge, 1994.

Racster, Olga. *The Master of the Russian Ballet: The Memoirs of Cav. Enrico Cecchetti*. Introduction by Anna Pavlova. London: Hutchinson & Co., [1922]; reprint New York: Da Capo Press, 1978.

DAV: 31-34. MOO/1: 176-182. MOO/2: 131-140. PAG: 24-29.

**Celeste, Mme** (see **Keppler, Celeste**)

**Cerrito, Fanny** (1817-1909)

Guest, Ivor. *Fanny Cerrito: The Life of a Romantic Ballerina.* London: Phoenix House, 1956.

"Le Quatuor dansè [i.e., dansé] à Londres par Taglioni, Charlotte Grisi, Cerrito et Fanny Elsler [sic]." *DI* 3, nos. 7-8 (July- August 1944). Portion on Cerrito, pp. 102, 120-123.

GUE: 23-29. MIG: 208-222. MOO/1: 136-146.

**Chabukiani, Vakhtang** (1910-1992)

SLO: 103-106. SMA: 313-321.

**Chaib, Elie** (1950– )

Newman, Barbara. "A Conversation with Elie Chaib." *BR* 19, no. 2 (Summer 1991): 81-90.

**Chappell, William** (1908-1994)

DAV: 34-37.

**Charlip, Remy** (1929– )

SIE: 38-43.

**Charnley, Michael** (1927– )

Jackson, Frank, text, with photography by Paul Wilson. "Michael Charnley." In his *They Make Tomorrow's Ballet: A Study of the Work of Jack Carter, Michael Charnley, John Cranko,* pp. 9-17. London: Meridian Books, 1953.

**Chase, Lucia** (1897-1986)

"Chase, Lucia." *CBY 1947*: 103-104.

"Chase, Lucia." *CBY 1975*: 71-74.

Louis, Murray. "Lucia Chase (1907-1986)." In *Murray Louis on Dance,* pp. 87-89. [Pennington, N.J.]: A Cappella Books, 1992.

"Lucia Chase Remembered." *BR* 18, no. 1 (Spring 1990): 54-66. Reminiscences by Oliver Smith, Sono Osato, Irina Baronova, Alicia Alonso, Nancy Zeckendorf, Morton Gould, Anna Kisselgoff, Mikhail Baryshnikov, Cynthia Gregory, Jerome Robbins, Eliot Feld, Dame Alicia Markova, Antony Tudor, Agnes de Mille, and Alexander Ewing.

**Chase, Lucia** *(continued)*

Payne, Charles. *American Ballet Theatre*. New York: Knopf, 1978. With contributions by Alicia Alonso, Erik Bruhn, Lucia Chase, and Nora Kaye.

GRU/1: 73-78.

**Chatfield, Philip** (1927– )

Swinson, Cyril. *Rowena Jackson and Philip Chatfield*. Dancers of To-Day, [No. 15]. London: Adam & Charles Black, 1958.

**C**

**Chauviré, Yvette** (1917– )

Chauviré, Yvette. "Career of a Ballerina Assoluta." In *Souvenirs de Ballet*, pp. 68-71. Edited by Duncan Melvin. London: Mayfair Publications, 1949.

Nemenschousky, Léon. *A Day with Yvette Chauviré*. London: Cassell & Company, 1960.

ATK: 23-27. DAV: 37-40. SWI/2: 54-56.

**Chen, Si-lan** (191?– )

Leyda, Si-lan Chen. *Footnote to History*. Edited by Sally Banes. New York: Dance Horizons, 1984.

**Childs, Lucinda** (1940– )

"Childs, Lucinda." *CBY 1984*: 75-78.

Childs, Lucinda. "Notes: '64 - '74." *TDR* 19, no. 1/T-65 (March 1975): 33-36.

Chin, Daryl, text, with dance notations by Lucinda Childs. "Talking with Lucinda Childs." *DS* 13, nos. 2&3 (Winter/Spring 1979): 70-81.

Wynne, Peter. *Judson Dance: An Annotated Bibliography of the Judson Dance Theater and of Five Major Choreographers—Trisha Brown, Lucinda Childs, Deborah Hay, Steve Paxton, and Yvonne Rainer*. Englewood, N.J.: author, May 1978.

BAN: 132-147. KRE: 94-109. LIV: 58-75.

**Chong, Ping** (1946– )

Carroll, Noël. "A Select View of Earthlings: Ping Chong (United States)." *TDR* 27, no. 1/T-97 (Spring 1983): 72-81.

Moynihan, D.S. "Ping Chong's *Nuit Blanche.*" *TDR* 25, no. 1/T-89 (March 1981): 101-105.

**Chouteau, Yvonne** (1929– )

ATK: 28-30.

**Christensen, Lew** (1909-1984)

MAY/1: 217-227. NEW/1: 28-42.

SCH/1: see Index of Choreographers, p. 135.

**Christensen, Willam** (1902– )

Dorris, George. "Willam Christensen Reminisces." In *Society of Dance History Scholars Proceedings*, p. 148. Twelfth Annual Conference, Arizona State University, 17-19 February 1989.

**Christensen Brothers (Willam** 1902– , **Harold** 1904-1989, and **Lew** 1909-1984)

Maynard, Olga. "The Christensens: An American Dance Dynasty." *Dance Magazine* 47, no. 6 (June 1973): 43-58. A Dance Magazine Portfolio.

**Chryst, Gary** (1949– )

GRU/2: 410-414.

**Chuma, Yoshiko** (1950– )

Fleming, Donald. "Yoshiko Chuma and the School of Hard Knocks." *TDR* 29, no. 2/T-106 (Summer 1985): 53-64.

**Cisneros, Evelyn** (1958– )

Simon, Charman. *Evelyn Cisernos: Prima Ballerina.* Chicago: Childrens Press, 1990.

**Clark, Michael** (1962– )

Glasstone, Richard. "Michael Clark's Use of Ballet Technique." *DN* 3, no. 4 (Winter 1994): 63-67.

## Clark, Michael *(continued)*

Nugent, Ann. "Dream Ticket." *DN* 3, no. 2 (Summer 1994): 16-23.

Parry, Jann. *"Mmm . . .* Michael Clark." *DN* 1, no. 2 (Summer 1992): 28-31, 33.

## Clarke, Martha (1944– )

"Clarke, Martha." *CBY 1989*: 114-117.

Jacobson, Daniel. "Martha Clarke's Imaginary Gardens." *BR* 12, no. 4 (Winter 1985): 8-14.

Kendall, Elizabeth, and Don Daniels. "A Conversation with Martha Clarke." *BR* 12, no. 4 (Winter 1985): 15-25.

## Clayton, Bessie (1878-1948)

Hardy, Camille. "Bessie Clayton: An American Genée." *DC* 2, no. 4 (1978-79): 251-278.

## Clifford, John (1947– )

"Clifford, John." *CBY 1972*: 79-81.

France, Charles Engell. "A Conversation with John Clifford." *BR* 4, no. 1 (1971): 3-33.

GRU/2: 359-364. MAS: 549-561. ROG: 149-168.

## Cohen, Yardena (191?– )

Ingber, Judith Brin. "The Priestesses." *DC* 18, no. 3 (1995): 453-465.

## Cole, Jack (1913-1974)

Loney, Glenn. *Unsung Genius: The Passion of Dancer-Choreographer Jack Cole*. New York & London: Franklin Watts, 1984.

Sotheby Parke Bernet & Co., London. *Catalogue of the Jack Cole Collection of Books and Pictures on the Dance*. 2 vols. London: Sotheby Parke Bernet & Co., 1979. Catalogue of a public auction, the property of John David Gray. Part I: Monday, 16th July 1979, and Tuesday, 17th July 1979. Part II: Monday, 12th November 1979.

SCH/1: see Index of Choreographers, p. 135.

## Coleman, Michael (1940– )

GRU/2: 147-152.

**Collier, Lesley** (1947– )

Nugent, Ann. "Images, Changes and Joy . . ." *DN*, no. 2 (Summer 1994): 2-3, 5-11.

**Collins, Richard** (1945-1991)

Collins, Richard. *Behind the Bolshoi Curtain.* London: William Kimber, 1974.

**Conrad, Gail** (1952– )

KRE: 230-249.

**Conrad, Karen** (1919-1976)

BEL: 24-27.

**Cook, Bart** (1949– )

GRE/3: 23-24.

**Coquillard, Albertine** (182?-1846; née **Albertine Constance Albrier**)

Guest, Ivor. "The Adventures of Albertine." In *The Ballet Annual 1963: A Record and Year Book of the Ballet*, pp. 49-54. Edited by Arnold L. Haskell and Mary Clarke. Seventeenth Issue. London: Adam & Charles Black, n.d.

**Corkle, Francesca** (1952– )

GRU/2: 404-409.

**Coronelli, Pietro** (1825-1902)

Ruyter, Nancy Lee Chalfa, with Hans C. Ruyter. "Pietro Coronelli: Dance Master of Zagreb." *DR* 7, no. 1 (Spring 1989): 78-83.

**Craft, Ben** (1963– )

Nugent, Ann. "A Craftsman in the Market Place." *DN* 3, no. 2 (Summer 1994): 48-54.

**Cragun, Richard** (1944– )

BLA: 156-159.

**Cranko, John** (1927-1973)

"Cranko, John." *CBY 1970*: 102-105.

Croce, Arlene. "John Cranko (1927-1973)." *BR* 4, no. 5 (1973): 101.

Jackson, Frank, text, with photography by Paul Wilson. "John Cranko." In his *They Make Tomorrow's Ballet: A Study of the Work of Jack Carter, Michael Charnley, John Cranko*, pp. 18-29. London: Meridian Books, 1953.

Percival, John. *Theatre in My Blood: A Biography of John Cranko*. London: The Herbert Press, 1983.

The Royal Ballet, London. *A Tribute to John Cranko*, Sadler's Wells Theatre, 3 October 1973. Souvenir program.

Williams, Peter. "John Cranko: Development of a Choreographer." In *The Ballet Annual 1954: A Record and Year Book of the Ballet*, pp. 90-95. Edited by Arnold L. Haskell. Eighth Issue. New York: Macmillan, n.d.

DAV: 40-41. FRA: 199-207. GRU/2: 169-175. HAL: 252-258.

**Craske, Margaret** (1898-1990)

Craske, Margaret. *The Dance of Love: My Life with Meher Baba*. North Myrtle Beach, S.C.: Sheriar Press, 1980.

———. *Still Dancing with Love: More Stories of Life with Meher Baba*. Myrtle Beach, S.C.: Sheriar Press, 1990.

———, and Cyril W. Beaumont. *The Theory and Practice of Allegro in Classical Ballet*. (Cecchetti Method). London: C.W. Beaumont, 1930.

———, and Friderica Derra de Moroda. *The Theory and Practice of Advanced Allegro in Classical Ballet*. (Cecchetti Method). Edited and with a Preface by Cyril Beaumont. rev. ed. London: Imperial Society of Teachers of Dancing, 1979.

GAL: 1-7.

**Crespé, Marie-Madeleine** (1760-1798)

MIG: 65-70.

**Cullberg, Birgit** (1908– )

"Cullberg, Birgit." *CBY 1982*: 75-78.

Cullberg, Birgit. "Ballet: Flight and Reality." Translated by Laura de la Torre Bueno. *DP* 29 (Spring 1967).

SOR/2: 169-176.

**Cummings, Blondell** (1948– )

Dixon-Stowell, Brenda. "Blondell Cummings: *The Ladies and Me.*" *TDR* 24, no. 4/T-88 (December 1980): 37-44.

**Cunningham, James** (1938– )

Carter, Curtis L. "A Dance-Choreographer Speaks: An Interview with James Cunningham." *Arts in Society* 13, no. 2 (Summer-Fall 1976): 256-261. Issue title: "Growth of Dance in America."

McGarrigle, Kevin. "Profile of a Choreographer." *YDR* [Issue #1] (Spring 1973): 12-13.

**Cunningham, Merce** (1919– )

Adam, Judy, ed. *Dancers on a Plane: Cage, Cunningham, Johns.* Contributions by Susan Sontag, Richard Francis, Mark Rosenthal, Anne Seymour, David Sylvester, and David Vaughan. London: Thames & Hudson, in association with Anthony d'Offay Gallery; New York: Knopf, 1990.

Anderson, Jack. "Dances About Everything and Dances About Some Things." *BR* 5, no. 4 (1975-1976): 56-60.

Banes, Sally. "Merce Cunningham's *Story.*" In *Society of Dance History Scholars Proceedings*, pp. 111-125. Twelfth Annual Conference, Arizona State University, 17-19 February 1989.

Brown, Carolyn. "On Chance." *BR* 2, no. 2 (1968): 7-25.

Brubach, Holly. "Cunningham Now." *BR* 6, no. 2 (1977-1978): 79-85.

Byrum, Mary Carolyn. "An Analysis of Three Non-Objective Choreographic Techniques." Unpublished dissertation, University of North Carolina at Greensboro, 1976. Ann Arbor, Mich.: University Microfilms International, 1976. Order No. 76-24,939. DAI 37-05A, p. 2716.

Cage, John. "Notes on Cunningham Choreography (1954-62)" and "Three Asides on the Dance (1959)." In *John Cage: Writer*, pp. 67-69 and 83-85. Previously uncollected pieces, selected and introduced by Richard Kostelanetz. New York: Limelight Editions, 1993.

Carroll, Noël, and Sally Banes. "Cunningham and Duchamp." *BR* 11, no. 2 (Summer 1983): 73-79.

Copeland, Roger. "Beyond Expressionism: Merce Cunningham's

**Cunningham, Merce** *(continued)*

Critique of 'The Natural.'" Chapter 12 in *Dance History: An Introduction*, pp. 182-197. Edited by Janet Adshead-Lansdale and June Layson. 2d ed., rev. and updated. London & New York: Routledge, 1994.

[Croce, Arlene]. "An Interview with Merce Cunningham." *BR* 1, no. 4 (1966): 3-6.

"Cunningham, Merce." *CBY 1966*: 61-64.

Cunningham, Merce. *Changes: Notes on Choreography*. Edited by Frances Starr. New York: Something Else Press, 1968.

——. "Choreography and the Dance." In *The Dance Anthology*, pp. 52-62. Edited by Cobbett Steinberg. New York, London, and Scarborough, Ontario: New American Library, 1980.

——. "A Collaborative Process Between Music and Dance." *Tri-Quarterly* 54 (Spring 1982): 173-186; reprinted in *A John Cage Reader: In Celebration of his 70th Birthday*, ed. by Peter Gena and Jonathan Brent. New York, London, Frankfurt: C.F. Peters, 1982.

——. "The Impermanent Art." In *7 Arts*, pp. 69-77. Dance, Music, Theatre, Painting, Sculpture, Literature, Architecture. No. 3. Edited by Fernando Puma. Indian Hills, Colo.: The Falcon's Wing Press, c. 1955; reprinted in *Esthetics Contemporary*, ed. by Richard Kostelanetz, Buffalo, N.Y.: Prometheus Books, 1978; rev. ed. 1989.

**Cunningham, Merce** *(continued)*

——. "Space, Time and Dance." *Trans/formation* 1, no. 3 (1952): 150-151.

——. "*Story*: Tale of a Dance and a Tour." Parts One, Two and Three. *Dance Ink* 6, no. 1 (Spring 1995): 14-21; *Dance Ink* 6, no. 2 (Summer 1995): 18-22; and *Dance Ink* 6, no. 3 (Fall 1995): 32-36.

——, with an Introduction by David Vaughan. "Thoughts on Dance, Music & The Visual Arts." In *Parallel Structures: Art, Dance, Music*, pp. 16-23. Guest edited by Clare Farrow. Art & Design Profile No. 33. London: Academy Editions, 1993.

——, in conversation with Jacqueline Lesschaeve. *The Dancer and the Dance*. New York & London: Marion Boyars, 1985.

—— et al. "Time to Walk in Space." *DP* 34 (Summer 1968).

"Cunningham and His Dancers." *BR* 15, no. 3 (Fall 1987): 19-40. Transcript of a dialogue among Carolyn Brown, Douglas Dunn, Viola Farber, Steve Paxton, Marianne Preger-Simon, Valda Setterfield, Gus Solomons, and David Vaughan, presented on March 7, 1987, as part of the festival "Merce Cunningham and the New Dance."

Damsholt, Inger. "The Impact of the 'Cunningham Concept': The Function of Music Within Contemporary Dance Performance in Denmark." In *Society of Dance History Scholars Proceedings*, pp. 169-173. Fifteenth Annual Conference, University of California, Riverside, 14-15 February 1992.

Daniels, Don. "Boutique Items and Risky Business: Cunningham, Wiener, Peters, Tomasson." *BR* 13, no. 2 (Summer 1985): 39-56.

"Decision Making Dancers." *BR* 20, no. 4 (Winter 1992): 86-97. The transcript of a symposium, moderated by Stephanie Woodard, about the working methods of modern dance pioneers Isadora Duncan, Merce Cunningham, and Twyla Tharp, with respective exponents Hortense Kooluris, Carolyn Brown, and Sara Rudner.

Dell, Cecily. "*Winterbranch* . . . and Hundreds of Years." *DS* 1, no. 2 (Spring 1965): 19-21.

Feldman, Elyn. "*Banjo*—Cunningham's Lost 'American' Piece." In *Dance: Current Selected Research*, Volume 1, pp. 89-96. Edited by Lynnette Y. Overby and James H. Humphrey. New York: AMS Press, 1989.

Fleming, Bruce. "Talking Merce." *DanceView* 11, no. 3 (Spring 1994): 19-22. A report on the conference, "Black Mountain

**Cunningham, Merce** *(continued)*

College and Merce Cunningham in the Fifties: New Perspectives," held at Russell Sage College, Troy, New York, 9-10 October 1993. For an opposing view of this conference, see article by Leslie Martin.

"The Forming of an Aesthetic: Merce Cunningham and John Cage." *BR* 13, no. 3 (Fall 1985): 23-40. The edited transcript of a panel discussion heard 16 June 1984 at the Dance Critics Association conference at The Kitchen in New York. Participants: Earle Brown, Remy Charlip, Marianne Simon, and David Vaughan.

Genter, Sandra. "*Ocean* in Brussels." *BR* 22, no. 4 (Winter 1994): 60-63.

Goldner, Nancy. "Cunningham Diary." *Bennington Review* No. 2 (September 1978): 75-81.

Greskovic, Robert. "Merce Cunningham as Sculptor." *BR* 11, no. 4 (Winter 1984): 88-95.

Grossman, Peter Z. "Talking with Merce Cunningham About Video." *DS* 13, nos. 2&3 (Winter/Spring 1979): 56-68.

Gruen, John, text, with photography by Feliciano. "Architectural Digest Visits: John Cage and Merce Cunningham." *Architectural Digest* 45, no. 11 (November 1988): 198-201, 272.

Johnston, Jill. "The New American Modern Dance." In *The New American Arts*, pp. 162-193. Edited by Richard Kostelanetz. New York: Collier Books, 1967; reprinted in *Salmagundi* No. 33-34 (Spring-Summer 1976): 149-174.

Jordan, Stephanie. "Freedom from the Music: Cunningham, Cage & Collaborations." *Contact* No. 20 (Autumn 1979): 16-19.

Kisselgoff, Anna. "Merce Cunningham: The Maverick of Modern Dance." *The New York Times Magazine*, March 21, 1982, pp. 22-25, 60-63.

Klosty, James, ed. *Merce Cunningham*. New York: Saturday Review Press, 1975; reprint New York: Proscenium, 1985; and reprint, with a new foreword and an additional photograph, New York: Limelight, 1986.

Kostelanetz, Richard, ed. *Merce Cunningham: Dancing in Space and Time*. Pennington, N.J.: A Cappella Books, 1992.

Kriegsman, Sali Ann. *Modern Dance in America: The Bennington Years*. Boston: G.K. Hall & Co., 1981.

**Cunningham, Merce** *(continued)*

Macaulay, Alastair. "Happy Hooligan." *The New Yorker* 68, no. 10 (April 27, 1992): 90-93.

———. "The Merce Experience." *The New Yorker* 64, no. 7 (April 4, 1988): 92-96.

Martin, Leslie. "Black Mountain College and Merce Cunningham in the Fifties: New Perspectives." *DRJ* 26, no. 1 (Spring 1994): 46-48. A report on the conference at Russell Sage College, Troy, New York, 9-10 October 1993. For an opposing view of this conference, see article by Bruce Fleming.

*Merce Cunningham & Dance Company.* New York: The Foundation for Contemporary Performance Arts, 1963. This booklet offers brief commentary by John Cage on the art of Merce Cunningham,

thumbnail descriptions of a dozen Cunningham works, short biographies of company members, and a sampling of statements from reviews.

Poster, William S. "'Something New, Simple and Fundamental.'" *BR* 1, no. 4 (1966): 6-10.

Potter, Michelle. "'A License to Do Anything': Robert Rauschenberg and the Merce Cunningham Dance Company." *DC* 16, no. 1 (1993): 1-43.

Ryman, Rhonda. "Cunningham, Brook, and Grotowski: New Concepts of Theatre." *YDR* [Issue #1] (Spring 1973): 23-29.

Sayers, Lesley-Anne. "Telling the Dancer from the Dance." *DN* 1, no. 4 (Winter 1992–93): 16-19, 21.

**Cunningham, Merce** *(continued)*

Silverman, Jill. "Merce Cunningham on Broadway." *PAJ* 2, no. 1 (Spring 1977): 93-96.

Snell, Michael. "Cunningham and the Critics." *BR* 3, no. 6 (1971): 16-39. Letters to the editor from Marcia Siegel, Deborah Jowitt, and Michael Snell in "Correspondence: Cunningham and the Critics." *BR* 4, no. 1 (1971): 76-85.

Tompkins, Calvin. "An Appetite for Motion." *The New Yorker* 44, no. 11 (May 4, 1968): 52-56, 58, 60, 63, 66, 69-70, 72, 75-76, 78, 83, 86, 89-90, 92, 97-98, 100, 103-104, 106, 111-112, 114, 117-120, 123-126. This profile also appears in Calvin Tompkin's *The Bride & the Bachelors: Five Masters of the Avant-Garde*. New York: Viking, 1968.

———, text, with photography by Richard Avedon. "Merce at Seventy-Five." *The New Yorker* 70, no. 3 (March 7, 1994): 74-75.

Tracy, Robert. "Bicycle in the Sky: Merce Cunningham on Decor." *BR* 20, no. 3 (Fall 1992): 57-58.

Vaughan, David. "Building an Archive: Merce Cunningham Dance Company." Archives of the Dance (2). *DR* 2, no. 1 (Spring 1984): 61-67.

———. "*Channels/Inserts*: Cunningham and Atlas (Continued)." *Millennium Film Journal* No. 12 (Fall-Winter 1982-1983): 126-130.

———. "Cunningham, Cage and Joyce: 'this longawaited messiagh of roaratorios.'" *C&D* 1, pt. 4 (1992): 79-89.

———. "From Diaghilev to Cunningham: Contemporary Artists Work with Dance." In *Das Ballett und die Künste (Ballet and the Arts)*, pp. 60-64. Cologne: Ballett-Bühnen-Verlag, 1981.

———. "*Locale*: The Collaboration of Merce Cunningham and Charles Atlas." *Millennium Film Journal* Nos. 10/11 (Fall-Winter 1981-1982): 18-22.

———. "Merce Cunningham: Retrospect and Prospect." *PAJ* 3, no. 3 (Winter 1979): 3-14.

———. "Merce Cunningham and the Northwest." In *Society of Dance History Scholars Proceedings*, pp. 111-125. Twelfth Annual Conference, Arizona State University, 17-19 February 1989.

———. "Merce Cunningham's *The Seasons*." *DC* 18, no. 2 (1995): 311-318.

———. "Notes on the Cunningham Repertory." *BR* 16, no. 1 (Spring 1988): 55-62.

**C**

**Cunningham, Merce** *(continued)*

------. "The Real Shock: The Merce Cunningham Dance Company's World Tour, 1964." In *Society of Dance History Scholars Proceedings*, pp. 21-27. Fifteenth Annual Conference, University of California, Riverside, 14-15 February 1992.

Yates, Peter. "Merce Cunningham Restores the Dance to Dance." *Arts & Architecture* 80, no. 11 (November 1963): 12-13, 40-41.

BRO: 88-91. COE: 160-178. FOS: 32-41; 41-57. HAS/2: 184-191. HOD: 84-119. LIV: 76-91. MAZ: 197-229. MCD: 52-76. ROG: 61-72. SOR/1: 250-255.

**Dalcroze, Jaques** (see **Jaques-Dalcroze, Emile**)

**d'Amboise, Carolyn George** (1927– )
SID: 55-63.

**d'Amboise, Christopher** (1960– )
d'Amboise, Christopher. *Leap Year: A Year in the Life of a Dancer.* Garden City, N.Y.: Doubleday, 1982.

**d'Amboise, Jacques** (1934– )
Barboza, Steven, text, with photography by Carolyn George d'Amboise. *I Feel Like Dancing: A Year with Jacques d'Amboise and the National Dance Institute.* New York: Crown Publishers, 1992.
"d'Amboise, Jacques (Joseph)." *CBY 1964*: 100-102.
d'Amboise, Jacques, Hope Cooke, and Carolyn George. *Teaching the Magic of Dance.* New York: Simon & Schuster, 1983.
Gelb, Barbara. "The Pied Piper of Dance." *New York Times Magazine*, April 12, 1981, pp. 50-53, 56, 58, 60, 62, 64, 66.
Rosen, Lillie F., text, with photography by Martha Swope. *Jacques d'Amboise.* Dance Horizons Spotlight Series. Brooklyn, N.Y.: Dance Horizons, 1975.
MAS: 263-269. SWI/3: 242-247.

**Danias, Starr** (1949– )
GRU/2: 399-403.

**Danieli, Fred** (1917– )
MAS: 209-213.

**Danielian, Leon** (1920– )
ATK: 31-34. GAL: 9-18. GRU/2: 83-90.

**Danilova, Alexandra** (1904– )
"Alexandra Danilova." *BR* 9, no. 4 (Winter 1982): 57-74. A portfolio
of photographs with a brief introduction by Baird Hastings.

Anderson, Jack. "Danilova and Franklin." *BR* 9, no. 4 (Winter
1982): 75-81. A chapter from Anderson's *The One and Only: The
Ballet Russe de Monte Carlo*. New York: Dance Horizons, 1981.

"The Art of Alexandra Danilova." *Chrysalis* 12, nos. 1-4/Issue 61
(1959): 3-18. A selection of brief reviews by Edwin Denby and
B.H. Haggin.

"A Conversation with Alexandra Danilova." Parts One and Two. *BR*
4, no. 4 (1973): 32-51 and *BR* 4, no. 5 (1973): 50-60. Letter to the
editor from Anthony Fay concerning this two-part conversation in
"Correspondence: Ballet Russe Retrospective." *BR* 4, no. 6
(1974): 91-97.

"Danilova, Alexandra." *CBY 1987*: 123-127.

Danilova, Alexandra. "*Choura*: A Memoir." Two Parts. *BR* 14, no. 2
(Summer 1986): 15-22 and *BR* 14, no. 3 (Fall 1986): 72-85.
Extracts from *Choura: The Memoirs of Alexandra Danilova*. New
York: Knopf, 1986.

———. *Choura: The Memoirs of Alexandra Danilova*. New York:
Knopf, 1986.

Fay, Anthony. "The Belle of the Ballets Russes: Alexandra Danilova." *Dance Magazine* 51, no. 10 (October 1977): 55-70. A
Dance Magazine Portfolio.

Twysden, A.E. *Alexandra Danilova*. London: C.W. Beaumont, 1945.
ATK: 35-41. BEL: 28-31. CRO: 43-64. DAV: 42-48. GRU/2: 29-35.
MAS: 1-8. MON: 24-25. SWI/2: 49-53. TRA: 18-27.

**d'Antuono, Eleanor** (1939– )
GRU/2: 232-236.

**Darling, Christopher** (1941– )
SID: 65-73.

**Dauberval, Jean** (1742-1806)

Guest, Ivor. "The Legacy of Dauberval." In *The Ballet Annual 1961: A Record and Year Book of the Ballet*, pp. 104-108. Edited by Arnold L. Haskell and Mary Clarke. Fifteenth Issue. New York: Macmillan, 1960.

**Davies, Siobhan** (1950– )

Kane, Angela. "Siobhan Davies: Family Connections." Dance Study Supplement, pt. 6. *The Dancing Times* 80, no. 954 (March 1990): 8 pp. (i-viii), between pp. 592 & 593.

Preston, Sophia. "Beyond Words." *DN* 1, no. 4 (Winter 1992-93): 11-15.

JOR: 131-159; 228-230.

**Dean, Laura** (1945– )

"Dean, Laura." *CBY 1988*: 140-143.

Dean, Laura. "Notes on Choreography." *DS* 9, no. 1 (Fall/Winter 1974-75): 8-13.

――. "7 Dances by Laura Dean and Company." *TDR* 19, no. 1/T-65 (March 1975): 18-25. The seven dances are *Stamping Dance* (1971), *Circle Dance* (1972), *Jumping Dance* (1973), *Walking Dance* (1973), *Changing Pattern Steady Pulse* (1973), *Spinning Dance* (1973), and *Response Dance* (1974).

LIV: 92-105.

**de Groat, Andrew** (194?– )

Flakes, Susan. "Robert Wilson's *Einstein on the Beach*." *TDR* 20, no. 4/T-72 (December 1976): 69-82. Detailed description of the action of this theater piece, which was choreographed by Andrew de Groat.

**De Keersmaeker, Anne Teresa** (1960– )

Roy, Sanjoy. "*Toccata*." *DN* 3, no. 2 (Summer 1994): 32-35, 37.

**Delarova, Eugenia** (1911-1990)

Louis, Murray. "Eugenia (Delarova) Doll (1911-1990)." In *Murray Louis on Dance*, pp. 90-92. [Pennington, N.J.]: A Cappella Books, 1992.

**de Lavallade, Carmen** (1931– )

Berman, Avis. "Architectural Digest Visits: Geoffrey Holder and Carmen de Lavallade." *Architectural Digest* 42, no. 11 (November 1985): 156-[161], 242.

"de Lavallade, Carmen (Paula)." *CBY 1967*: 92-95.

**Delsarte, François** (1811-1871)

Dasgupta, Gautam. "Commedia Delsarte." *PAJ* 15, no. 3 (#45, September 1993): 95-102.

Kirby, E.T. "The Delsarte Method: 3 Frontiers of Actor Training." *TDR* 16, no. 1/T-53 (March 1972): 55-69.

Morgan, Anna. *An Hour with Delsarte: A Study of Expression.* Boston: Lee and Shepard, 1892.

Ruyter, Nancy Lee Chalfa. "American Delsarteans Abroad." In *Society of Dance History Scholars Proceedings*, pp. 275-282. Fifteenth Annual Conference, University of California, Riverside, 14-15 February 1992.

———. "Appendix 2: A Tentative List of Delsartian Books in English in Chronological Order." In her *Reformers and Visionaries: The Americanization of the Art of Dance*, pp. 134-137. New York: Dance Horizons, 1979.

———. "A Sampling of Exercise Materials from American Delsarte Manuals." In *Society of Dance History Scholars Proceedings*, p. 232. Sixth Annual Conference, The Ohio State University, 11-13 February 1983.

Shawn, Ted. *Every Little Movement: A Book About François Delsarte.* Pittsfield, Mass.: Eagle Print and Binding Co., 1954; 2d ed., rev. and enl., 1963; reprint Brooklyn, N.Y.: Dance Horizons, 1968? MAY/2: 17-19.

**de Mille, Agnes** (1905-1993)

Barker, Barbara. "Agnes de Mille's Heroines of the Forties." In *Society of Dance History Scholars Proceedings*, pp. 140-147. Twelfth Annual Conference, Arizona State University, 17-19 February 1989.

———. "In Memoriam: Agnes de Mille, September 18, 1904-October 7, 1993." *DRJ* 26, no. 1 (Spring 1994): 62.

"de Mille, Agnes." *CBY 1943*: 165-167.

"de Mille, Agnes." *CBY 1985*: 79-83.

**de Mille, Agnes** *(continued)*

de Mille, Agnes. *America Dances*. New York: Macmillan; London: Collier Macmillan, 1980.

——. *And Promenade Home*. Boston & Toronto: Little, Brown & Company, 1958; reprint, with a new Preface by Cynthia Gregory, New York: Da Capo Press, 1980.

——, text, with photography by Peter Vitale. "Architectural Digest Visits: Agnes de Mille." *Architectural Digest* 41, no. 12 (December 1984): 174-179, 210.

——. *The Book of the Dance*. New York: Golden Press; London: Paul Hamlyn, 1963.

——. *Dance to the Piper*. Boston: Little, Brown & Company, 1952; reprint, with a new Preface by Cynthia Gregory, New York: Da Capo Press, 1980.

——. *Lizzie Borden: A Dance of Death*. Boston: Little, Brown & Company, 1968.

——. *Portrait Gallery*. Boston: Houghton Mifflin, 1990.

——. *Reprieve: A Memoir*. Garden City, N.Y.: Doubleday, 1981.

——. "Russian Journals." *DP* 44 (Winter 1970).

——. *Speak to Me, Dance with Me*. Boston: Little, Brown & Company, 1973.

——. *To A Young Dancer: A Handbook*. Boston & Toronto: Little, Brown and Company, 1962.

——, comp. *Walter's Book: In Memoriam*. Memorial Service, Reminiscences, Letters, & Journal Entries, compiled by Agnes de Mille Prude. New York: the author, 1991. A volume devoted to Agnes de Mille's late husband, Walter Prude, who died August 28, 1988. Book packaged with an audiocassette of the memorial service for Walter Prude.

——. *Where the Wings Grow*. Garden City, N.Y.: Doubleday, 1978.

Easton, Carol. *No Intermissions: The Life of Agnes de Mille*. New York, London, Toronto: Little, Brown and Company, 1996.

Edwards, Anne. *The DeMilles: An American Family*. New York: Abrams, 1988.

Gere, David. "A Conversation with Agnes de Mille." *BR* 22, no. 1 (Spring 1994): 52-60.

Gherman, Beverly. *Agnes de Mille: Dancing Off the Earth*. New York: Atheneum, 1990.

Museum of the City of New York, Friends of the Theatre and Music Collection. *A Memorable Evening of Dance Honoring Agnes de Mille, May 16, 1983*. Souvenir program.

**D**

**de Mille, Agnes** *(continued)*

Rosen, Lillie F. "Talking with Agnes de Mille." *DS* 11, no. 1 (Fall/Winter 1976-77): 8-17.

Shearer, Sybil. "Agnes de Mille." *BR* 22, no. 4 (Winter 1994): 10-12.

Speaker-Yuan, Margaret. *Agnes de Mille: Choreographer.* American Women of Achievement. New York & Philadelphia: Chelsea House Publishers, 1988.

FOW: 52-75. FRA: 155-166. HAL: 228-239. LYL: 46-58. MAY/1: 241-263. MCC: 117-132. MUI: 115-124. SCH/1: see Index of Choreographers, p. 135 and Index of Directors, p. 175.

**Dendy, Mark** (1961– )

"A Conversation with Mark Dendy." *BR* 18, no. 3 (Fall 1990): 55-76.

**Denisova, Alexandra** (1922– )

Windreich, Leland. "The Career of Alexandra Denisova: Vancouver, de Basil, Cuba." *DC* 3, no. 1 (1979): 1-21.

**Derman, Vergie** (1942– )

Clarson-Leach, Robert. *Vergie Derman: Dancing with the Royal Ballet.* London: Artmusique Publishing, 1986.

**de Valois, Ninette** (1898– )

Clarke, Mary. *The Sadler's Wells Ballet: A History and an Appreciation.* New York: Macmillan, 1955.

Dale, Margaret. "When the Morning Stars Sang Together." *BR* 19, no. 1 (Spring 1991): 68-77. Background to the creation of *Job*.

"de Valois, Ninette." *CBY 1949*: 146-148.

de Valois, Ninette. *Come Dance with Me: A Memoir 1898-1956.* Cleveland & New York: The World Publishing Company, 1957; reprint New York: Da Capo Press, 1980.

——. *"The Cycle" and Other Poems.* London: Sadler's Wells Trust, 1985.

**de Valois, Ninette** *(continued)*

———. *Invitation to the Ballet.* London: John Lane The Bodley Head, 1937.

———. *Step by Step: The Formation of an Establishment.* London: W.H. Allen, 1977.

Farjeon, Annabel. "Choreographers: Dancing for de Valois and Ashton." *DC* 17, no. 2 (1994): 195-206.

Jordan, Stephanie. "A Conversation with Ninette de Valois." *BR* 18, no. 1 (Spring 1990): 74-80.

Lawson, Joan. *Ninette de Valois.* Makers of English Ballet, No. 1. London: Fitzroy Publications, n.d.

———, James Laver, Geoffrey Keynes, and Frank Howes. *"Job" and "The Rake's Progress."* Edited by Arnold L. Haskell. Sadler's Wells Books, No. 2. London: The Bodley Head, 1949.

Marshall, Norman. "Ninette de Valois and the English Ballet." Chapter 10 in his *The Other Theatre*, pp. 139-161. London: John Lehmann, 1947; reprint London: Theatre Book Club, [1950].

Neatby, Kate. *Ninette de Valois and the Vic-Wells Ballet.* Edited by Edwin Evans. Artists of the Dance. London: British- Continental Press, 1934.

Ries, Frank W.D. "Sir Geoffrey Keynes and the Ballet *Job.*" *DR* 2, no. 1 (Spring 1984): 19-34.

Sayers, Lesley-Anne. "An Enigma More Than a Landmark." *DN* 2, no. 3 (Autumn 1993): 41-47, 49. De Valois' *Job* and its place in British artistic traditions.

Sorley Walker, Kathrine. "The Festival and the Abbey: Ninette de Valois' Early Choreography, 1925-1934." Parts One and Two. *DC* 7, no. 4 (1984-85): 379-412 and *DC* 8, nos. 1 & 2 (1985): 51-100.

———, with contributions by Dame Ninette. *Ninette de Valois: Idealist Without Illusions.* London: Hamish Hamilton, 1987.

Taplin, Diana Theodores. "Dame Ninette at York." *YDR* Issue #6 (Spring 1977): 6-8.

Wiles, Patricia Joyce Wade. "A Study of *Job, a Masque for Dancing* by Ralph Vaughan Williams." Unpublished dissertation, Texas Tech University, 1988. Ann Arbor, Mich.: University Microfilms International, 1989. Order No. 890,8533. DAI 50-02A, p. 0300.

Zoete, Beryl de. "Three British Choreographers." In her *The Thunder and the Freshness*, pp. 43-55. London: Neville Spearman; New York: Theatre Arts Books, 1963. Portion on de Valois, pp. 44-47.

**de Valois, Ninette** *(continued)*
    DAV: 296-304. FRA: 74-92. HAL: 152-159. HUR: 264-268. MAS:
    85-87. NOB: 191-195.

**Deveson, Rosemary** (1921– )
    Deveson, Rosemary. *Dancing for De Basil: Letters to Her Parents
    from Rosemary Deveson, 1938-1940.* Selected, edited and with
    connecting text and notes by Leland Windreich. Toronto: Arts
    Inter-Media Canada/Dance Collection Danse, 1989. Published on
    three floppy diskettes (text equivalent to a book-length manu-
    script), MS DOS, 5 ¼″ or 3.5″, will operate on most IBM Personal
    Computers or compatibles and
    also the Macintosh.

*A Loftier Flight*

THE LIFE AND ACCOMPLISHMENTS OF
Charles-Louis Didelot, Balletmaster

*by* MARY GRACE SWIFT

THE DE LA TORRE BUENO PRIZE: 1973

**Didelot, Charles-Louis** (1767-
1837)
    Swift, Mary Grace. *A Loftier
    Flight: The Life and Accom-
    plishments of Charles-Louis
    Didelot, Balletmaster.* Middle-
    town, Conn.: Wesleyan Uni-
    versity Press; London: Pitman
    Publishing, 1974.
    ROS: 38-54. WIL: 5-49.

**Dolgushin, Nikita** (1938– )
    Greskovic, Robert. "Dancing in
    the Dark—Discovering Nikita
    Dolgushin." *Dance Theatre
    Journal* 5, no. 4 (Spring 1988): 10-13.
    SMA: 275-281.

**Dolin, Anton** (1904-1983)
    The Anton Dolin International Gala Committee. *A Pictorial Tribute
    to Sir Anton Dolin: The First British Ballet Star, 1904-1983,* book
    of the gala, Royal Opera House, Covent Garden, 24th June 1984.
    [London: Gala Committee, 1984].
    "Celebrating Anton Dolin," arranged by Donald Saddler. *BR* 13, no.
    1 (Spring 1985): 74-91. An edited selection of remarks made at

**Dolin, Anton** *(continued)*

the program of memoirs, held at the Library and Museum of the Performing Arts, 21 January 1984.

"Dolin, Anton." *CBY 1946*: 149-151.

Dolin, Anton. *Alicia Markova: Her Life and Art*. New York: Hermitage House, 1953.

——. *Autobiography*. London: Oldbourne, 1960.

——. *Ballet Go Round*. London: Michael Joseph, 1938.

——. *Divertissement*. London: Sampson Low, Marston & Co., [1931].

——. *Last Words: A Final Autobiography*. London: Century Publishing, 1985.

——. *Pas de Deux: The Art of Partnering*. New York: Kamin Dance Publishers, 1949.

——. *The Sleeping Ballerina*. With a Foreword by Dame Marie Rambert. London: Frederick Muller, 1966; reprint London: Dance Books, 1974. A biography of Olga Spessivtzeva.

Haskell, Arnold L. *Anton Dolin: The "First Chapter."* Artists of the Dance. London: British-Continental Press, 1929.

Lowndes, Joan Selby. *The Blue Train: The Story of Anton Dolin*. London: Collins, 1953.

Wheatcroft, Andrew, comp. *Dolin: Friends and Memories*. London: Routledge & Kegan Paul, 1982.

Williams, Peter. *Alicia Markova and Anton Dolin: A Legend of British Ballet*. London: Hall Publications, n.d.

ATK: 42-47. BEL: 32-37. BLA: 114-117. DAV: 57-63. GRU/2: 52-58. HUR: 204-207. MCC: 49-61. SCH/1: see Index of Choreographers, p. 135.

**Donn, Jorge** (1947-1992)

BLA: 170-172. GRU/2: 187-189.

**Doone, Rupert** (1903-1966)

Medley, Robert. *Drawn from the Life: A Memoir*. London & Boston: Faber & Faber, 1983.

**Doubrovska, Felia** (1896-1981)

Ackerman, Gerald. "Eternally Elegant: Felia Doubrovska (1896-1981)." *BR* 9, no. 4 (Winter 1982): 6.

**Doubrovska, Felia** *(continued)*
Huckenpahler, Victoria. "Felia Doubrovska: Imperial Ballerina."
  *DC* 5, no. 4 (1982-83): 361-437.
GAL: 19-28. GRU/2: 23-28. NEW/1: 1-10. TRA: 36-45.

**Dove, Ulysses** (1947– )
Barton, Peter. "Ulysses Dove: Alvin Ailey American Dance The-
  atre." In his *Staying Power: Performing Artists Talk About Their
  Lives*, pp. 126-137. New York: Dial Press, 1980.
Williams, Julinda Lewis. "*Inside*: A Dance." *DS* 14, no. 3 (Septem-
  ber 1980): 22-28.

**Dowell, Anthony** (1943– )
*Anthony Dowell*. Dance Horizons Spotlight Series. Brooklyn, N.Y.:
  Dance Horizons, 1976.
"Dowell, Anthony." *CBY 1971*: 106-108.
Rosen, Lillie F., text, with photography by Anthony Crickmay.
Spatt, Leslie, photography, with text by Nicholas Dromgoole. *Sibley
  & Dowell*. London: Collins, 1976.
BLA: 152-155. GRU/2: 117-124. PET: 12-33.

**Driver, Senta** (1942– )
Daly, Ann. "Interview with Senta Driver." *W&P* 3, no. 2/Issue #6
  (1987-1988): 90-96.

**Dudinskaya, Natalia** (1912– )
SLO: 95-97. SMA: 72-78.

**Dudley, Jane** (1912– )
Dudley, Jane. "The Early Life of an American Modern Dancer." *DR*
  10, no. 1 (Spring 1992): 3-20.
Sears, David. "Breaking Down *Harmonica Breakdown*." *BR* 11, no.
  4 (Winter 1984): 58-67.
Tobias, Anne. "Jane Dudley Retrospective." *BR* 16, no. 4 (Winter
  1989): 50.
LLO: 179-182; 190-192.

**Duell, Daniel** (1952– )
MAS: 577-581.

## Duell, Joseph (1956-1986)

Gurewitsch, Matthew. "Remembering Joseph Duell." *BR* 17, no. 2 (Summer 1989): 61-67.

L'Engle, Madeleine. "What Can Any Of Us Say?" *BR* 13, no. 4 (Winter 1986): 47. L'Engle's one-page tribute is followed by a portfolio of photographs of Joseph Duell, captioned by Marilyn Hunt with quotations from her interviews with him from 1983 through 1985 (pp. 48-59).

Mason, Francis. "Joseph Duell (1956-1986)." *BR* 13, no. 4 (Winter 1986): 45-46.

SWI/3: 153-158.

## Duncan, Irma (1897-1977)

Duncan, Irma. *Duncan Dancer: An Autobiography.* Middletown, Conn.: Wesleyan University Press, 1966.

——. "Follow Me! The Autobiography of Irma Duncan." Parts One and Two. *DP* 21 (1965) and *DP* 22 (1965).

## Duncan, Isadora (1878-1927)

Adler, Norma. "Reconstructing the Dances of Isadora Duncan." *TDR* 28, no. 3/T-103 (Fall 1984): 59-66.

Artists Guild of America and The California Palace of the Legion of Honor. *Isadora Duncan,* catalogue of the memorial exhibition of drawings by Jules Grandjouan, December 1, 1956 to January 1, 1957. San Francisco: The California Palace of the Legion of Honor, 1956.

*Ballet Review* 6, no. 4 (1977-1978). A special issue celebrating the art of Isadora Duncan. Articles: Jill Silverman. "André Levinson on Isadora Duncan" (pp. 1-5). André Levinson. "The Art and Meaning of Isadora Duncan" (pp. 5-14). André Levinson. "In Memoriam" (pp. 14-20). Elizabeth Kendall. "Before the World Began" (pp. 21-32). Debra Goldman. "Mothers and Fathers: A View of Isadora and Fokine" (pp. 33-43). Julia Levien. "Sources of Style in the Dances of Isadora Duncan" (pp. 44-49). Annabelle Gamson. "On Dancing Isadora's Dances" (pp. 50-54). Don Daniels. "Duncan Revived" (pp. 55-65).

Bardsley, Kay. "The Duncans at Carnegie Hall." *BR* 19, no. 3 (Fall 1991): 85-96.

**Duncan, Isadora** *(continued)*

——. "Isadora Duncan and the Russian Ballet." In *Society of Dance History Scholars Proceedings*, pp. 121-130. Eleventh Annual Conference, North Carolina School of the Arts, 12-14 February 1988.

——. "Isadora Duncan's First School: The First Generation Founders of the Tradition." *DRA X* (1979): 219-249.

——. "Re-animations of Duncan Masterworks: Imbued with the Fire of Maria-Theresa Duncan—A Four-year Project, 1976-1980." In *Proceedings of the Conference "Dance Reconstructed: Modern Dance Art Past, Present, Future,"* pp. 191-200. Rutgers University, New Brunswick, New Jersey, October 16 and 17, 1992.

——. "Social Cause as Dance, Enter Isadora." *BR* 22, no. 2 (Summer 1994): 73-83.

Beiswanger, Barbara Page. "The Ideational Sources of the Modern Dance in America as Expressed in the Work of Two Leading Exponents, Isadora Duncan and Ruth St. Denis." Unpublished dissertation, New York University, 1944. Ann Arbor, Mich.: University Microfilms International, 1973. Order No. 73-08,423. No DAI abstract available.

Blair, Fredrika. *Isadora: Portrait of the Artist as a Woman.* New York: McGraw-Hill, 1986.

Bloch, Alice. "Isadora Duncan and Vaslav Nijinsky: Dancing on the Brink." Unpublished dissertation, Temple University, 1991. Ann Arbor, Mich.: University Microfilms International, 1991. Order No. 91-34,920. DAI 52-07A, p. 2301.

Bolitho, William. "Isadora Duncan." Chapter 11 in his *Twelve Against the Gods: The Story of Adventure*, pp. 305-327. New York: Simon & Schuster, 1929.

**Duncan, Isadora** *(continued)*

Craig, Gordon. "Gordon Craig and the Dance." *DI* 2, no. 8 (August 1943).

——. "Memories of Isadora Duncan." In *Gordon Craig on Movement and Dance*, pp. 247-252. Edited and with an Introduction by Arnold Rood. New York: Dance Horizons, 1977; reprinted from *The Listener* 47, no. 1214 (June 5, 1952): 913-914.

Daly, Ann. "Dance History and Feminist Theory: Reconsidering Isadora Duncan and the Male Gaze." In Laurence Senelick's *Gender in Performance: The Presentation of Difference in the Performing Arts*, pp. 239-259. Hanover, N.H. & London: University Press of New England for Tufts University, 1992.

——. "Isadora Duncan's Dance Theory." *DRJ* 26, no. 2 (Fall 1994): 24-31.

*Dance Magazine* 51, no. 7 (July 1977). Special Isadora Duncan centennial issue. Articles: Paul Hertelendy. "Isadora's Childhood: Clearing Away the Clouds" (pp. 48-50). Nesta Macdonald. "Isadora Reexamined: Lesser-known Aspects of the Great Dancer's Life—Part One: 1877-1900" (pp. 51-66). A Dance Magazine Portfolio. Lois Draegin. "After Isadora: Her Art as Inspiration" (pp. 67-71).

*Dance at the Temple of the Wings: The Boynton-Quitzow Family in Berkeley*. Berkeley: Regional Oral History Office, The Bancroft Library, University of California, 1973. Vol. I: Charles Quitzow and Sülgwynn Boynton Quitzow, interview by Suzanne Riess and Margaretta Mitchell, with an Afterword by Rhea Boynton Hildebrand. Vol. II: OElóel Quitzow Braun and Durevol Boynton Quitzow, interview by Suzanne Riess.

de Mille, Agnes. "Duncan." In her *The Book of the Dance*, pp. 134-137. New York: Golden Press; London: Paul Hamlyn, 1963.

——. "Isadora Duncan." Chapter 5 in her *America Dances*, pp. 43-50. New York: Macmillan; London: Collier Macmillan, 1980.

Desti, Mary. *The Untold Story: The Life of Isadora Duncan 1921-1927*. New York: Horace Liveright, 1929; reprint, with a new Preface by Dale Harris, New York: Da Capo Press, 1981. The English edition of this book appeared as *Isadora Duncan's End*. London: Victor Gollancz, 1929.

de Wilde, Nancy. "Isadora Duncan's *Seventh Symphony* in the Netherlands: Reactions to Her Choice and Interpretation of the Music." In *Society of Dance History Scholars Proceedings*, pp.

**D**

**Duncan, Isadora** *(continued)*

166-176. Tenth Annual Conference, University of California, Irvine, 13-15 February 1987.

Dienes, Gedeon P. "Isadora Duncan in Hungary." In *Society of Dance History Scholars Proceedings*, pp. 147-158. Tenth Annual Conference, University of California, Irvine, 13-15 February 1987.

Dillon, Millicent. *After Egypt: Isadora Duncan & Mary Cassatt*. New York: Dutton, 1990.

Drewal, Margaret Thompson. "Isis and Isadora." In *Society of Dance History Scholars Proceedings*, pp. 185-194. Tenth Annual Conference, University of California, Irvine, 13-15 February 1987.

Dumesnil, Maurice. *An Amazing Journey: Isadora Duncan in South America*. New York: Ives Washburn Publisher, 1932.

Duncan, Anna, talks to Parker Tyler. "Isadora and Vanessa." *BR* 3, no. 1 (1969): 20-36. Anna Duncan, one of the original Duncan dancers, discusses the film *The Loves of Isadora*.

Duncan, Dorée, Carol Pratl, and Cynthia Splatt, eds. *Life Into Art: Isadora Duncan and Her World*. Text by Cynthia Splatt. Foreword by Agnes de Mille. New York & London: W.W. Norton, 1993.

Duncan, Irma. *Duncan Dancer: An Autobiography*. Middletown, Conn.: Wesleyan University Press, 1966.

———. *Isadora Duncan: Pioneer in the Art of Dance*. New York: New York Public Library, 1959.

———. *The Technique of Isadora Duncan*. New York: Kamin Publishers, 1937; reprint Brooklyn, N.Y.: Dance Horizons, c. 1970.

———, and Allan Ross Macdougall. *Isadora Duncan's Russian Days & Her Last Years in France*. New York: Covici-Friede, 1929.

Duncan, Isadora. *The Art of the Dance*. Edited by Sheldon Cheney. New York: Theatre Arts Books, 1969.

———. *Isadora Speaks*. Edited and introduced by Franklin Rosemont. San Francisco: City Lights Books, c. 1981. Author's Note: "The principal aim of this book has been to collect as many as possible of Isadora Duncan's writings and speeches that are not included in *My Life* and *The Art of the Dance*."

———. *My Life*. Garden City, N.Y.: Garden City Publishing Company, c. 1927.

Eynat-Confino, Irène. "Movement: Isadora Duncan." The first section of Chapter 7 in her *Beyond the Mask: Gordon Craig, Movement, and the Actor*, pp. 62-71. Carbondale & Edwardsville: Southern Illinois University Press, 1987.

**Duncan, Isadora** *(continued)*

Genthe, Arnold. *Isadora Duncan.* New York & London: Mitchell Kennerley, 1929.

Gold, Sylvia. *A Selection of Isadora Duncan Dances: The Schubert Selection.* Newport Beach, Calif.: Sutton Movement Writing Press, 1984.

Graff, Ellen. "Walt Whitman and Isadora Duncan: The Construction of a Personal Mythology." In *Society of Dance History Scholars Proceedings*, pp. 177-184. Tenth Annual Conference, University of California, Irvine, 13-15 February 1987.

Hansen, Martha Alice. "Isadora Duncan: A Literary Inquiry into the Somatic Foundations of Her Art, Life, and Ideology During the Early Years." Unpublished dissertation, Temple University, 1988. Ann Arbor, Mich.: University Microfilms International, 1988. Order No. 881,8795. DAI 49-09A, p. 2429.

Hayes, Richard. "Isadora and Lola: The Tone of Time." *BR* 3, no. 1 (1969): 36-47. A lengthy review of the film *The Loves of Isadora.*

*Isadora.* [Hollywood]: Universal Studios, 1968. The souvenir program of the film *The Loves of Isadora*, starring Vanessa Redgrave.

Jeschke, Claudia. *"The Dance of the Future."* In *Society of Dance History Scholars Proceedings*, pp. 106-118. Tenth Annual Conference, University of California, Irvine, 13-15 February 1987.

——, and Gabi Vettermann. "Isadora Duncan, Berlin and Munich in 1906: Just an Ordinary Year in a Dancer's Career." *DC* 18, no. 2 (1995): 217-229.

Jowitt, Deborah. "Images of Isadora: The Search for Motion." *DRJ* 17, no. 2 & 18, no. 1 (Fall 1985/Spring 1986): 21-29.

——. "The Impact of Greek Art on the Style and Persona of Isadora Duncan." In *Society of Dance History Scholars Proceedings*, pp. 195-201. Tenth Annual Conference, University of California, Irvine, 13-15 February 1987.

Kendall, Elizabeth. "Europe and Isadora." Chapter 3 in her *Where She Danced*, pp. 53-69. New York: Knopf, 1979.

Kozodoy, Ruth. *Isadora Duncan.* American Women of Achievement. New York: Chelsea House Publishers, 1988.

Layson, June. "Isadora Duncan: Her Influence on the Founding and Development of British Modern Dance." In *Society of Dance History Scholars Proceedings*, pp. 126-132. Tenth Annual Conference, University of California, Irvine, 13-15 February 1987.

**Duncan, Isadora** *(continued)*

———. "Isadora Duncan: A Preliminary Analysis of her Work." *DR* 1, no, 1 (Spring 1983): 39-49.

———. "Mixed Blessings: Isadora Duncan's Legacy to British Early Modern Dance." In *Society of Dance History Scholars Proceedings*, pp. 299-304. Fifteenth Annual Conference, University of California, Riverside, 14-15 February 1992.

Levien, Julia. *Duncan Dance: A Guide for Young People Ages Six to Sixteen.* Pennington, N.J.: Princeton Book Company, Publishers, 1994.

———. "Isadora Duncan and the Spanish Dance." In *Society of Dance History Scholars Proceedings*, pp. 162-164. Fourteenth Annual Conference, New World School of the Arts, Miami, Florida, 8-10 February 1991.

Levine, Judy. "Nineteenth Century Scientism as an Organizer of Belief: The Role of Evolutionism on the Philosophy of Isadora Duncan." In *Society of Dance History Scholars Proceedings*, pp. 119-125. Tenth Annual Conference, University of California, Irvine, 13-15 February 1987.

Loewenthal, Lillian. "Isadora Duncan and her Relationship to the Music of Chopin." In *Society of Dance History Scholars Proceedings*, pp. 159-165. Tenth Annual Conference, University of California, Irvine, 13-15 February 1987.

———. "Isadora Duncan in the Netherlands." *DC* 3, no. 3 (1979-80): 227-253.

———. *The Search for Isadora: The Legend & Legacy of Isadora Duncan.* Princeton, N.J.: Princeton Book Company, Publishers, 1993.

Macdonald, Nesta. "Isadora Reexamined: Lesser-known Aspects of the Great Dancer's Life." Part One: 1877-1900; Part Two: Paris and After; Part Three: Isadora and Gordon Craig; Part Four: Isadora and London, 1908; Part Five: Isadora and Paris Singer; and Part Six: Isadora in London, 1921. *Dance Magazine* 51, no. 7 (July 1977): 51-66; *Dance Magazine* 51, no. 8 (August 1977): 42-46; *Dance Magazine* 51, no. 9 (September 1977): 60-63; *Dance Magazine* 51, no. 10 (October 1977): 79-81; *Dance Magazine* 51, no. 11 (November 1977): 45-47; and *Dance Magazine* 51, no. 12 (December 1977): 71-73. Part One of this series is a Dance Magazine Portfolio.

Macdougall, Allan Ross. "Isadora Duncan and the Artists." *DI* 5, no. 3 (March 1946).

**Duncan, Isadora** *(continued)*

——. *Isadora: A Revolutionary in Art and Love*. New York: Thomas Nelson & Sons, 1960.

Magriel, Paul David. "Bibliography of Isadora Duncan: A List of References in American Libraries." *Bulletin of Bibliography* 16, no. 9 (May-August 1939): 173-175.

——, ed. *Isadora Duncan*. New York: Henry Holt, 1947; reprinted in Magriel's *Nijinsky, Pavlova, Duncan*. New York: Da Capo Press, 1977.

Martin, John. "Isadora Duncan and Basic Dance: Project for a Textbook." *DI* 1, no. 1 (January 1942).

May, Antoinette. "Isadora Duncan: A Force of Nature." Chapter 3 in her *Different Drummers: They Did What They Wanted*, pp. 58-80. Millbrae, Calif.: Les Femmes, 1976.

Maynard, Lorraine. "Dancing Rebel." Chapter 7 in her *Genius in Chrysalis: Locked Doors on Greatness Within*, pp. 142-157. New York, London, Toronto: Longmans, Green & Co., 1936.

McVay, Gordon. *Isadora & Esenin*. Ann Arbor, Mich.: Ardis, 1980.

Mitchell, Margaretta K. "Dance for Life: Isadora Duncan and her California Dance Legacy at the Temple of the Wings." In *Society of Dance History Scholars Proceedings*, pp. 133-144. Tenth Annual Conference, University of California, Irvine, 13-15 February 1987.

Ostrom, Nicki N. "The Gordon Craig - Isadora Duncan Collection: A Register." In *Bulletin of the New York Public Library* 76 (1972): 181-198.

Potter, Michelle. "Designed for Dance: The Costumes of Léon Bakst and the Art of Isadora Duncan." *DC* 13, no. 2 (1990): 154-169.

Pruett, Diane Milhan. "A Study of the Relationship of Isadora Duncan to the Musical Composers and Mentors Who Influenced Her Musical Selection for Choreography." Unpublished dissertation, University of Wisconsin-Madison, 1978. Ann Arbor, Mich.: University Microfilms International, 1979. Order No. 791,8929. DAI 40-05A, p. 2346.

Rather, Lois. *Lovely Isadora*. Oakland, Calif.: Rather Press, 1976.

Roslavleva, Natalia. "Prechistenka 20: The Isadora Duncan School in Moscow." *DP* 64 (Winter 1975).

Ruyter, Nancy Lee Chalfa. "Passionate Revolt: Isadora Duncan." In her *Reformers and Visionaries: The Americanization of the Art of Dance*, pp. 33-54. New York: Dance Horizons, 1979.

**Duncan, Isadora** *(continued)*

Schneider, Ilya Ilyich. *Isadora Duncan: The Russian Years*. Translated by David Magarshack. London: Macdonald, 1968.

Seroff, Victor. *The Real Isadora*. New York: Dial Press, 1971.

Souritz, Elizabeth. "Isadora Duncan's Influence on Dance in Russia." *DC* 18, no. 2 (1995): 281-291.

Splatt, Cynthia. *Isadora Duncan & Gordon Craig: The Prose & Poetry of Action*. San Francisco: Book Club of California, 1988.

Steegmuller, Francis. *"Your Isadora": The Love Story of Isadora Duncan & Gordon Craig*. New York: Random House & The New York Public Library, 1974.

Stokes, Sewell. *Isadora Duncan: An Intimate Portrait*. London: Brentano's, 1928.

———. *Recital in Paris*. A Novel. London: Peter Davies, [1954]. Author's Note: "Anyone who identifies Sarah Menken with the late Isadora Duncan will not be altogether wrong."

Terry, Walter. *Isadora Duncan: Her Life, Her Art, Her Legacy*. New York: Dodd, Mead & Company, 1964.

———. "The Legacy of Isadora Duncan and Ruth St. Denis." *DP* 5 (Winter 1960).

Thorpe, Edward. *Creating a Ballet: MacMillan's "Isadora."* London: Evans Brothers, 1981.

Villazana-Ruiz, Maria. "Isadora Duncan's Legacy: Influences and Development in the United States and Russia." In *Proceedings of the Conference "Dance Reconstructed: Modern Dance Art Past, Present, Future,"* pp. 201-210. Rutgers University, New Brunswick, New Jersey, October 16 and 17, 1992.

Wagenknecht, Edward. "The Dance of Life as Art and as Orgy: Isadora Duncan." In his *Seven Daughters of the Theater*, pp. 137-158. Norman: University of Oklahoma Press, 1964.

Walkowitz, Abraham. *Isadora Duncan in Her Dances*. Girard, Kans.: Haldeman-Julius Publications, 1945.

Weiss, David. *The Spirit and the Flesh*. Garden City, N.Y.: Doubleday, 1959. A novel inspired by the life of Isadora Duncan.

ARM: 16-19. AUS/1: 66-94. BRO: 7-11. CAF: 46-69. DAV: 63-68. DEM/3: 3-18. DRU: 67-91. FOW: 6-27. HUR: 28-36. LLO: 3-11. MAG: 190-201. MAR: 129-148. MAY/2: 30-69. MAZ: 35-60. MOO/1: 271-280. MUI: 57-70. PAL: 11-25. SOR/1: 170-181. TER: 39-45. VAN: 15-28.

**Duncan, Maria-Theresa** (1896-1987)

Bardsley, Kay. "A Dancing 'Isadorable': Maria-Theresa." *DS* 11, no. 2 (Spring/Summer 1977): 47-52.

**Dunham, Katherine** (1912– )

Aschenbrenner, Joyce, with Notations of the Dunham Method and Technique by Lavinia Williams. "Katherine Dunham: Reflections on the Social and Political Contexts of Afro-American Dance." *DRA XII* (1980): xiii, 161 [3].

Beckford, Ruth. *Katherine Dunham: A Biography.* New York & Basel: Marcel Dekker, 1979.

Biemiller, Ruth. *Dance: The Story of Katherine Dunham.* Garden City, N.Y.: Doubleday, 1969.

Buckle, Richard. *Katherine Dunham: Her Dancers, Singers, Musicians.* London: Ballet Publications, n.d. Bilingual: English/French.

Clark, VèVè, and Margaret B. Wilkerson, eds. *KAISO! Katherine Dunham, an Anthology of Writings.* Berkeley, Calif.: Institute for the Study of Social Change, 1978.

Cluzel, Magdeleine E. "Katherine Dunham Seen Through the Eyes of the Artist André Quellier." In her *Glimpses of the Theatre and Dance*, pp. 63-69. Translated from the French by Lily and Baird Hastings. New York: Kamin Publishers, 1953.

"Dunham, Katherine." *CBY 1941*: 245-246.

Dunham, Katherine. *Dances of Haiti.* Los Angeles: Center for Afro-American Studies (University of California), 1983.

———. *Journey to Accompong.* New York: Henry Holt, 1946.

**Dunham, Katherine** *(continued)*

———. *Kasamance: A Fantasy.* New York: Third Press, c. 1974.

———. *A Touch of Innocence.* New York: Harcourt, Brace & Company, 1959.

Gwynn, Eleanor W. Faucette. "A Key Determinant of Dance Style: The Structural Use of the Dance Instrument as Illustrated by the Choreography of Katherine Dunham's *Rites de Passage.*" Unpublished dissertation, University of Wisconsin-Madison, 1978. Ann Arbor, Mich.: University Microfilms International, 1978. Order No. 781,5412. DAI 39-06A, p. 3190.

Harnan, Terry. *African Rhythm American Dance: A Biography of Katherine Dunham.* New York: Knopf, 1974.

Haskins, James. *Katherine Dunham.* New York: Coward, McCann & Geoghegan, 1982.

Hill, Constance Valis. "Katherine Dunham's *Southland*: Protest in the Face of Repression." *DRJ* 26, no. 2 (Fall 1994): 1-10.

Rose, Albirda. *Dunham Technique: "A Way of Life."* Dubuque, Iowa.: Kendall/Hunt Publishing Company, 1990.

DEM/3: 38-50. LLO: 243-253. MAS: 189-193. MCC: 133-142. SCH/1: see Index of Choreographers, p. 135.


**Dunleavy, Rosemary** (1940– )

MAS: 529-535.


**Dunn, Douglas** (1942– )

Banes, Sally. "Cool Symmetries/Douglas Dunn." *DS* 12, no. 2 (Spring/Summer 1978): 50-62.

Brown, Trisha, and Douglas Dunn. "Dialogue: On Dance." *PAJ* 1, no. 2 (Fall 1976): 76-83.

BAN: 186-201. KRE: 56-71.


**Dunn, Judith** (1934?-1983)

Dunn, Judith. "My Work and Judson's." *BR* 1, no. 6 (1967): 22-26.

Poster, Constance H. "Judith Dunn as Teacher." *BR* 1, no. 6 (1967): 27-30.

BRO: 134-140. SIE: 44-49.

**Dunn, Robert** (1928– )

    Banes, Sally. *Democracy's Body: Judson Dance Theater 1962-1964.* Studies in the Fine Arts: The Avant-Garde, No. 43. Ann Arbor, Mich.: UMI Research Press, c. 1983.

    MCD: 77-94.

**Dupond, Patrick** (1959– )

    PET: 56-73.

**Duport, Louis** (1781 or 1783-1853)

    Moore, Lillian. "The Duport Mystery." *DP* 7 (1960).

**Duport, Pierre Landrin** (ca. 1762-1853)

    Moore, Lillian. "The Duport Mystery." *DP* 7 (1960).

**Dupré, Louis** (1697?-1774)

    MOO/2: 18-25.

**Durang, John** (1768-1822)

    Durang, John. *The Memoir of John Durang: American Actor 1785-1816.* Edited by Alan S. Downer. [Pittsburgh, Pa.]: University of Pittsburgh Press, 1966.

    Moore, Lillian. "John Durang: The First American Dancer." *DI* 1, no. 8 (August 1942).

    MAG: 15-37.

**Duvernay, Pauline** (1813-1894)

    Beaumont, Cyril W. "Pauline Duvernay." In his *Three French Dancers of the 19th Century*, pp. 9-18. Essays on Dancing and Dancers, No. 9. London: C.W. Beaumont, 1935.

    Guest, Ivor. "Dandies and Dancers." *DP* 37 (Spring 1969). "The Perils of Pauline," pp. 36-41.

    MOO/1: 119-126.

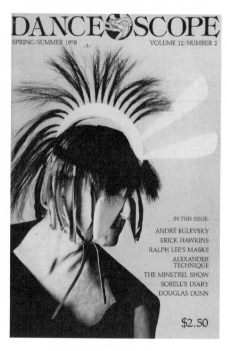

SPRING/SUMMER 1978 — VOLUME 12/NUMBER 2

IN THIS ISSUE:
ANDRÉ EGLEVSKY
ERICK HAWKINS
RALPH LEE'S MASKS
ALEXANDER TECHNIQUE
THE MINSTREL SHOW
SORELL'S DIARY
DOUGLAS DUNN

$2.50

**Early, Fergus** (1946– )

Huxley, Michael. "Approaches to New Dance: An Analysis of Two Works." An analysis of Fergus Early's *Are You Right There Michael Are You Right?* (1982) in Chapter 9 of *Dance Analysis: Theory and Practice*, pp. 162-169. Edited by Janet Adshead. London: Dance Books, 1988.

**Edwards, Leslie** (1916– )

DAV: 69-71.

**Eglevsky, André** (1917-1977)

"Eglevsky, André." *CBY 1953*: 174-176.

Hastings, Baird, comp. "André Eglevsky: A Photograph Portfolio." *BR* 8, no. 1 (1980): 1-32. With an introductory essay by Baird Hastings.

Horwitz, Dawn Lille, and Don McDonagh. "Conversations with André Eglevsky." *BR* 8, no. 1 (1980): 33-74. Article appended by two lists: Performances by André Eglevsky on "The Kate Smith Show" (NBC-TV) (p. 75). André Eglevsky: A General Chronology (p. 76).

**Eglevsky, André** *(continued)*

Manchester, P.W. "André Eglevsky, 1917-1977." *BR* 7, no. 1 (1978-1979): 66-69.

Rosen, Lillie F. "Remembering André Eglevsky (1917-1977)." *DS* 12, no. 2 (Spring/Summer 1978): 7-13.

Sheridan, Hope. "André Eglevsky: The Great Classic Dancer." *Chrysalis* 2, nos. 3-5 [1949]: [1]-31.

ATK: 48-51. DAV: 72-75. MCC: 143-149.

**Egorova, Lubov** (1880-1972)

SMA: 19-25.

**Eiko & Koma (Eiko** 1952– & **Koma** 1948– )

Windham, Leslie. "A Conversation with Eiko & Koma." *BR* 16, no. 2 (Summer 1988): 47-59.

**Elkins, Doug** (1960– )

Mason, Francis, and Don Daniels. "A Conversation with Doug Elkins." *BR* 22, no. 3 (Fall 1994): 50-63.

**Elssler, Fanny** (1810-1884)

Arkin, Lisa C. "Spanish Seductress or Sublime Stylist: Authenticity or Exoticism in Fanny Elssler's *La Cachucha.*" In *Proceedings of the Conference "Dance Reconstructed: Modern Dance Art Past, Present, Future,"* pp. 65-72. Rutgers University, New Brunswick, New Jersey, October 16 and 17, 1992.

Aschengreen, Erik. "The Beautiful Danger: Facets of the Romantic Ballet." *DP* 58 (Summer 1974). "Fanny Elssler and the Disappointed Romantics," pp. 16-24.

Beaumont, Cyril W. *Fanny Elssler (1810-1884)*. Essays on Dancing and Dancers, No. 10. London: C.W. Beaumont, 1931.

**Elssler, Fanny** *(continued)*

Costonis, Maureen Needham. "Fanny Elssler in Havana." In *Society of Dance History Scholars Proceedings*, pp. 214-233. Fourteenth Annual Conference, New World School of the Arts, Miami, Florida, 8-10 February 1991. Reprinted in *C&D* 3, pt. 4 (1994): 37-46.

------. "The Personification of Desire: Fanny Elssler and American Audiences." *DC* 13, no. 1 (1990): 47-67.

Crow, Duncan. "Fanny Elssler." Chapter 5 in his *Henry Wikoff: The American Chevalier*, pp. 49-57. London: MacGibbon & Kee, 1963.

Delarue, Allison. *The Chevalier Henry Wikoff: Impresario, 1840.* Princeton, N.J.: Privately printed at Princeton University Press, 1968.

*Fanny Elssler in America.* Introduction and Notes by Allison Delarue. New York: Dance Horizons, 1976.

Guest, Ivor. *Fanny Elssler.* London: Adam & Charles Black, 1970.

Heiberg, Johanne Luise. "Memories of Taglioni and Elssler." Translated by Patricia McAndrew. *DC* 4, no. 1 (1981): 14-18.

Hutchinson, Ann. *Fanny Elssler's "Cachucha."* New York: Theatre Arts, 1981.

Meglin, Joellen A. "Fanny Elssler's *Cachucha* and Women's Lives: Domesticity and Sexuality in France in the 1830s." In *Proceedings of the Conference "Dance Reconstructed: Modern Dance Art Past, Present, Future,"* pp. 73-96. Rutgers University, New Brunswick, New Jersey, October 16 and 17, 1992.

"Le Quatuor dansè [i.e., dansé] à Londres par Taglioni, Charlotte Grisi, Cerrito et Fanny Elsler [sic]." *DI* 3, nos. 7-8 (July- August 1944). Portion on Elssler, pp. 108-117.

Weissenböck, Jarmila. *Fanny Elssler: Materialien.* Translated by Stefanie Winkelbauer. Vienna: Hermann Böhlaus Nachf., 1984. Bilingual: German/English.

Wikoff, Henry. *The Reminiscences of an Idler.* New York: Fords, Howard & Hulbert, 1880.

GUE: 91-98. MIG: 145-167. MOO/1: 91-109. MOO/2: 104-112. SWI/1: 207-228.

**Elvin, Violetta** (1925– ; née **Violetta Prokhorova**)

Elvin, Harold. *The Gentle Russian.* London: The Pacific Press, 1976.

**Elvin, Violetta** *(continued)*

A novel loosely based on the author's experiences in the U.S.S.R., where he met the dancer Violetta Prokhorova, who later became his wife.

Fisher, Hugh. *Violetta Elvin.* Dancers of To-Day, No. 3. London: Adam & Charles Black, 1953.

CRO: 114-136. DAV: 76-78. HUR: 294-295.

**Enters, Angna** (1897-1989)

Cocuzza, Ginnine. "Angna Enters: American Dance-Mime." *TDR* 24, no. 4/T-88 (December 1980): 93-102.

——, commentary. "'First Person Plural': A Portfolio from the Theatre of Angna Enters." *W&P* 1, no. 1/[Issue #1] (Spring-Summer 1983): 36-39.

——. "The Theater of Angna Enters: American Dance-Mime." Unpublished dissertation, New York University, 1987. Ann Arbor, Mich.: University Microfilms International, 1987. Order No. 871,2740. DAI 48-03A, p. 0515.

"Enters, Angna." *CBY 1940*: 279-281.

"Enters, Angna." *CBY 1952*: 173-176.

Enters, Angna. *Artist's Life.* New York: Coward-McCann, 1958.

——. *First Person Plural.* New York: Stackpole Sons, 1937; reprint New York: Da Capo Press, 1978.

——. *Love Possessed Juana [Queen of Castile]: A Play in 4 Acts.* New York: Twice a Year Press, 1939.

——. *On Mime.* Middletown, Conn.: Wesleyan University Press, 1965.

——. *Silly Girl: A Portrait of Personal Remembrance.* Cambridge, Mass.: Houghton Mifflin, 1944.

Mandel, Dorothy. *Uncommon Eloquence: A Biography of Angna Enters.* Denver, Colo.: Arden Press, 1986.

SOR/1: 83-96.

**Erdman, Jean** (1917– )

"Erdman, Jean." *CBY 1971*: 115-118.

LLO: 192-193. SOR/1: 197-212.

**Espinosa, Edouard** (1872-1950)

Espinosa, Edouard. *And Then He Danced: The Life of Espinosa by Himself.* London: Sampson Low, Marston & Co., [1948].

**Espinosa, Léon** (1825-1903)
MOO/2: 119-123.

**Evan, Blanche** (1909-1982)
Benov, Ruth Gordon, comp. *Collected Works By and About Blanche Evan: Dancer, Teacher, Writer, Dance/Movement/Word Therapist.* San Francisco: Blanche Evan Dance Foundation, 1991.

**Evanitsky, Stephanie** (1944– )
Carroll, Noël. "Air Dancing." *TDR* 19, no. 1/T-65 (March 1975): 5-12.

**Evans, Bill** (1946– )
Evans, Bill. "Choreographer of Regions." In *Society of Dance History Scholars Proceedings*, pp. 44-50. Twelfth Annual Conference, Arizona State University, 17-19 February 1989.

**Evdokimova, Eva** (1948– )
Kleinert, Annemarie. *Portrait of an Artist: Eva Evdokimova.* Berlin: Stapp Verlag, 1982.

**Fagan, Garth** (1950– )
Mason, Francis. "A Conversation with Garth Fagan." *BR* 23, no. 1 (Spring 1995): 19-28.

**Falco, Louis** (1942-1993)
KRE: 40-55.

**Farber, Viola** (1931– )
Smoliar, Stephen. "Impressions of Viola Farber." *BR* 3, no. 6 (1971): 45-50.
LIV: 106-119.

**Farrell, Suzanne** (1945– )
Croce, Arlene. "Farrell and Farrellism." *The New Yorker* 50, no. 50 (February 3, 1975): 87-90; reprinted in Arlene Croce's *Afterimages*, pp. 120-125. New York: Knopf, 1977.
Daniel, David. "A Conversation with Suzanne Farrell." *BR* 7, no. 1 (1978-1979): 1-15.
———. "Diana Adams on Suzanne Farrell," *BR* 9, no. 4 (Winter 1982): 9-19.

**Farrell, Suzanne** *(continued)*

———. "In Mr. B's Steps." *The New Yorker* 69, no. 13 (May 17, 1993): 56-59.

"Farrell, Suzanne." *CBY 1967*: 112-115.

Farrell, Suzanne, with Toni Bentley. *Holding On to the Air: An Autobiography*. New York: Summit Books, 1990.

"Farrell Dancing, Year by Year." *BR* 9, no. 4 (Winter 1982): 20-47. A portfolio of photographs.

Kriegsman, Alan M., text, with photography by Martha Swope. *Suzanne Farrell*. Dance Horizons Spotlight Series. Brooklyn, N.Y.: Dance Horizons, 1975.

McDonagh, Don. "Suzanne Farrell." *BR* 17, no. 4 (Winter 1990): 62-68.

GRE/2: 23-34. GRU/2: 190-195. MON: 80-83. SWI/3: 219-223. TRA: 148-159.

**Fedorova, Sofia** (1879-1963)

SMA: 110-117.

**Feld, Eliot** (1942– )

"Feld, Eliot." *CBY 1971*: 126-128.

Cowser, R.L., Jr. "Eliot Feld Talks." *DS* 14, no. 3 (September 1980): 16-21.

Emerson, Ken. "Feld's Foster." *BR* 22, no. 3 (Fall 1994): 82-84.

France, Charles Engell. "A Conversation with Eliot Feld." *BR* 3, no. 6 (1971): 7-15.

COE: 102-107. GRU/2: 433-439. HOD: 156-191. ROG: 169-183.

**Fenley, Molissa** (1954– )

Banes, Sally. "'Drive,' She Said: The Dance of Molissa Fenley." *TDR* 24, no. 4/T-88 (December 1980): 3-14.

Fenley, Molissa. "Engram." *TDR* 27, no. 4/T-100 (Winter 1983): 38-39.

KRE: 210-229.

**Ferri, Alessandra** (1963– )

GRU/1: 17-22.

**Field, John** (1921-1991)

Field, Anne Heaton, comp. *John Field, CBE: A Memorial Tribute*. London: the author, 1992.

**Fifield, Elaine** (1930– )

Fifield, Elaine, with Kevin Perkins. *In My Shoes*. London: W.H. Allen, 1967.

ATK: 52-54.

**Fokine, Michel** (1880-1942)

Beaumont, Cyril W. *Michel Fokine & His Ballets*. London: C.W. Beaumont, 1935.

de Mille, Agnes. "Fokine." In her *The Book of the Dance*, pp. 138-145. New York: Golden Press; London: Paul Hamlyn, 1963.

Fokine, Michel. *"The Dying Swan."* New York: J. Fischer & Brother, 1925. Includes Camille Saint-Saëns's music for the dance.

——. *Fokine: Memoirs of a Ballet Master*. Translated by Vitale Fokine. Edited by Anatole Chujoy. Boston: Little, Brown & Company, 1961.

Garafola, Lynn. *Diaghilev's Ballets Russes*. New York & Oxford: Oxford University Press, 1989.

——. "Fokine's *Paganini* Reconstructed." *BR* 14, no. 1 (Spring 1986): 69-71.

Goldman, Debra. "Mothers and Fathers: A View of Isadora and Fokine." *BR* 6, no. 4 (1977-1978): 33-43.

Gregory, John. *Les Sylphides—Chopiniana*. Croesor, Penrhyndeudraeth, Gwynedd, Wales, U.K.: Zena Publications, 1989. [On cover: *Les Sylphides—Chopiniana*: Personal Reflections on Michel Fokine's Masterpiece].

Horwitz, Dawn Lille. "A Ballet Class with Michel Fokine." *DC* 3, no. 1 (1979): 36-45.

——. "Fokine and the American Musical." *BR* 13, no. 2 (Summer

**Fokine, Michel** *(continued)*

1985): 57-72. An extract from Dawn Lille Horwitz's *Michel Fokine*. Boston: Twayne Publishers, 1985.

——. *Michel Fokine*. Boston: Twayne Publishers, 1985.

——. "Michel Fokine—Choreography of the Thirties." In *Society of Dance History Scholars Proceedings*, pp. 194-199. Eleventh Annual Conference, North Carolina School of the Arts, 12-14 February 1988.

——. "Panel: Michel Fokine's Style." In *Society of Dance History Scholars Proceedings*, p. 216. Ninth Annual Conference, City College, City University of New York, 14-17 February 1986.

——. "Two Bacchanales on Broadway—Choreographed by Fokine." In *Society of Dance History Scholars Proceedings*, pp. 166-175. Sixth Annual Conference, The Ohio State University, 11-13 February 1983.

Kirstein, Lincoln, Arnold L. Haskell, and Stewart Deas. *"Carnaval," "Le Spectre de la Rose," and "Les Sylphides."* Edited by Arnold L. Haskell. Sadler's Wells Ballet Books, No. 4. London: The Bodley Head, 1949.

——. *Fokine*. Artists of the Dance. London: British-Continental Press, 1934.

Koner, Pauline. "With Fokine." *BR* 17, no. 1 (Spring 1989): 16-26. An extract from the first chapter of Pauline Koner's *Solitary Song*. Durham, N.C. & London: Duke University Press, 1989.

Lomax, Sondra. "Fokine's Manifesto and *Les Sylphides*." In *New Directions in Dance*, pp. 113-120. Edited by Diana Theodores Taplin. Toronto: Pergamon Press, 1979. Collected writings from the Seventh Dance in Canada Conference, University of Waterloo, Canada, June 1979.

"Michel Fokine 1880-1942: Illustrated Checklist of the Centenary Exhibition organized by the Dance Collection of the New York Public Library at Lincoln Center." *BR* 9, no. 3 (Fall 1981): 53-69.

Nelson, Karen. "Bringing Fokine to Light." *DRJ* 16, no. 2 (Fall 1984): 3-12.

Perron, Wendy. "The Far-Flung Fokine Family." *BR* 18, no. 2 (Summer 1990): 48-58. Article includes a Fokine family tree.

Pudełek, Janina. "Fokine in Warsaw, 1908-1914." *DC* 15, no. 1 (1992): 59-71.

**Fokine, Michel** *(continued)*

Sokolov-Kiminsky, Arkady. "Mikhail Fokine in St. Petersburg 1912-18." *DR* 10, no. 1 (Spring 1992): 53-58.

DAV: 78-84. DRU: 92-113. FRA: 1-19. HAL: 87-96. HAS/1: 83-91, 100. HAS/2: 105-114. HUR: 92-104. KON: 7-21. MOO/1: 183-192. PAL: 123-126. SCH/2: 58-67.

**Fontaine, Mlle de la** (ca. 1655-ca. 1738)

MIG: 7-9.

**Fonteyn, Margot** (1919-1991)

Anthony, Gordon. *Ballerina: Further Studies of Margot Fonteyn.* London: Home & Van Thal, 1945.

——. *Margot Fonteyn.* 2d ed. London: Gordon Anthony, 1941.

——. *Margot Fonteyn.* London: Phoenix House, 1950.

Beaumont, Cyril W. *Margot Fonteyn.* Essays on Dancing and Dancers, No. 11. London: C.W. Beaumont, 1948.

——. "Margot Fonteyn." In *The Ballet Annual 1954: A Record And Year Book of the Ballet*, pp. 73-77. Edited by Arnold L. Haskell. Eighth Issue. New York: Macmillan, 1953.

Bland, Alexander. *Fonteyn & Nureyev: The Story of a Partnership.* New York: Times Books, 1979.

Chappell, William. *Fonteyn: Impressions of a Ballerina.* London: Spring Books, [1950].

Clarke, Mary, text, with photography by Anthony Crickmay. *Margot Fonteyn.* Dance Horizons Spotlight Series. Brooklyn, N.Y.: Dance Horizons, 1976.

Como, William, ed. *Margot Fonteyn.* New York: DANAD Publishing Company, c. 1973. Includes an essay by Tobi Tobias: "She Was Only a Girl Named Peggy, but Oh How She Could Dance."

**Fonteyn, Margot** *(continued)*

*Dance & Dancers* 6, no. 4 (April 1955). A special issue celebrating Margot Fonteyn's twenty-one years as a dancer. Articles: "Snowflake to Firebird" (pp. 7-8). "Fonteyn's First Roles" (p. 9). "The Career of Fonteyn" (p. 10). "War-time Roles" (pp. 11-12). "Post-war Roles" (pp. 13-14). "Fonteyn from the Other Side of the Footlights" (pp. 14-15). "Margot Fonteyn Throws a Party" (pp. 16-17).

Fisher, Hugh. *Margot Fonteyn.* 3d rev. ed. Dancers of To-Day, No. 1. London: Adam & Charles Black, 1964.

"Fonteyn, Margot." *CBY 1949*: 206-207.

"Fonteyn, Margot." *CBY 1972*: 149-151.

Fonteyn, Margot. *Autobiography.* London: W.H. Allen, 1975.

——. *A Dancer's World: An Introduction.* London: W.H. Allen, 1978.

——. *The Magic of Dance.* New York: Knopf, 1979.

——, text, with illustrations by Trina Schart Hyman. *Swan Lake.* New York: Harcourt, Brace, Jovanovich, 1989.

Frank, Elizabeth. *Margot Fonteyn.* London: Chatto & Windus, 1958.

Harris, Dale. "Snowflake to Superstar." *BR* 4, no. 6 (1974): 67-79.

Hastings, Baird. "Margot Fonteyn (1919-1991)." *BR* 19, no. 1 (Spring 1991): 20-35.

Ludden, Ken. "Fonteyn on Video." BR 19, no. 3 (Fall 1991): 83-84.

Moiseiwitsch, Maurice, and Eric Warman, eds. "Margot Fonteyn." In their *The Royal Ballet on Stage and Screen: The Book of the Royal Ballet Film*, pp. 29-38. London, Melbourne, Toronto: Heinemann, 1960.

Monahan, James. *Fonteyn: A Study of the Ballerina in her Setting.* New York: Pitman, 1957.

Money, Keith. *The Art of Margot Fonteyn.* New York: Reynal & Company, 1965.

——. *Fonteyn and Nureyev: The Great Years.* London: Harvill Press, 1994.

——. *Fonteyn: The Making of a Legend.* London: Collins, 1973.

"Remembering Margot Fonteyn." *BR* 21, no. 2 (Summer 1993): 21-43. A symposium hosted by the Dance Collection in Bruno Walter Auditorium on 16 June 1991. The panel was introduced and moderated by Francis Mason. Participants: Clive Barnes, Joy Brown, Robert Gottlieb, Dale Harris, Baird Hastings, Doris

**Fonteyn, Margot** *(continued)*

Hering, Oleg Kerensky, Georgina Parkinson, Valda Setterfield, and David Vaughan.

Tobias, Tobi. "Margot Fonteyn: She Was Only a Girl Named Peggy, but Oh How She Could Dance." *Dance Magazine* 47, no. 7 (July 1973): 43-58. A Dance Magazine Portfolio.

Vernon, Gilbert. "Margot Fonteyn: A Personal Tribute." *DC* 14, nos. 2 & 3 (1991): 221-233.

Williams, Peter. "Margot Fonteyn: English Ballerina." In *Souvenirs de Ballet*, pp. 24-27. Edited by Duncan Melvin. London: Mayfair Publications, 1949.

ATK: 55-60. AUS/2: 93-104. CLA: 158-190. CRO: 92-113. DAV: 85-91. DRU: 175-192. GRU/2: 101-108. HUR: 254-259. MCC: 86-94. MON: 36-39. MUI: 135-145. NOB: 60-64.

**Foregger, Nikolai** (1892-1939)

Foregger, Nikolai. "Experiments in the Art of the Dance." *TDR* 19, no. 1/T-65 (March 1975): 74-77.

Gordon, Mel. "Foregger and The Dance of the Machines." *TDR* 19, no. 1/T-65 (March 1975): 68-73.

**Fornaroli, Cia** (see **Toscanini, Cia Fornaroli**)

**Forsythe, William** (1949– )

Driver, Senta. "2 or 3 Things That Might Be Considered Primary." *BR* 18, no. 1 (Spring 1990): 81-85.

——, and the Editors of *Ballet Review*. "A Conversation with William Forsythe." *BR* 18, no. 1 (Spring 1990): 86-97.

Jeschke, Claudia. "American Theatricality in Contemporary German Theater Dancing: John Neumeier and William Forsythe." In *Society of Dance History Scholars Proceedings*, pp. 201-206. Fifteenth Annual Conference, University of California, Riverside, 14-15 February 1992.

Stuart, Otis. "Forsythe's Follies." *BR* 15, no. 3 (Fall 1987): 41-44.

Wilkins, Darrell A. "Aesthetics and Cultural Criticism in William Forsythe's *Impressing the Czar*." *BR* 22, no. 1 (Spring 1994): 61-66.

**Forti, Simone** (1935– )

Forti, Simone. *Angel*. New York: the author, 1978. *Angel* is a poem in twenty-three paragraphs and is a restatement of a performance

**Forti, Simone** *(continued)*

    piece originally presented in the Fine Arts Building in New York, 1976.

——. "Bicycles." *DS* 13, no. 1 (Fall 1978): 44-51.

——. "A Chamber Dance Concert." *TDR* 19, no. 1/T-65 (March 1975): 37-39.

——. *Handbook in Motion.* Halifax: The Press of the Nova Scotia College of Art and Design; New York: New York University, 1974.

Sommers, Pamela. "Simone Forti's *Jackdaw Songs.*" *TDR* 25, no. 2/T-90 (Summer 1981): 124-126.

BAN: 20-39.

**Fracci, Carla** (1936– )

"Fracci, Carla." *CBY 1975*: 139-141.

Tobias, Tobi. "Visiting Fracci." *Dance Magazine* 48, no. 1 (January 1974): 51-66. A Dance Magazine Portfolio.

GRU/2: 196-201. MON: 56-59.

**Frame, Peter** (1957– )

SWI/3: 168-172.

**Franca, Celia** (1921– )

Bell, Ken, photography, and a memoir by Celia Franca. *The National Ballet of Canada: A Celebration.* Toronto & London: University of Toronto Press, c. 1978.

"Franca, Celia." *CBY 1956*: 186-188.

DAV: 91-94.

**Frankel, Emily** (1930– )

Jackson, Teague. *Encore: The Private and Professional Triumph of Emily Frankel.* Englewood Cliffs, N.J.: Prentice-Hall, 1978.

**Frankenberg, Ellen von** (1906– )

Bell-Kanner, Karen. *The Life and Times of Ellen von Frankenberg.* Choreography and Dance Studies, Vol. 1. Chur, Switzerland: Harwood Academic Publishers, 1991.

**Franklin, Frederic** (1914– )

Anderson, Jack. "Danilova and Franklin." *BR* 9, no. 4 (Winter 1982): 75-81. A chapter from Anderson's *The One and Only: The Ballet Russe de Monte Carlo.* New York: Dance Horizons, 1981.

**Franklin, Frederic** *(continued)*

"Franklin, Frederic." *CBY 1943*: 213-214.

Maynard, Olga. "Frederic Franklin: A Life in the Theater." *Dance Magazine* 48, no. 6 (June 1974): 43-58. A Dance Magazine Portfolio.

ATK: 61-64. DAV: 94-98.

**Fraser, Moyra** (ca. 1925– )

DAV: 98-102.

**Friedman, Judith** (1940; now **Judith R. F. Kupersmith, M.D.**)

SID: 93-103.

**Fuchs, Caroline Augusta Josephine Thérèse** (1806-1901; known as **Madame Augusta**)

SWI/1: 109-127.

**Fuente, Luis** (1946– )

COH/1: 34-37.

**Fuller, Loïe** (1862-1928)

Doughty, Heather. "The Choreographer in the Courtroom: Loïe Fuller and Leonide Massine." In *Society of Dance History Scholars Proceedings*, pp. 35-39. Fifth Annual Conference, Harvard University, 13-15 February 1982.

The Fine Arts Museums of San Francisco. *In Celebration of Loïe Fuller*, a festival of performing arts complemented by an exhibition, December 10, 1977 - February 26, 1978. San Francisco: [The] California Palace of the Legion of Honor, [1977]. A flyer about the exhibition and festival events.

Fuller, Loïe. *Fifteen Years of a Dancer's Life*. Boston: Small, Maynard & Company Publishers, 1913; reprint New York: Dance Horizons, 1978?

**Fuller, Loïe** *(continued)*

Harris, Margaret Haile. *Loïe Fuller: Magician of Light*. Richmond: Virginia Museum, 1979.

Kermode, Frank. "Loïe Fuller and the Dance Before Diaghilev." *Theatre Arts* 46, no. 9 (September 1962): 6-21.

Morinni, Clare de. "Loïe Fuller: The Fairy of Light." *DI* 1, no. 3 (March 1942).

Sommer, Sally R. "Loïe Fuller." *TDR* 19, no. 1/T-65 (March 1975): 53-67.

———. "Loïe Fuller's Art of Music and Light." *DC* 4, no. 4 (1981): 389-401.

———. "The Stage Apprenticeship of Loïe Fuller." *DS* 12, no. 1 (Fall/Winter 1977-78): 23-34.

BRO: 12-19. HUR: 37-39. MAG: 202-220. MAZ: 17-34. TER: 45-47. VAN: 32-34.

# G

**Gable, Christopher** (1940– )
NEW/1: 266-284.

**Galli, Rosina** (1896-1940)
Limarzi, Tullia. "'She Trills with her Toes'—The Metropolitan Opera Ballet Career of Rosina Galli." In *Society of Dance History Scholars Proceedings*, pp. 80-89. Ninth Annual Conference, City College, City University of New York, 14-17 February 1986.

**Gambarelli, Maria** (1901?-1990)
BEL: 38-41.

**Gardel, Pierre** (1758-1840)
Chapman, John V. "Forgotten Giant: Pierre Gardel." *DR* 5, no. 1 (Spring 1987): 3-20.

**Gardie, Anna** (ca. 1760-1798)
MOO/2: 58-60.

**Geltzer, Ekaterina** (1872-1962)
SLO: 69-72. SMA: 80-88.

**Genée, Adeline** (1878-1970)
Guest, Ivor. *Adeline Genée: A Lifetime of Ballet under Six Reigns*. London: Adam & Charles Black, 1958.

**Genée, Adeline** *(continued)*

———. *Ballet in Leicester Square: The Alhambra and the Empire, 1860-1915*. London: Dance Books, 1992.

———. "Dame Adeline Genée." In *The Ballet Annual 1956: A Record and Year Book of the Ballet*, pp. 54-61. Edited by Arnold L. Haskell. Tenth Issue. New York: Macmillan, 1955.

———. *The Empire Ballet*. London: The Society for Theatre Research, 1962.

Hardy, Camille. "The American Debut of Adeline Genée." In *New Directions in Dance*, pp. 121-133. Edited by Diana Theodores Taplin. Toronto: Pergamon Press, 1979. Collected writings from the Seventh Dance in Canada Conference, University of Waterloo, Canada, June 1979.

CAF: 128-145. DAV: 102-108. GUE: 45-51.

**Gentry, Eve** (1910?-1994)

Adler-Friess, Aanya. "Three Grand Ladies of Modern Dance: Eve Gentry, Eleanor King and Elizabeth Waters." In *Society of Dance History Scholars Proceedings*, pp. 147-155. Eighth Annual Conference, University of New Mexico, 15-17 February 1985.

**George, Carolyn** (see **d'Amboise, Carolyn George**)

**Gerdt, Pavel** (1844-1917)

SMA: 254-259.

**Gert, Valeska** (1892-1978)

de Keersmaeker, Anne Teresa. "Valeska Gert." *TDR* 25, no. 3/T-91 (Fall 1981): 55-66.

**Geva, Tamara** (1908– )

Geva, Tamara. *Split Seconds: A Remembrance*. New York: Harper & Row, 1972.

MAS: 9-17. TRA: 28-35.

**Gillis, Christopher** (1951-1993)

Lobenthal, Joel. "Christopher Gillis: Dancing for Paul Taylor." *BR* 13, no. 2 (Summer 1985): 10-22.

**Gilmour, Sally** (1921– )
DAV: 109-111.

**Gilpin, John** (1930-1983)
Gilpin, John. *A Dance with Life*. London: William Kimber, 1982.
Swinson, Cyril. *John Gilpin*. Dancers of To-Day, No. 12. London:
Adam & Charles Black, 1957.
DAV: 111-113. GRU/2: 52-58.

**Glasco, Kimberly** (1960– )
Carreiro, Assis. *Kimberly Glasco*.
Profiles of Canadian Dance, No.
1. Toronto: Press of Terpsichore,
1987.

**Godunov, Alexander** (1949-1995)
"Godunov, Alexander." *CBY 1983*:
148-151.
PET: 94-113.

**Goleizovsky, Kasian** (1892-1970)
Banes, Sally. "Goleizovsky's Ballet
Manifestos." *BR* 11, no. 3 (Fall
1983): 64-75.
Leyda, Si-lan Chen. *Footnote to
History*. Edited by Sally Banes.
New York: Dance Horizons, 1984.
Manor, Giora. "Goleizovsky's *Jo-
seph the Beautiful*: A Modern
Ballet Before Its Time." *C&D* 2, pt. 3 (1992): 63-70.
———. "Kasyan Goleizovsky's Russian Revolution." Part One and
Part Two. *Dance Magazine* 63, no. 1 (January 1989): 56-60 and
*Dance Magazine* 63, no. 2 (February 1989): 60-64.
Souritz, Elizabeth. "Kasian Yaroslavich Goleizovsky." Chapter 4 in
her *Soviet Choreographers in the 1920s*, pp. 154-215. Translated
from the Russian by Lynn Visson. Edited, with additional
translation, by Sally Banes. Durham, N.C. & London: Duke
University Press, 1990.

**Goleizovsky, Kasian** *(continued)*

———. "Soviet Choreographers in the 1920s: Kasian Yaroslavich Goleizovsky." *DRJ* 20, no. 2 (Winter 1988): 9-22.

**Golikova, Tatyana** (1945– )

ZHD: 272-291.

**Gollner, Nana** (1920-1980)

BEL: 42-45. DAV: 113-115.

**Golovine, Serge** (1927– )

Reiss, Françoise. "Serge Golovine." *Chrysalis* 5, nos. 1-2 (1952): [3]-[7].

**Gordeyev, Vyacheslav** (1948– )

GRE/1: 13-15.

**Gordon, David** (1936– )

Barr, Burt. "David Gordon's *What Happened.*" *TDR* 23, no. 3/T-83 (September 1979): 33-48.

Croce, Arlene. "Making Work." *The New Yorker* 58, no. 41 (November 29, 1982): 51-52, 55-56, 59-60, 63-64, 67-68, 73-74, 76, 78-86, 88, 93-94, 96, 98-103, 105-107.

"Gordon, David." *CBY 1994*: 217-221.

Gordon, David. "It's About Time." *TDR* 19, no. 1/T-65 (March 1975): 43-52.

Setterfield, Valda. "The Making of *Field, Chair & Mountain.*" *BR* 13, no. 1 (Spring 1985): 5-21.

Smith, Karen. "David Gordon's *The Matter.*" *TDR* 16, no. 3/T-55 (September 1972): 117-127.

BAN: 96-110.

**Gore, Walter** (1910-1979)

"Walter Gore: A Tribute in Four Parts." *DR* 6, no. 1 (Spring 1988). The four parts: Clement Crisp. "Introduction" (pp. 3-6). Walter Gore. "Up Till Now" (pp. 7-16). Paula Hinton Gore. "Walter Gore" (pp. 17-22). Paula Hinton Gore and Clement Crisp. "Walter Gore's Choreographies: A First Listing" (pp. 23-29).

DAV: 115-119. FRA: 122-131.

**Gorsky, Alexander** (1871-1924)

Beaumont, Cyril W. "Alexander Gorski." Chapter 10 in his *The Ballet Called "Swan Lake,"* pp. 64-68. London: C.W. Beaumont, 1952.

Souritz, Elizabeth. "Alexander Alexeyevich Gorsky." Chapter 3 in her *Soviet Choreographers in the 1920s*, pp. 85-153. Translated from the Russian by Lynn Visson. Edited, with additional translation, by Sally Banes. Durham, N.C. & London: Duke University Press, 1990.

ROS: 155-166. SCH/2: 56-58.

**Gould, Diana** (see **Menuhin, Diana Gould**)

**Gould, Norma** (1888?-1980)

Prevots, Naima. "Norma Gould: Forgotten Pioneer." In *Society of Dance History Scholars Proceedings*, pp. 87-93. Fifth Annual Conference, Harvard University, 13-15 February 1982.

PRE: 21-51.

**Govrin, Gloria** (1942– )

GRE/3: 21-22.

**Graham, Martha** (1894-1991)

Ackerman, Gerald. "Photography and the Dance: Soichi Sunami and Martha Graham." *BR* 12, no. 2 (Summer 1984): 32-66.

Alderson, Evan. "Metaphor in Dance: The Example of Graham." In *Society of Dance History Scholars Proceedings*, pp. 111-118. Sixth Annual Conference, The Ohio State University, 11-13 February 1983.

Anderson, Jack. "Some Personal Grumbles About Martha Graham." *BR* 2, no. 1 (1967): 25-30.

Armitage, Merle, ed. *Martha Graham*. Los Angeles: Merle Armitage, 1937; reprint New York: Da Capo Press, 1978.

Bliss, Paula M. "A Natural Collaboration." In *Society of Dance History Scholars Proceedings*, pp. 82-87. Twelfth Annual Conference, Arizona State University, 17-19 February 1989. The collaboration of Martha Graham and Isamu Noguchi.

**Graham, Martha** *(continued)*

Cohen, Selma Jeanne. "The Achievement of Martha Graham." *Chrysalis* 11, nos. 5-6 (1958): 3-11.

Corey, Frederick Charles. "Principles for the Use of Stylized Movement During the Interpretation and Performance of Literature Based on Martha Graham's Use of Classical Tragedy in Modern Dance." Unpublished dissertation, University of Arizona, 1987. Ann Arbor, Mich.: University Microfilms International, 1987. Order No. 872,6813. DAI 48-09A, p. 2193.

Costonis, Maureen Needham. "*American Document*: A Neglected Graham Work." In *Society of Dance History Scholars Proceedings*, pp. 72-81. Twelfth Annual Conference, Arizona State University, 17-19 February 1989.

Croce, Arlene. "Tell Me, Doctor." *BR* 2, no. 4 (1968): 12-18.

*Dance Magazine* 65, no. 7 (July 1991). A special memorial issue celebrating the art of Martha Graham. Feature articles: Joseph H. Mazo. "Martha Remembered" (pp. 34-45). Marian Horosko. "Martha's Prince" (pp. 46-47). Tim Wengerd. "Martha's Men" (pp. 48-52). Walter Sorell. "Martha and Myth" (pp. 53-55). "Martha's Dances: A Catalogue of Graham's Works from 1926 to 1990" (pp. 56-57). Gary Parks. "Martha Affirmed" (p. 58).

Daniel, Oliver. "*Rite of Spring*, First Staging in America: Stokowski-Massine-Graham." *BR* 10, no. 2 (Summer 1982): 67-71. An extract, in somewhat different form, from Oliver Daniel's *Stokowski: A Counterpoint of View*. New York: Dodd, Mead, 1982.

Dell, Cecily. "Random Graham." *DS* 2, no. 2 (Spring 1966): 21-26.

de Mille, Agnes. *Martha: The Life and Work of Martha Graham*. New York: Random House, 1991.

Dendy, Mark. "Graham's Season." *BR* 19, no. 1 (Spring 1991): 36-42.

———. "Graham Without Graham, 1991." *BR* 20, no. 3 (Fall 1992): 29-35.

Dixon-Stowell, Brenda. "Ethnic and Exotic Aspects in the Choreography of Selected Works by Ted Shawn and Martha Graham." In *Society of Dance History Scholars Proceedings*, pp. 21-28. Seventh Annual Conference, Goucher College, Towson, Maryland, 17-19 February 1984.

Fischer, Barry. "Graham's Dance 'Steps in the Street' and Selected Early Technique: Principles for Reconstructing Choreography

**Graham, Martha** *(continued)*

from Videotape." Unpublished dissertation, New York University, 1986. Ann Arbor, Mich.: University Microfilms International, 1986. Order No. 862,5670. DAI 47-10A, p. 3595.

Foreman, Donlin. *Out of Martha's House.* Foreword by Jacques d'Amboise. Italian translation by Elisa Rondoni. Rimini, Italy: Guaraldi/Nuova Compagnia Editrice, 1992. Bilingual: English/ Italian.

Fraser, John. "Martha Graham: Into the Cool Lucid Light of a Seer." *YDR* Issue #2 (Fall 1973): 23-29.

Gardner, Howard. "Martha Graham: Discovering the Dance of America." *BR* 22, no. 1 (Spring 1994): 67-93. Reprinted from *Creating Minds: An Anatomy of Creativity Seen Through the Lives of Freud, Einstein, Picasso, Stravinsky, Eliot, Graham and Gandhi* by Howard Gardner. New York: Basic Books, 1993.

Garfunkel, Trudy. *Letter to the World: The Life and Dances of Martha Graham.* Boston, New York, London, Toronto: Little, Brown and Company, 1995.

Gibbs, Angelica. "The Absolute Frontier." *The New Yorker* 23, no. 45 (December 27, 1947): 28-32, 34-37.

Goldberg, Marianne. "She Who Is Possessed No Longer Exists Outside: Martha Graham's *Rite of Spring.*" *W&P* 3, no. 1/ Issue #5 (1986): 17-27.

"Graham." *Dance Magazine* 48, no. 7 (July 1974). A four-part Dance Magazine Portfolio. Tobi Tobias. "The Graham Season: April 15-May 4, 1974" (pp. 44-45). Jean Nuchtern. "Martha Graham's Women Speak" (pp. 46-49). Doris Hering. "But Not for Clytemnestra: Comments on *The Notebooks of Martha Graham*" (pp. 52-55). Joel Shapiro. "Martha Graham at the Eastman School" (pp. 55-57).

**Graham, Martha** *(continued)*

"Graham, Martha." *CBY 1944*: 251-253.

"Graham, Martha." *CBY 1961*: 182-185.

Graham, Martha. *Blood Memory*. New York: Doubleday, 1991.

——. *The Notebooks of Martha Graham*. New York: Harcourt Brace Jovanovich, 1973.

Helpern, Alice. *The Technique of Martha Graham*. Dobbs Ferry, N.Y.: Morgan & Morgan, 1994. Originally published in *SDH* 2, no. 2 (Spring/Summer 1991).

Hodes, Stuart. "Three Brides in *Spring*." *BR* 18, no. 4 (Winter 1990-1991): 91-94.

Holder, Geoffrey. "Martha Graham: American Original." *Show* 3, no. 11 (November 1963): 86-87, 118-120.

Horan, Robert. "The Recent Theater of Martha Graham." *DI* 6, no. 1 (January 1947).

Horosko, Marian, comp. *Martha Graham: The Evolution of Her Dance Theory and Training 1926-1991*. Pennington, N.J.: A Cappella Books, 1991.

Jackson, Graham. "The Roots of Heaven: Sexuality in the Work of Martha Graham." In *Dance Spectrum: Critical and Philosophical Enquiry*, pp. 50-60. Edited by Diana Theodores Taplin. Waterloo, Ontario: Otium Publications; Dublin: Parsons Press, 1983.

Johnston, Jill. "Martha Graham: An Irresponsible Study . . . The Head of Her Father." *BR* 2, no. 4 (1968): 6-12.

Jowitt, Deborah. "In Memory: Martha Graham, 1894-1991." *TDR* 35, no. 4/T-132 (Winter 1991): 14-16.

Kriegsman, Sali Ann. *Modern Dance in America: The Bennington Years*. Boston: G.K. Hall & Co., 1981.

Leabo, Karl, ed. *Martha Graham*. New York: Theatre Arts Books, 1961.

Leatherman, LeRoy. *Martha Graham: Portrait of the Lady as an Artist*. New York: Knopf, 1966.

Lepczyk, Billie. "Martha Graham's Movement Invention Viewed through Laban Analysis." In *Dance: Current Selected Research*, Volume 1, pp. 45-64. Edited by Lynnette Y. Overby and James H. Humphrey. New York: AMS Press, 1989.

"Martha Graham (1894-1991)." *BR* 19, no. 3 (Fall 1991): 18-31. Reminiscences by Marian Seldes, May O'Donnell, Stuart Hodes, and Francis Mason.

## Graham, Martha *(continued)*

McDonagh, Don. "A Chat with Martha Graham." *BR* 2, no. 4 (1968): 18-28.

———. *Martha Graham: A Biography*. New York: Praeger, 1973.

McGehee, Helen. "Working for Martha Graham." *DR* 3, no. 2 (Autumn 1985): 56-64.

Morgan, Barbara. *Martha Graham: Sixteen Dances in Photographs.* New York: Duell, Sloan & Pearce, 1941; 1st rev. ed. Dobbs Ferry, N.Y.: Morgan & Morgan, c. 1980. This edition includes a "Complete chronological list of dances composed by Martha Graham from April 1926 to December 1980."

Noguchi, Isamu. "Noguchi: Collaborating with Graham." In *Isamu Noguchi: Essays and Conversations*, pp. 80-89. Edited by Diane Apostolos-Cappadona and Bruce Altshuler. New York: Abrams, in association with The Isamu Noguchi Foundation, 1994.

Oswald, Genevieve. "Myth and Legend in Martha Graham's *Night Journey*." *DRA XIV* (1983): 42-49.

———. "A Vision of Paradise: Myth and Symbol in *The Embattled Garden*." *C&D* 2, pt. 3 (1992): 27-37.

Polcari, Stephen. "Martha Graham and Abstract Expressionism." *Smithsonian Studies in American Art* 4, no. 1 (Winter 1990): 3–27.

Propper, Herbert. "Space/Symbol: The Spatial Concepts in Selected Dances of Martha Graham." Unpublished dissertation, University of Michigan, 1977. Ann Arbor, Mich.: University Microfilms International, 1977. Order No. 77-26,338. DAI 38-06A, p. 3147.

Purcell, J.M. "Notes on *Dark Meadow*: In Print, On Tour." *BR* 5, no. 2 (1975-1976): 97-100.

Sears, David. "Graham Masterworks in Revival." *BR* 10, no. 2 (Summer 1982): 25-34.

———. "Martha Graham: The Golden Thread." *BR* 14, no. 3 (Fall 1986): 44-64.

Shelton, Suzanne. "Jungian Roots of Martha Graham's Dance Imagery." In *Society of Dance History Scholars Proceedings*, pp. 119-132. Sixth Annual Conference, The Ohio State University, 11-13 February 1983.

Sherman, Jane. "Martha and Doris in Denishawn: A Closer Look." *DC* 17, no. 2 (1994): 179-193.

**Graham, Martha** *(continued)*

Snyder, Diana Maria. "'The Most Important Lesson for Our Theater.'" *BR* 10, no. 4 (Winter 1983): 7-20.

——. "Theatre as Verb: The Theatre Art of Martha Graham, 1923-1958." Unpublished dissertation, University of Illinois at Urbana-Champaign, 1980. Ann Arbor, Mich.: University Microfilms International, 1981. Order No. 810,8668. DAI 41-11A, p. 4545.

Soares, Janet Mansfield. *Louis Horst: Musician in a Dancer's World.* Durham, N.C. & London: Duke University Press, 1992.

Stodelle, Ernestine. *Deep Song: The Dance Story of Martha Graham.* New York: Schirmer Books; London: Collier Macmillan Publishers, 1984.

——. "Graham: 'I Am A Dancer.'" *BR* 12, no. 3 (Fall 1984): 59-71. An extract from *Deep Song: The Dance Story of Martha Graham.* New York: Schirmer Books; London: Collier Macmillan, 1984.

Terry, Walter. *Frontiers of Dance: The Life of Martha Graham.* Women of America. New York: Thomas Y. Crowell Company, 1975.

Tracy, Robert. "Noguchi: Collaborating with Graham." *BR* 13, no. 4 (Winter 1986): 9-17.

Trowbridge, Charlotte. *Dance Drawings of Martha Graham.* New York: Dance Observer, 1945.

ARM: 55-58. BRO: 48-53. COE: 134-153. DEM/2: 144-160. FOS: 23-32; 41-57. FOW: 28-51. HAL: 141-149. HAS/2: 176-184. LLO: 35-76. MAG: 238-259. MAR: 187-205. MAY/2: 105-125. MAZ: 153-196. MOO/1: 298-303. MUI: 89-97. PAL: 43-57. ROG: 25-40. SOR/1: 170-181. TER: 83-99.


**Grahn, Lucile** (1819-1907)

MIG: 168-178.


**Grand Union, The** (1970-1976; later **Rio Grande Union, The**)

Banes, Sally. "Grand Union: The Presentation of Everyday Life as Dance." *DRJ* 10, no. 2 (Spring-Summer 1978): 43-49.

——. *Terpsichore in Sneakers: Post-Modern Dance.* Boston: Houghton Mifflin, 1980; reprint with a new introduction and an updated chronology, Middletown, Conn.: Wesleyan University Press, 1987.

**Grand Union, The** *(continued)*

Kendall, Elizabeth. "The Grand Union: Our Gang." *BR* 5, no. 4 (1975-1976): 44-55.

Lorber, Richard. "The Problem with Grand Union." *DS* 7, no. 2 (Spring/Summer 1973): 32-34.

Paxton, Steve. "The Grand Union." *TDR* 16, no. 3/T-55 (September 1972): 128-134.

Ramsay, Margaret Hupp. *The Grand Union (1970-1976): An Improvisational Performance Group*. Artists and Issues in the Theatre, No. 2. New York: Peter Lang, c. 1991.

Robbins, Karen. "The Grand Union." *DS* 7, no. 2 (Spring/Summer 1973): 28-31.

FOS: 191-200; 220-227.

**Grant, Alexander** (1925– )

Crabb, Michael. "Alexander Grant: New Director for the National Ballet of Canada." *YDR* Spring 1976 (Issue #5): 26-29.

Willis, Margaret. "Russian Squats and Chinese Chequers." *DN* 4, no. 1 (Spring 1995): 71-76.

DAV: 119-122. NEW/1: 72-86.

**G**

**Grant, Gail** (1910– )

Grant, Gail. *The Technical Manual and Dictionary of Classical Ballet*. New York: Kamin Dance Publishers, 1950.

Rennie, Karen. *Moon Magic: Gail Grant and the 1920's Dance in Regina*. Toronto: Dance Collection Danse, 1992.

**Gray, Harriette Ann** (1913–1968)

Bonali, Gloria Ann. "Harriette Ann Gray: Her Life and Her Career as a Dancer, Choreographer, and Teacher 1913-1968." Unpublished dissertation, Texas Woman's University, 1971. On file, but not available from UMI. Order No. 02-36,311. Available from Microform. ADD X1971, p. 0207.

**Gregory, Cynthia** (1946– )

"Gregory, Cynthia." *CBY 1977*: 174-177.

Gregory, Cynthia, text, with photography by Martha Swope. *Cynthia Gregory Dances "Swan Lake"*. New York: Simon & Schuster, 1990.

**Gregory, Cynthia** *(continued)*

Péres, Louis, text and photography. *Cynthia Gregory.* Dance Horizons Spotlight Series. Brooklyn, N.Y.: Dance Horizons, 1975. GRU/1: 106-110. GRU/2: 221-226. MON: 88-91. PET: 154-177. SWI/3: 237-241.

**Grey, Beryl** (1927– )

Anthony, Gordon. *Beryl Grey.* London: Phoenix House, 1952.

Crowle, Pigeon. *Beryl Grey: The Progress of a Ballerina.* London: Faber & Faber, 1952.

Fisher, Hugh. *Beryl Grey.* Dancers of To-Day, No. 8. New York: Macmillan, 1955.

Gillard, David. *Beryl Grey: A Biography.* London: W.H. Allen, 1977.

Grey, Beryl, ed. *My Favourite Ballet Stories.* Guildford & London: Lutter Worth Press, 1981.

——. *Red Curtain Up.* New York: Dodd, Mead & Company, 1958.

——. *Through the Bamboo Curtain.* London: Collins, 1965.

ATK: 65-68. DAV: 122-124. HUR: 292-294. NEW/1: 112-127. SWI/2: 33-38.

DANCE RESEARCH

The Journal of the Society for Dance Research

Volume II   Number 1   Spring 1984

**Gries, Lance** (1963– )

Johnson, Robert. "It Isn't Easy Being Gries." *BR* 22, no. 3 (Fall 1994): 85-87.

**Grigorovich, Yuri** (1927– )

"Grigorovich, Yuri (Nikolaevich)." *CBY 1975*: 179-182.

Jennings, Luke. "The Czar's Last Dance." *The New Yorker* 71, no. 5 (March 27, 1995): 70-77, 79-86.

GRE/1: 1-10. DEM/1: 139-165.

**Gripenberg, Maggie** (1881-1976)

Ambegaokar, Saga M. "Maggie Gripenberg (1881-1976): A Finnish Pioneer in Modern Dance—The Early Years, and an Overview." In

**Gripenberg, Maggie** *(continued)*

> *Society of Dance History Scholars Proceedings*, pp. 75-84. Tenth Annual Conference, University of California, Irvine, 13-15 February 1987.

**Grisi, Carlotta** (1819-1899)

> Lifar, Serge. *Carlotta Grisi*. Translated by Doris Langley Moore. London: John Lehmann, 1947.
>
> "Le Quatuor dansè [i.e., dansé] à Londres par Taglioni, Charlotte Grisi, Cerrito et Fanny Elsler [sic]." *DI* 3, nos. 7-8 (July- August 1944). Portion on Grisi, pp. 106-107.
>
> MIG: 194-207. MOO/1: 127-135.

**Gross, Sally** (1933– )

> Satin, Leslie. *"One and Another*: Dancing with Sally Gross." *W&P* 5, no. 2/Issue #10 (1992): 148-165.

**Guest, Ann Hutchinson** (1918– )

> Guest, Ann Hutchinson. "The Golden Age of the Broadway Musical: A Personal Reminiscence." *DC* 16, no. 3 (1993): 323-371.

**Guillem, Sylvie** (1965– )

> Stuart, Otis. "Who is Sylvie?" *BR* 19, no. 3 (Fall 1991): 32-35.

**Guimard, Madeleine** (1743-1816)

> Beaumont, Cyril W. "Madeleine Guimard." In his *Three French Dancers of the 18th Century*, pp. 26-31. Essays on Dancing and Dancers, No. 6. London: C.W. Beaumont, 1934.
>
> Craig, Gordon. "Mademoiselle Guimard and Her Private Theatres." In *Gordon Craig on Movement and Dance*, pp. 172-178. Edited and with an Introduction by Arnold Rood. New York: Dance Horizons, 1977; reprinted from *The Dancing Times* 24, no. 279 (December 1933): 251-254.
>
> Guest, Ivor. "Letters from London: Guimard's Farewell to the Stage." *DC* 18, no. 2 (1995): 207-215.
>
> Perugini, Mark Edward. "Guimard the Grand, 1743-1816." Chapter 18 in his *A Pageant of the Dance & Ballet*, pp. 151-162. London: Jarrolds Publishers, 1935.
>
> MIG: 71-89. MOO/1: 51-56.

**Guyot, Marie-Catherine** (fl. 1705-1725)

Whitley-Bauguess, Paige. "The Search for Mlle Guyot." In *Society of Dance History Scholars Proceedings*, pp. 32-67. Eleventh Annual Conference, North Carolina School of the Arts, 12-14 February 1988.

## Haakon, Paul (1912-1992)

Gruen, John. "Paul Haakon." *Dance Magazine* 51, no. 11 (November 1977): 51-66. A Dance Magazine Portfolio.

Ware, Walter. "Paul Haakon." In his *Ballet Is Magic: A Triple Monograph*, pp. 21-36. New York: IHRA Publishing Company, 1936.

SCH/1: see Index of Choreographers, p. 135.

## Hadassah (1909?-1992)

LLO: 193-196.

## Haller, Lelia (1903– )

Scott, Harold George. *Lelia: The Compleat Ballerina.* Gretna, La.: Pelican Publishing Company, 1975.

## Halprin, Anna (1920– )

Halprin, Anna. "Ages of the Avant-Garde." *PAJ* 16, no. 1/Issue #46 (January 1994): 44-47.

———. *"Planetary Dance." TDR* 33, no. 2/T-122 (Summer 1989): 51-66.

Hartman, Rose. "Talking with Anna Halprin." *DS* 12, no. 1 (Fall/Winter 1977-78): 57-66.

Jean, Norma, and František Deák. "Anna Halprin's Theatre and Therapy Workshop." *TDR* 20, no. 1/T-69 (March 1976): 50-54.

**Halprin, Anna** *(continued)*

Maletic, Vera. "The Process Is the Purpose: An Interview with Anna Halprin." *DS* 4, no. 1 (Fall/Winter 1967-68): 11-18.

Rainer, Yvonne. "Yvonne Rainer Interviews Anna Halprin." In *The Drama Review: Thirty Years of Commentary on the Avant-Garde*, pp. 101-121. Edited by Brooks McNamara and Jill Dolan. Theater and Dramatic Studies, No. 35. Ann Arbor, Mich.: UMI Research Press, 1986; reprinted from *TDR* 10, no. 2 (Winter 1965): 142-167.

Ross, Janice. "Innocence Abroad: The 1965 Stockholm Premiere of Anna Halprin's *Parades and Changes*." In *Society of Dance History Scholars Proceedings*, pp. 159-168. Fifteenth Annual Conference, University of California, Riverside, 14-15 February 1992.

Schechner, Richard. "Anna Halprin: A Life in Ritual." *TDR* 33, no. 2/T-122 (Summer 1989): 67-73.

Turner, Diane M. "Anna Halprin: An Artist and an Influence." In *Dance: Current Selected Research*, Volume 1, pp. 97-113. Edited by Lynnette Y. Overby and James H. Humphrey. New York: AMS Press, 1989.

BRO: 126-133.

**Hamel, Martine van** (see **van Hamel, Martine**)

**Hamilton, Gordon** (1918-1959)

DAV: 124-126.

**Harrington, Rex** (1962– )

Carreiro, Assis. *Rex Harrington*. Profiles of Canadian Dance, No. 2. Toronto: Press of Terpsichore, 1987.

**Hart, Evelyn** (1956– )

Wyman, Max. *Evelyn Hart: An Intimate Portrait*. Toronto: McClelland & Stewart, 1991.

**Hart, John** (1921– )

DAV: 126-128.

**Harvey, Cynthia** (1957– )

Harvey, Cynthia, with David Vaughan. "Working with Ashton." *BR* 17, no. 3 (Fall 1989): 33-37.

**Hawkins, Erick** (1909–1994)

Brown, Beverly. "Training to Dance with Erick Hawkins." *DS* 6, no. 1 (Fall/Winter 1971-72): 6-30.

*The Dance of Choreographer Erick Hawkins, The Music of Composer Lucia Dlugoszewski, The Designs of Sculptor Ralph Dorazio.* New York: The Guinn Company, 1964. Essays by Robert Sabin, Faubion Bowers, F.S.C. Northrop, Dale McConathy, Erick Hawkins, Mary Norton, Ben Moore, Ned O'Gorman, Robert Crowley, Lawrence Witchel, Lois Balcom, Alfred Frankenstein, and Dinah Maggie.

Dlugoszewski, Lucia. "*8 Clear Places.*" *BR* 21, no. 4 (Winter 1993): 60-65.

*Erick Hawkins: Theory and Training.* New York: American Dance Guild, 1979.

*5 Essays on the Dance of Erick Hawkins.* New York: Foundation for Modern Dance, Inc., n.d. Essays by Mark Woodworth, Parker Tyler, Lucia Dlugoszewski, Beverly Brown, and Robert Sabin.

"Hawkins, Erick." *CBY 1974*: 169-171.

Hawkins, Erick. *The Body Is a Clear Place and Other Statements on Dance.* Princeton, N.J.: Princeton Book Company, Publishers, 1992.

———. "Machines Versus Tools." *BR* 21, no. 4 (Winter 1993): 54-59.

Keefer, Julia L. "Erick Hawkins, Modern Dancer: History, Theory, Technique, and Performance." Unpublished dissertation, New York University, 1979. Ann Arbor, Mich.: University Microfilms International, 1979. Order No. 792,5478. DAI 40-06A, p. 2992.

Mason, Francis. "A Conversation with Erick Hawkins and Lucia Dlugoszewski." *BR* 21, no. 4 (Winter 1993): 47-53.

Penella, Florence. "The Vision of Erick Hawkins." *DS* 12, no. 2 (Spring/Summer 1978): 14-23.

Popkin, Sheryl S. "The Influence of Eastern Thought in the Dance of Erick Hawkins." Unpublished dissertation, Temple University, 1978. Ann Arbor, Mich.: University Microfilms International, 1978. Order No. 781,7401. DAI 39-04A, p. 1896.

Triebe, Sheryl Popkin. "Erick Hawkins: A New Perspective." In *Dance: Current Selected Research*, Volume 3, pp. 39-55. Edited by Lynnette Y. Overby and James H. Humphrey. New York: AMS Press, c. 1992.

**Hawkins, Erick** *(continued)*
BRO: 92-96. COH/2: 38-51. MAS: 137-139. ROG: 41-60.
SOR/2: 242-244.


**Hay, Deborah** (1941– )

Chin, Daryl. "Deborah Hay: A Brief Introduction." *DS* 12, no. 1 (Fall/Winter 1977-78): 17-18.

Daly, Ann. "The Play of Dance: An Introduction to *Lamb, lamb, lamb, lamb, lamb* . . . " *TDR* 36, no. 4/T-136 (Winter 1992): 54-57.

Hay, Deborah. "Ages of the Avant-Garde." *PAJ* 16, no. 1/Issue #46 (January 1994): 26-27.

——. "Dance Talks." *DS* 12, no. 1 (Fall/Winter 1977-78): 18-22.

——. *Lamb at the Altar: The Story of a Dance.* Durham, N.C. & London: Duke University Press, 1994.

——. "*Lamb, lamb, lamb, lamb, lamb* . . . : A Movement Libretto for 42 Individuals." *TDR* 36, no. 4/T-136 (Winter 1992): 58-81.

——, with drawings by Donna Jean Rogers. *Moving Through the Universe in Bare Feet: Ten Circle Dances for Everybody.* Chicago: Swallow Press, 1975.

——. "Playing Awake: Letters to My Daughter." *TDR* 33, no. 4/T-124 (Winter 1989): 70-76.

Jeffers, Bill. "Leaving the House: The Solo Performance of Deborah Hay." *TDR* 23, no. 1/T-81 (March 1979): 79-86.

Wynne, Peter. *Judson Dance: An Annotated Bibliography of the Judson Dance Theater and of Five Major Choreographers—Trisha Brown, Lucinda Childs, Deborah Hay, Steve Paxton, and Yvonne Rainer.* Englewood, N.J.: author, May 1978.

BAN: 112-130. FOS: 5-14; 41-57. LIV: 120-133. MCD: 134-147.


**Haydée, Marcia** (1937– )

"Haydée, Marcia." *CBY 1977*: 197-200.
GRU/2: 176-180. MON: 68-71.


**Hayden, Melissa** (1923– )

Gustaitis, Rasa. *Melissa Hayden: Ballerina.* London: Thomas Nelson & Sons, 1967.

"Hayden, Melissa." *CBY 1955*: 271-272.

**Hayden, Melissa** *(continued)*

Hayden, Melissa. *Melissa Hayden: Off Stage and On*. Garden City, N.Y.: Doubleday, 1963.

GRU/2: 371-377. MAS: 355-360. TRA: 110-119.

**Healy, Katherine** (1969– )

Healy, Katherine. "The Baby Ballerina on Trial." *DN* 2, no. 2 (Summer 1993): 19-27.

———. "Why a Career in Dance?" *DN* 2, no. 1 (Spring 1993): 13-19.

**Heinel, Anna** (1753-1808)

MIG: 59-64.

**Helpmann, Robert** (1909-1986)

Anthony, Gordon. *Robert Helpmann: Studies*. London: Home & Van Thal, 1946.

Benthall, Michael, Clemence Dane, M.H. Middleton, Arnold L. Haskell, and Eric Blom. *"Hamlet" and "Miracle in the Gorbals."* Edited by Arnold L. Haskell. Sadler's Wells Ballet Books, No. 3. London: The Bodley Head, 1949.

Brahms, Caryl. *Robert Helpmann: Choreographer*. London: B.T. Batsford, 1943.

Gibbon, Monk. *The Red Shoes Ballet*. London: Saturn Press, 1948; reprint New York: Garland Publishing, 1977.

Gourlay, J. Logan, ed. *Robert Helpmann Album*. Glasgow: Stage and Screen Press; London: Personal Presentations, 1948. With contributions by Arnold Haskell and Alan Dent, and photography by Angus McBean, Edward Mandinian, Baron, and Roger Wood.

"Helpmann, Robert." *CBY 1950*: 228-230.

Salter, Elizabeth. *Helpmann: The Authorised Biography of Sir Robert Helpmann, CBE*. Brighton: Angus & Robertson Publishers, 1978.

Sorley Walker, Kathrine. *Robert Helpmann*. Theatre World Monograph No. 9. London: Rockliff, 1957.

ATK: 69-73. BLA: 122-125. DAV: 128-137. FRA: 132-141. GIB: 74-77. HUR: 282-286. SWI/2: 76-80.

**Hendel, Henriette** (1772-1894)

MOO/2: 26-33.

**Hendl, Susan** (1949– )

GRE/3: 19-20.

**Hewitt, Ernest** (1917-1976)
DAV: 138-139.

**Higgins, Elizabeth Twistington** (1925-1990)
Alexander, Marc. *The Dance Goes On: The Life and Art of Elizabeth Twistington Higgins.* Kingsley, Hampshire: Leader Books, 1980.

**Hightower, Rosella** (1920– )
ATK: 74-76. DAV: 139-142. GRU/2: 75-82.

**Hijikata, Tatsumi** (1929-1986)
Stein, Bonnie Sue. "Tatsumi Hijikata (1929-1986)." *TDR* 30, no. 2/T-110 (Summer 1986): 126.
Tanaka, Min. "from *I Am an Avant-Garde Who Crawls the Earth.*" *TDR* 30, no. 2/T-110 (Summer 1986): 153-155.

**Hoctor, Harriet** (1907-1977)
Cocuzza, Ginnine. "An American Premiere Danseuse." *DS* 14, no. 3 (September 1980): 36-51.
Ware, Walter. "Harriet Hoctor." In his *Ballet Is Magic: A Triple Monograph,* pp. 1-19. New York: IHRA Publishing Company, 1936.
SCH/1: see Index of Choreographers, p. 135.

**Hoffmann, Gertrude** (1886?-1966)
Cohen, Barbara Naomi. *The Borrowed Art of Gertrude Hoffmann.* Dance Data No. 2. Brooklyn: Dance Horizons, n.d.
———. "Gertrude Hoffmann: Salome Treads the Boards." *DRA IX* (1978): 23-32.

**Holder, Geoffrey** (1930– )
Berman, Avis. "Architectural Digest Visits: Geoffrey Holder and Carmen de Lavallade." *Architectural Digest* 42, no. 11 (November 1985): 156-[161], 242.
"Holder, Geoffrey." *CBY 1957*: 263-264.
Holder, Geoffrey. *Adam.* New York: Viking, 1986. This is not a work about dance or this artist's career. It is a book of magnificent photography—a study of the human nude as sculpture—which shows another facet of Geoffrey Holder's talent.

**Holder, Geoffrey** *(continued)*

——, with illustrations by the author. *Geoffrey Holder's Caribbean Cookbook.* New York: Viking, [1973].

**Holm, Hanya** (1893-1992)

*Ballett International* 16, no. 3 (March 1993). A special memorial issue celebrating the art of Hanya Holm. Feature articles: Isa Partsch-Bergsohn. "Hanya Holm: A Missing Link Between German and American Modern Dance" (pp. 14-17). Murray Louis. "No Dead Eyes or Lazy Minds: Some Thoughts on Hanya Holm" (pp. 18-19). Susan Manning. "You Have to Hear What Isn't on the Surface: An Interview with Hanya Holm" (pp. 20-23).

Cristofori, Marilyn. "Hanya Holm Resource Videotapes" (Stanford University Libraries). *DRJ* 22, no. 1 (Spring 1990): 56-57.

——. "In Memoriam: Hanya Holm, March 3, 1893-November 3, 1992." *DRJ* 25, no. 1 (Spring 1993): 70.

Fisher, Betsy. "Preserving the Solo and Duet from Hanya Holm's *Homage to Mahler.*" In *Proceedings of the Conference "Dance Reconstructed: Modern Dance Art Past, Present, Future,"* pp. 41-46. Rutgers University, New Brunswick, New Jersey, October 16 and 17, 1992.

"Hanya Holm: The Life and Legacy." *The Journal for Stage Directors & Choreographers* 7, no. 1 (Spring-Summer 1993). Contents: Aria Edry. Preface/From the Editor (p. 6). Marilyn Cristofori. "Homage to Hanya Holm: A Hundred Years of Dance" (pp. 9-12). Mimi Kagan, Louise Kloepper, Alfred Brooks, Carolyn Brooks, and Eve Gentry. "Company Stories: Notes From the Early Days" (pp. 15-25). This article is adapted from a longer version which first appeared in "Hanya Holm: A Pioneer in American Dance," Marilyn Cristofori, Issue Editor. *Choreography and Dance* 2, pt. 2 (1992). Barbara Morgan. "Hanya Through the Lens: A Portfolio of *Trend*" (pp. 26-32). Hanya Holm. "Hanya Speaks: A Philosophy of Dance—Comments & Excerpts" (pp. 35-37). Hanya Holm. "Two Students Remembered: Joan Karlen and Susan Osberg" (pp. 37-38). Crandall Diehl, Murray Gitlin, Don Redlich, Marcia B. Siegel, and Harry Woolever. "Hanya Holm: From Concert to Broadway Stage" (pp. 41-49). "Hanya Holm: Chronology of Works" (pp. 52-54). Andrea Sferes, comp. "Hanya Holm: Bibliography & Research Sources" (pp. 56-60).

**Holm, Hanya** *(continued)*

"Hanya Holm: A Pioneer in American Dance." *C&D* 2, pt. 2 (1992). Marilyn Cristofori, Issue Editor. Contents: Marilyn Cristofori. "Hanya Holm: A Pioneer in American Dance" (pp. 5-6). Eve Gentry. "The 'Original' Hanya Holm Company" (pp. 9-39). Mary Anthony. "The Hanya Holm New York Studio in the Early 1940s" (pp. 41-45). Glen Tetley. "Hanya: Mentor, Friend and Muse" (pp. 47-52). Alwin Nikolais. "Hanya Holm" (pp. 53-61). Margery J. Turner. "Hanya: The Colorado Summers and Beyond" (pp. 63-71). Crandall Diehl. "*My Fair Lady* and Other Broadway Memories" (pp. 73-87). Kathryn Appleby. "Hanya Holm in the 1980s" (pp. 89-92).

"Holm, Hanya." *CBY 1954*: 340-342.

Kriegsman, Sali Ann. *Modern Dance in America: The Bennington Years*. Boston: G.K. Hall & Co., 1981.

Miller, Raphael Francis. "The Contributions of Selected Broadway Musical Theatre Choreographers: Connolly, Rasch, Balanchine, Holm, and Alton." Unpublished dissertation, University of Oregon, 1984. Ann Arbor, Mich.: University Microfilms International, 1984. Order No. 842,2855. DAI 45-07A, p. 1922.

Redlich, Don, and Ilene Fox. "Problems in the Process of Setting Down the Notation Score for Hanya Holm's *RATATAT!*" In *Proceedings of the Conference "Dance Reconstructed: Modern Dance Art Past, Present, Future,"* pp. 47-51. Rutgers University, New Brunswick, New Jersey, October 16 and 17, 1992.

Shearer, Sybil. "My Hanya Holm." *BR* 21, no. 4 (Winter 1993): 4-7.

Siegel, Marcia B. "A Conversation with Hanya Holm." *BR* 9, no. 1 (Spring 1981): 5-30.

Sorell, Walter. *Hanya Holm: The Biography of an Artist*. Middletown, Conn.: Wesleyan University Press, 1969; reprint 1979.

BRO: 70-82. LLO: 155-172. MAY/2: 151-156. SCH/1: see Index of Choreographers, p. 135. TER: 120-129.

**Hong, Sin Cha** (195?– )

Hong, Sin Cha. *Dance of Silence*. [New York? printed by] Shinko Printing Co., Japan, 1983.

**Horosko, Marian** (1927– )

MAS: 371-379. SID: 75-84.

**Horst, Louis** (1884-1946)

Dalbotten, Ted. "The Teaching of Louis Horst." *DS* 8, no. 1 (Fall/ Winter 1973-74): 26-40.

Kriegsman, Sali Ann. *Modern Dance in America: The Bennington Years.* Boston: G.K. Hall & Co., 1981.

Pischl, A.J., and Selma Jeanne Cohen, eds. "Composer/ Choreographer." *DP* 16 (1963): 6-8.

Sears, David, ed. "Louis Horst: A Centennial Compendium." *BR* 12, no. 2 (Summer 1984): 77-98.

Soares, Janet Mansfield. *Louis Horst: Musician in a Dancer's World.* Durham, N.C. & London: Duke University Press, 1992.

——. "Musician Louis Horst (1884-1964): His Influence on Concepts of Modernism in American Dance." In *Society of Dance History Scholars Proceedings*, pp. 88-94. Twelfth Annual Conference, Arizona State University, 17-19 February 1989.

**Horton, Lester** (1906-1953)

Bizot, Richard. "Lester Horton's *Salome*, 1934-1953 and After." DRJ 16, no. 1 (Spring 1984): 35-40.

Perces, Marjorie B., Ana Marie Forsythe, and Cheryl Bell. *The Dance Technique of Lester Horton.* Princeton, N.J.: Princeton Book Company, Publishers, 1992.

Warren, Larry. *Lester Horton: Modern Dance Pioneer.* New York & Basel: Marcel Dekker, c. 1977; reprint Princeton, N.J.: Princeton Book Company, Publishers, 1991.

——, Frank Eng, Bella Lewitzky, and Joyce Trisler. "The Dance Theater of Lester Horton." *DP* 31 (Autumn 1967).

LLO: 277-292. PRE: 223-244.

**House, Christopher** (1954– )

Mason, Francis. "A Conversation with Christopher House." *BR* 22, no. 1 (Spring 1994): 43-51.

**Hoving, Lucas** (1912– )

SIE: 6-11.

**Howard, Andrée** (1910-1968)

Gilmour, Sally. "Remembering Andrée Howard." *DR* 2, no. 1 (Spring 1984): 48-60.

Pritchard, Jane. "The Choreography of Andrée Howard: Some Further Information." *DC* 15, no. 1 (1992): 77-87.

**Howard, Andrée** *(continued)*

Sorley Walker, Kathrine. "The Choreography of Andrée Howard." *DC* 13, no. 3 (1990-91): 265-358.

Zoete, Beryl de. "Three British Choreographers." In her *The Thunder and the Freshness*, pp. 43-55. London: Neville Spearman; New York: Theatre Arts Books, 1963. Portion on Howard, pp. 47-51.

DAV: 142-145. FRA: 142-154.

**Howard, David** (1937– )

Rosen, Lillie F. "Two Ballet Teachers: Finis Jhung & David Howard." *DS* 15, no. 1 (March 1981): 33-51.

**Huang, Al Chung-liang** (1937– )

Huang, Al Chung-liang. *Embrace Tiger, Return to Mountain: The Essence of T'ai Chi.* Moab, Utah: Real People Press, 1973.

**Hübbe, Nikolaj** (1967– )

Daniels, Don. "Newborns: Hübbe's *Apollo* and New York Choreographies." *BR* 22, no. 3 (Fall 1994): 88-97.

Kaplan, Larry. "A Conversation with Nikolaj Hübbe." *BR* 21, no. 3 (Fall 1993): 52-64.

**Hughes, Russell Meriwether** (see **La Meri**)

**Humphrey, Doris** (1895-1958)

Becker, Svea. "From Humphrey to Limón: A Modern Dance Tradition." *DNJ* 2, no. 1 (Spring 1984): 37-52.

——, and Joenine Roberts. "A Reaffirmation of the Humphrey-Weidman Quality." *DNJ* 1, no. 1 (January 1983): 3-17.

Dance Notation Bureau. *Doris Humphrey: The Collected Works.* Vol. 1. "Water Study," "Shakers," "Partita V." New York: Dance Notation Bureau Press, 1978.

——. *Doris Humphrey: The Collected Works.* Vol. 2. "Air for the G String," "Two Ecstatic Themes," "Day on Earth." New York: Dance Notation Bureau Press, 1992.

Davis, Martha Ann, and Claire Schmais. "An Analysis of the Style and Composition of *Water Study.*" *DRA I* (1967): 105-113.

Dils, Ann. "Performance Practice and Humphrey Reconstruction." In *Proceedings of the Conference "Dance Reconstructed: Modern Dance Art Past, Present, Future,"* pp. 223-227. Rutgers University, New Brunswick, New Jersey, October 16 and 17, 1992.

**Humphrey, Doris** *(continued)*

Evan, Blanche. "Inquest: Historic in Setting, Modern in Form, Timeless in Content." In *Collected Works By and About Blanche Evan: Dancer, Teacher, Writer, Dance/Movement/Word Therapist*, pp. 46-48. Compiled by Ruth Gordon Benov. San Francisco: Blanche Evan Dance Foundation, 1991. Reprinted from *Dance Observer* 12, no. 1 (January 1945): 4-5.

"Humphrey, Doris." *CBY 1942*: 398-400.

Humphrey, Doris. *The Art of Making Dances*. Edited by Barbara Pollack. New York & Toronto: Rinehart & Company, 1959.

———. *Doris Humphrey: An Artist First*. Edited by Selma Jeanne Cohen. Middletown, Conn.: Wesleyan University Press, 1972.

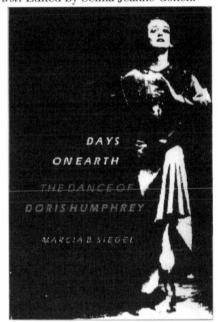

———. "New Dance: An Unfinished Autobiography." *DP* 25 (Spring 1966).

Jordan, Stephanie. "Music as Structural Basis in the Choreography of Doris Humphrey, with Reference to Humphrey's Use of Music Visualization Techniques and Musical/Choreographic Counterpoint and to the Historical Context of Her Work." Unpublished dissertation, University of London, Goldsmiths' College, 1986.

———. "The Musical Key to Dance Reconstruction." In *Proceedings of the Conference "Dance ReConstructed: Modern Dance Art Past, Present, Future,"* pp. 185-190. Rutgers University, New Brunswick, New Jersey, October 16 and 17, 1992.

Kagan, Elizabeth. "Towards the Analysis of a Score: A Comparative Study of *Three Epitaphs* by Paul Taylor and *Water Study* by Doris Humphrey." *DRA IX* (1978): 75-92.

Kaye, Meli Davis. "Doris Humphrey at Green Mansions, 1947." *DC* 18, no. 3 (1995): 405-418.

King, Eleanor. *Transformations: The Humphrey-Weidman Era*. New York: Dance Horizons, 1978.

**Humphrey, Doris** *(continued)*

Koner, Pauline. "Working with Doris Humphrey." *DC* 7, no. 3 (1984-85): 235-278.

Kriegsman, Sali Ann. *Modern Dance in America: The Bennington Years.* Boston: G.K. Hall & Co., 1981.

Marion, Sheila. "Studying *Water Study.*" *DRJ* 24, no. 1 (Spring 1992): 1-11.

Martin, John, with photography by Thomas Bouchard. "Days of Divine Indiscipline." *DP* 12 (Autumn 1961).

Savery, Helen. "Dancing in the Depression." *DC* 7, no. 3 (1984-85): 279-293.

Sherman, Jane. "Martha and Doris in Denishawn: A Closer Look." *DC* 17, no. 2 (1994): 179-193.

Siegel, Marcia B. *Days on Earth: The Dance of Doris Humphrey.* New Haven, Conn. & London: Yale University Press, 1987; reprint Durham, N.C. & London: Duke University Press, 1992.

——. "Four Works by Doris Humphrey." *BR* 7, no. 1 (1978-1979): 16-36. An extract from Marcia B. Siegel's *The Shapes of Change: Images of American Dance.* Boston: Houghton Mifflin, 1979.

Stodelle, Ernestine. "*Air for the G String.*" *BR* 11, no. 4 (Winter 1984): 86-87.

——. *The Dance Technique of Doris Humphrey and Its Creative Potential.* Princeton, N.J.: Princeton Book Company, Publishers, 1978; 2d ed., 1990.

Venable, Lucy, text, with drawings by Susie Watts Margolin. "*Passacaglia*, 1938-1965: The Art of Remaking a Dance." *DS* 1, no. 2 (Spring 1965): 6-14.

Wentink, Andrew Mark. "The Doris Humphrey Collection: An Introduction and Guide." In *Bulletin of the New York Public Library* 77 (1973): 80-142.

——. "'From the Orient . . . Oceans of Love, Doris': The Denishawn Tour of the Orient as seen through the Letters of Doris Humphrey." *DC* 1, no. 1 (1977): 22-45.

Youngerman, Suzanne. "The Translation of a Culture into Choreography: A Study of Doris Humphrey's *The Shakers* Based on Labananalysis." *DRA IX* (1978): 93-110.

BRO: 54-64. KON: 149-189. LLO: 76-131. MAR: 206-226. MAY/2: 125-151. MAZ: 117-152. MOO/1: 287-297. PAL: 58-74. SCH/1: see Index of Choreographers, p. 135. SOR/1: 20-27. TER: 100-113.

**Hutchinson, Ann** (see **Guest, Ann Hutchinson**)

**Idzikowski, Stanislas** (1894-1977)

*The Art of Stanislas Idzikowski*. London: C.W. Beaumont, 1926.

**Inglesby, Mona** (1918– )

Franks, A.H. "The Inglesby Legend." In *The Ballet Annual 1950: A Record and Year Book of the Ballet*, pp. 104-108. Edited by Arnold L. Haskell. Fourth Issue. London: Adam & Charles Black, n.d.

Handley-Taylor, Geoffrey. *Mona Inglesby: Ballerina and Choreographer*. London: Vawser & Wiles, 1947.

Inglesby, Mona. "From the Cradle of British Ballet." *DN* 4, no. 1 (Spring 1995): 35-45. An extract from Mona Inglesby's as yet unpublished autobiography, *Tour de Force*.

DAV: 146-152. NOB: 233-239.

**Istomina, Avdotia** (1799-1848)

Schmidt, Paul. "Pushkin and Istomina: Ballet in Nineteenth-Century Russia." *DRJ* 20, no. 2 (Winter 1988): 3-7.

**Ito, Michio** (1894-1961)

Caldwell, Helen. *Michio Ito: The Dancer and His Dances*. Berkeley: University of California Press, 1977.

Cowell, Mary-Jean, and Satoru Shimazaki, Research Assistant. "East and West in the Work of Michio Ito." *DRJ* 26, no. 2 (Fall 1994): 11-23.

KON: 23-38. PRE: 179-195.

**Ivanov, Lev** (1834-1901)

Beaumont, Cyril W. "Lev Ivanov." Chapter 7 in his *The Ballet Called "Swan Lake,"* pp. 51-56. London: C.W. Beaumont, 1952.

Slonimsky, Yury. "Writings on Lev Ivanov." *DP* 2 (Spring 1959).

Wiley, Roland John. *Tchaikovsky's Ballets: "Swan Lake," "Sleeping Beauty," "Nutcracker."* Oxford: Clarendon Press, 1985.

ROS: 124-138.

**Ivanova, Lydia** (1903-1924)

SMA: 89-97.

**Jackson, Rowena** (1926– )
Swinson, Cyril. *Rowena Jackson and Philip Chatfield*. Dancers of To-Day. London: Adam & Charles Black, 1958.
HUR: 296-297.

**Jamison, Judith** (1944– )
"Jamison, Judith." *CBY 1973*: 202-205.
Jamison, Judith, with Howard Kaplan. *Dancing Spirit: An Autobiography*. New York, London, Toronto: Doubleday, 1993.
Maynard, Olga. *Judith Jamison: Aspects of a Dancer*. Garden City, N.Y.: Doubleday, 1982.
LYL: 96-106.

**Jaques-Dalcroze, Emile** (1865-1950)
Bachmann, Marie-Laure. *Dalcroze Today: An Education Through and Into Music*. Translated by David Parlett. Oxford: Clarendon Press, 1991.
Balance, John. "Jacques Dalcroze [sic] and His School." In *Gordon Craig on Movement and Dance*, pp. 227-230. Edited and with an

**Jaques-Dalcroze, Emile** *(continued)*

Introduction by Arnold Rood. New York: Dance Horizons, 1977; reprinted from *The Mask* 5, no. 1 (July 1912): 32-36.

*The Eurhythmics of Jaques-Dalcroze.* Introduction by Professor M.E. Sadler. Boston: Small Maynard and Company, 1915.

Jaques-Dalcroze, Emile. *Eurhythmics, Art and Education.* Translated from the French by Frederick Rothwell. Edited and prepared for the press by Cynthia Cox. New York: A.S Barnes & Co., 1930.

———. *Rhythm, Music and Education.* Translated from the French by Harold F. Rubinstein. London: Chatto & Windus, 1921; reprint [London]: The Dalcroze Society, 1967.

Odom, Selma Landen. "Choreographing *Orpheus*: Hellerau 1913 and Warwick 1991." In *Proceedings of the Conference "Dance Reconstructed: Modern Dance Art Past, Present, Future,"* pp. 127-136. Rutgers University, New Brunswick, New Jersey, October 16 and 17, 1992.

Ruyter, Nancy Lee Chalfa. "Appendix 1: Dalcroze Eurythmics." In her *Reformers and Visionaries: The Americanization of the Art of Dance*, pp. 131-133. New York: Dance Horizons, 1979.

Spector, Irwin. *Rhythm and Life: The Work of Emile Jaques-Dalcroze.* Dance and Music Series, No. 3. Stuyvesant, N.Y.: Pendragon Press, 1990.

Zoete, Beryl de. "A Tribute to My Master, Jaques-Dalcroze." In her *The Thunder and the Freshness*, pp. 13-26. London: Neville Spearman; New York: Theatre Arts Books, 1963.

MAY/2: 20-21.

**Jarvis, Judy** (1942-1986)

Anderson, Carol. *Judy Jarvis, Dance Artist: A Portrait.* Toronto: Dance Collection Danse Press, 1993.

**Jeanmaire, Renée** (1926– )

Beaumont, Cyril. "Hommage à Jeanmaire." In *The Ballet Annual 1950: A Record and Year Book of the Ballet*, pp. 67-74. Edited by Arnold L. Haskell. Fourth Issue. London: Adam & Charles Black, [1949].

"Jeanmaire, Renée." *CBY 1952*: 289-290.

ATK: 77-79. DAV: 152-155. MCC: 150-156.

**Jenner, Ann** (1944– )
GRU/2: 153-156.

**Jhung, Finis** (1937– )
Rosen, Lillie F. "Two Ballet Teachers: Finis Jhung & David Howard." *DS* 15, no. 1 (March 1981): 33-51.

**Jillana** (1934– )
MAS: 303-306.

**Job, Lenore Peters** (1890-1984)
Job, Lenore Peters. *Looking Back While Surging Forward*. San Francisco: Peters Wright Creative Dance, 1984.

**Joffrey, Robert** (1930-1988)
Dorris, George. "The Choreography of Robert Joffrey: A Preliminary Checklist." *DC* 12, no. 1 (1989): 105-139.
——. "The Choreography of Robert Joffrey: A Supplement." *DC* 12, no. 3 (1989): 383-385.
"Joffrey, Robert." *CBY 1967*: 201-203.
Joffrey, Robert. "Past and Present: The Vital Connection." In *Visions: Ballet and Its Future*, pp. 143-150. Edited by Michael Crabb. Essays from the International Dance Conference to commemorate the 25th anniversary of the National Ballet of Canada, held at the Town Hall, St. Lawrence Centre for the Arts, Toronto, November 15-16, 1976. Foreword by Sir Frederick Ashton. Introduction by Vincent Tovell. Toronto: Simon & Pierre, c. 1978.
GRU/2: 378-384.

**Johnson, Virginia** (1950– )
"Johnson, Virginia." *CBY 1985*: 208-211.

**Jonas, Joan** (194?– )
Jonas, Joan, with Rosalind Krause. "Seven Years." *TDR* 19, no. 1/T-65 (March 1975): 13-17.
Reiring, Janelle. "Joan Jonas' *Delay Delay*." *TDR* 16, no. 3/T-55 (September 1972): 142-150.

J

**Jones, Bill T.** (1952– )

Gates, Henry Louis, Jr. "The Body Politic." *The New Yorker* 70, no. 39 (November 28, 1994): 112-118, 120-124.

"Jones, Bill T." *CBY 1993*: 285-289.

Wallach, Maya. "A Conversation with Bill T. Jones." *BR* 18, no. 4 (Winter 1990-91): 73-75.

Zimmer, Elizabeth. "Bill T. Jones: Preparing *The Last Summer at Uncle Tom's Cabin.*" In *Breakthroughs: Avant-Garde Artists in Europe and America, 1950-1990*, pp. 258-263. Wexner Center for the Arts, The Ohio State University, [Columbus]. New York: Rizzoli, 1991.

——, and Susan Quasha, eds. *Body Against Body: The Dance and Other Collaborations of Bill T. Jones & Arnie Zane*. Barrytown, N.Y.: Station Hill Press, 1989.

KRE: 110-133.

**Jooss, Kurt** (1901-1979)

Blum, Odette. "*The Green Table* Project." *DRJ* 21, no. 1 (Spring 1989): 38-42.

Coton, A.V. *The New Ballet: Kurt Jooss and His Work*. London: Dennis Dobson, 1946.

"The Dance Theatre of Kurt Jooss." *C&D* 3, pt. 2 (1993). Suzanne K. Walther, Issue Editor. Contents: Sorell, Walter. "The Times that Gave Birth to Kurt Jooss" (pp. 1-6). Suzanne K. Walther. "Kurt Jooss: The Evolution of an Artist" (pp. 7-24). Suzanne Schlicher. "The West German Dance Theatre: Paths from the Twenties to the Present" (pp. 25-43). Anna Markard. "Jooss the Teacher: His Pedagogical Aims and the Development of the Choreographic Principles of Harmony" (pp. 45-51). Suzanne K. Walther. "The Dance of Death: Description and Analysis of *The Green Table*" (pp. 53-77). Christian Holder. "Dancing for Jooss: Recreating the Role of Death in *The Green Table*" (pp. 79-91). Jooss Ballets: Chronological List (pp. 93-94). Jooss Ballets: Alphabetical List (pp. 94-102). Notes on Contributors (pp. 103-104). Index (pp. 105-108).

"Jooss, Kurt." *CBY 1976*: 206-209.

Maris, Laura. "Jooss' *The Green Table* and *The Big City*: Musical

**Jooss, Kurt** *(continued)*

Forms and Devices as Choreographic Tools." *DC* 19, no. 2 (1996): pages not yet set.

Markard, Anna, and Hermann Markard. *Jooss.* Cologne: Ballett-Bühnen Verlag, 1985.

——. "Kurt Jooss and His Work." *BR* 10, no. 1 (Spring 1982): 15-67.

Nugent, Ann. *"The Green Table* and *Café Müller." DN* 1, no. 3 (Autumn 1992): 34-41.

Siegel, Marcia B. *"The Green Table*—Sources of a Classic." *DRJ* 21, no. 1 (Spring 1989): 15-21.

Walther, Suzanne K. *The Dance of Death: Kurt Jooss and the Weimar Years.* Choreography and Dance Studies, Vol. 7. Chur, Switzerland: Harwood Academic Publishers, 1994.

——. "The Form of Content: The Dance-Drama of Kurt Jooss." Unpublished dissertation, New York University, 1990. Ann Arbor, Mich.: University Microfilms International, 1990. Order No. 90-25,189. DAI 51-04A, p. 1031.

Winearls, Jane. *Modern Dance: The Jooss-Leeder Method.* 2d ed. London: Adam & Charles Black, 1968.

DAV: 155-160. HAL: 149-152. LLO: 223-232. MOO/1: 304-307.

**Judson (Judson Dance Theater)** (1962-1972)

*Ballet Review* 1, no. 6 (1967). A special issue that assesses the accomplishments of Judson Dance Theater. Feature articles: Arlene Croce. "After Five Years" (pp. 3-4). Jill Johnston. "Judson 1964: End of an Era" (pp. 7-14). Constance H. Poster. "Making It New—Meredith Monk and Kenneth King" (pp. 14-21). Judith Dunn. "My Work and Judson's" (pp. 22-26). Constance H. Poster. "Judith Dunn as Teacher" (pp. 27-30). James Waring, John Herbert McDowell, Judith Dunn, Arlene Croce, and Don McDonagh. "Judson: A Discussion" (pp. 30-53). "Judson: A Dance Chronology" (pp. 54-72). Jack Anderson. "The Other Theater at Judson" (pp. 73-77).

Banes, Sally. "The Birth of the Judson Dance Theatre: 'A Concert of Dance' at Judson Church, July 6, 1962." *DC* 5, no. 2 (1982): 167-212.

——. *Democracy's Body: Judson Dance Theater 1962-1964.* Studies in the Fine Arts: The Avant-Garde, No. 43. Ann Arbor, Mich.: UMI Research Press, c. 1983.

J

**Judson (Judson Dance Theater)** *(continued)*

——. "Icons of the Ordinary: Judson Dance Theatre and Pop Art." In *Society of Dance History Scholars Proceedings*, pp. 190-198. Sixth Annual Conference, The Ohio State University, 11-13 February 1983.

Carmines, Al. "In the Congregation of Art." *DS* 4, no. 1 (Fall/ Winter 1967-68): 25-31.

Johnston, Jill. *Marmalade Me*. New York: Dutton, 1971. A mix of critical commentary and autobiography from the 1960s, with a particular emphasis on Judson Dance Theater.

*Judson Dance Theater: 1962-1966*. Project Director: Wendy Perron. Curatorial Coordinator: Daniel J. Cameron. Bennington, Vt.: Bennington College, 1981. This exhibition catalogue includes essays by Jill Johnston and Sally Banes, as well as brief statements by numerous Judson artists.

McDonagh, Don. *The Rise and Fall and Rise of Modern Dance*. New York: Outerbridge & Dienstfrey, 1970; paperback reprint, New York & Scarborough, Ontario: New American Library, 1971; rev. ed. with new photographs, but without the choreochronicles, Pennington, N.J.: A Cappella Books, 1990.

Sears, David. "A Trisha Brown - Robert Rauschenberg Collage." *BR* 10, no. 3 (Fall 1982): 47-51.

Siegel, Marcia B. "The Death of Some Alternatives." *BR* 10, no. 3 (Fall 1982): 76-80.

Wynne, Peter. *Judson Dance: An Annotated Bibliography of the Judson Dance Theater and of Five Major Choreographers — Trisha Brown, Lucinda Childs, Deborah Hay, Steve Paxton, and Yvonne Rainer*. Englewood, N.J.: author, May 1978.

## Kai, Una (1928– )

Caverly, Sandra. "Notes on a Conversation with Una Kai." *YDR* Issue #2 (Fall 1973): 42-45.

MAS: 277-280.

## Kain, Karen (1951– )

"Kain, Karen." *CBY 1980*: 174-177.

Kain, Karen, with Stephen Godfrey and Penelope Reed Doob. *Karen Kain, Movement Never Lies: An Autobiography*. Toronto: McClelland & Stewart, 1994.

Street, David, photography, with text by David Mason. *Karen Kain: Lady of Dance*. Toronto: McGraw-Hill Ryerson, 1978.

MON: 92-93.

## Karsavina, Tamara (1885-1978)

Barrie, James M., with an Introduction by Tamara Karsavina. "The Truth about the Russian Dancers." *DP* 14 (Spring 1962).

Bruce, H.J. *Silken Dalliance*. London: Constable, 1946.

———. *Thirty Dozen Moons*. London: Constable, 1949.

Hartnoll & Eyre Ltd., London. *Nijinsky, Karsavina and the Diaghilev Ballet 1909-1914*, catalogue of the exhibition of drawings by Valentine Gross, October 16 - November 2, 1973.

Haskell, Arnold L. *Tamara Karsavina*. Artists of the Dance. London: British-Continental Press, 1930.

**Karsavina, Tamara** *(continued)*

Karsavina, Tamara. *Classical Ballet: The Flow of Movement.* London: Adam & Charles Black, 1962.

———. *Theatre Street.* rev. and enl. ed. London: Constable, 1948.

Lifar, Serge. "Tamara Karsavina." In his *The Three Graces: The Legends and the Truth,* pp. 114-158. Translated by Gerard Hopkins. London: Cassell, 1959.

Macdonald, Nesta. "Tamara Karsavina." *BR* 7, nos. 2 & 3 (1978-1979): 136-172.

Svetlov, Valerien. *Thamar Karsavina.* Translated by H. de Vere Beauclerk and Nadia Evrenov. Edited by Cyril W. Beaumont. London: C.W. Beaumont, 1922.

AUS/1: 96-122. CLA: 95-126. CRO: 15-42. DAV: 160-168. HAS/1: 111-117. MCC: 14-26. MON: 18-21. MOO/1: 203-209. SMA: 188-199.


**Kaye, Nora** (1920-1987)

*The Herbert and Nora Kaye Ross Collection.* Los Angeles: Butterfield & Butterfield, 1988. Catalogue of a public auction held December 5, 6 and 7, 1988.

"Kaye, Nora." *CBY 1953*: 308-310.

Kaye, Nora. "The Lure of Ballet Theatre." In *American Ballet Theatre,* pp. 309-316, by Charles Payne. New York: Knopf, 1978.

Taras, John. "Nora Kaye: A Tribute." *BR* 14, no. 4 (Winter 1987): 36-48.

ATK: 80-83. DAV: 169-171. MON: 40-41. NEW/2: 78-87. SWI/2: 67-70.


**Kaye, Pooh** (1951– )

Levine, Mindy N. "An Interview with Pooh Kaye." *Millennium Film Journal,* Nos. 10-11 (Fall-Winter 1981-82): 33-42.


**Kchessinska, Mathilda** (1872-1971)

Kschessinska, Mathilde (H.S.H. The Princess Romanovsky-Krassinsky). *Dancing in Petersburg: The Memoirs of Kschessinska.* Translated by Arnold Haskell. Garden City, N.Y.: Doubleday, 1961; reprint New York: Da Capo Press, 1977.

MUI: 31-39. SMA: 54-63.

**Keen, Elizabeth** (1938– )
MCD: 270-282.

**Kehlet, Niels** (1938– )
Hunt, Marilyn. "A Conversation with Niels Kehlet." *BR* 16, no. 2 (Summer 1988): 76-96.

**Kelly, Desmond** (1942– )
NEW/1: 312-327.

**Kemp, Lindsay** (1939– )
Carter, Gary. "Happy Valley." *DN* 4, no. 1 (Spring 1995): 29-33. The pantomime world of Lindsay Kemp's *Cinderella*.
Wilms, Anno, photography. *Lindsay Kemp and Company*. Introduction by David Haughton. Preface by Derek Jarman. London: GMP Publishers, 1987.

**Kemp, Travis** (1914-1995)
Benari, Naomi. *Vagabonds and Strolling Dancers: The Lives and Times of Molly Lake and Travis Kemp*. London: Imperial Society of Teachers of Dancing, [1990].

**Kent, Allegra** (1938– )
"Kent, Allegra." *CBY 1970*: 219-221.
Kent, Allegra, text and captions, with exercise photography by Hank O'Neal and ballet photography by Martha Swope. *Allegra Kent's Water Beauty Book*. Introduction by Edward Villella. New York: St. Martin's Press; London: St. James Press, 1976.

**Kent, Allegra** *(continued)*

———, with James and Constance Camner. *The Dancers' Body Book.* New York: Morrow, 1984.

GRE/3: 16-17. GRU/2: 319-324. MAS: 361-365. TRA: 128-133.

**Keppler, Celeste** (1814?-1882; known as **Madame Celeste**)

SWI/1: 87-107.

**Kidd, Michael** (1919– )

"Kidd, Michael." *CBY 1960*: 213-215.

FRA: 178-179. SCH/1: see Index of Choreographers, p. 135.

**King, Eleanor** (1906-1991)

Adler-Friess, Aanya. "Three Grand Ladies of Modern Dance: Eve Gentry, Eleanor King and Elizabeth Waters." In *Society of Dance History Scholars Proceedings*, pp. 147-155. Eighth Annual Conference, University of New Mexico, 15-17 February 1985.

Fort, Charles. "Interview with Eleanor King." *Xavier Review* 2 (1982): 1-17.

Hoak, Gail. "Eleanor King Retrospective: Solo Works from 1935-1963." In *Society of Dance History Scholars Proceedings*, p. 95. Twelfth Annual Conference, Arizona State University, 17-19 February 1989. Description and program of a lecture/performance.

King, Eleanor. *Transformations: The Humphrey-Weidman Era.* New York: Dance Horizons, 1978.

Mantell-Seidel, Andrea. "Eleanor King in Japan: Dance Bridging East-West." In *Society of Dance History Scholars Proceedings*, pp. 115-122. Fifteenth Annual Conference, University of California, Riverside, 14-15 February 1992.

———. "Recreation and Revival: Eleanor King's *She*: The Mothers Create." In *Proceedings of the Conference "Dance Reconstructed: Modern Dance Art Past, Present, Future,"* pp. 211-218. Rutgers University, New Brunswick, New Jersey, October 16 and 17, 1992.

Plett, Nicole, ed. *Eleanor King: Sixty Years in American Dance.* Santa Cruz, N. Mex.: Moving Press, 1988.

LLO: 292-300.

## King, Kenneth (1948– )

[Howell, John]. "Interview: Kenneth King." *PAJ* 3, no. 2 (Fall 1978): 16-24.

Howell, John. "Kenneth King: Dancer/Choreographer." *PAJ* 3, no. 2 (Fall 1978): 12-15.

Poster, Constance H. "Making It New—Meredith Monk and Kenneth King." *BR* 1, no. 6 (1967): 14-21.

BAN: 168-185. KRE: 148-175.

## Kirby, Charles (1926– )

SID: 85-92.

## Kirkland, Gelsey (1952– )

Harris, Dale. "Gelsey Kirkland at Covent Garden." *BR* 8, nos. 2&3 (1980): 267-271.

"Kirkland, Gelsey." *CBY 1975*: 221-224.

Kirkland, Gelsey, with Greg Lawrence. *Dancing on My Grave*. Garden City, N.Y.: Doubleday, 1986.

——, and Greg Lawrence. *The Shape of Love*. New York: Doubleday, 1990.

FOW: 98-121. GRE/3: 10-12. MON: 96-99.

## Kistler, Darci (1964– )

Acocella, Joan. "Balanchine's Last Princess." *Connoisseur* 219, no. 929 (June 1989): 104-109.

Greskovic, Robert. "The Arrival of Darci Kistler." *BR* 9, no. 2 (Summer 1981): 83-90.

"Kistler, Darci." *CBY 1991*: 334-337.

Kistler, Darci, with Alicia Kistler. *Ballerina: My Story*. Books for Young Readers. New York, London, Toronto: Pocket Books, 1993.

Mason, Francis. "A Conversation with Darci Kistler." *BR* 21, no. 3 (Fall 1993): 37-44.

MAS: 591-594. TRA: 182-187.

## Kivitt, Ted (1942– )

GRU/2: 237-243. LYL: 22-34.

**Klevtsov, Yuri** (196?– )

Kaplan, Larry. "The Bolshoi: Klevtsov and Posokhov." *BR* 18, no. 4 (Winter 1990-1991): 26-37.

**Kobeleff, Constantin** (1885-1966)

PAG: 30-34.

**Kolpakova, Irina** (1933– )

SMA: 172-179.

**Koma** (see **Eiko & Koma**)

**Koner, Pauline** (1912– )

"Koner, Pauline." *CBY 1964*: 237-239.

Koner, Pauline. *Elements of Performance: A Guide for Performers in Dance, Theatre and Opera*. Choreography and Dance Studies, Vol. 3. Chur, Switzerland: Harwood Academic Publishers, 1993.

——. "Russia!" *BR* 17, no. 3 (Fall 1989): 81-99. An extract from Pauline Koner's *Solitary Song*. Durham, N.C. & London: Duke University Press, 1989.

——. *Solitary Song*. Durham, N.C. & London: Duke University Press, 1989. An autobiography.

Kriegsman, Sali Ann. "Interview with a Maverick Modern: Pauline Koner." *DS* 13, no. 4 (Summer 1979): 36-53.

Maynard, Olga. "Pauline Koner: A Cyclic Force." *Dance Magazine* 47, no. 4 (April 1973): 55-70. A Dance Magazine Portfolio.

COH/2: 76-89. SOR/2: 128-136.

**Kosloff, Theodore** (ca. 1883-1956)

PRE: 119-132.

**Kosmovska, Irina** (192?-1993)

MAS: 485-487.

**Kovach, Nora** (1931– )

Kovach, Nora, and Istvan Rabovsky, with George Mikes. *Leap Through the Curtain: The Story of Nora Kovach & Istvan Rabovsky*. New York: Dutton, 1955.

**Kovach, Nora** *(continued)*
Walther, Suzanne K. "From Behind the Iron Curtain." *Dance Research Monograph One 1971–1972*, pp. 153-161. Co-edited by Patricia A. Rowe and Ernestine Stodelle. New York: Committee on Research in Dance (CORD), 1973.

**Kramarevsky, Andrei** (1928– )
MAS: 595-598.

**Kraul, Earl** (1929– )
Lomax, Sondra. "Earl Kraul Tells Almost All." *YDR* Spring 1977 (Issue #6): 22-27.

**Kraus, Gertrud** (1903-1977)
Manor, Giora. *The Life and Dance of Gertrud Kraus*. Tel-Aviv: Hakibbutz Hameuchad Publishing House, 1978. Hebrew text, with English summary.

**Kreutzberg, Harald** (1902-1968)
Forster, Marianne. "Reconstructing European Modern Dance: Boden-wieser, Chladek, Leeder, Kreutzberg, Hoyer." In *Proceedings of the Conference "Dance Reconstructed: Modern Dance Art Past, Present, Future,"* pp. 137-149. Rutgers University, New Brunswick, New Jersey, October 16 and 17, 1992.
Turbyfill, Mark. *Ruth Page [and] Kreutzberg*. [Chicago?, 1934]. PAG: 96-112.

**Kriza, John** (1919-1975)
ATK: 84-87.

**Kronstam, Henning** (1934-1995)
Tomalonis, Alexandra. "Dancing for Ashton and Balanchine: Talking with Henning Kronstam." *DanceView* 11, no. 4 (Summer 1994): 24-55.

**Kudelka, James** (1955– )
"Kudelka, James." *Current Biography* 56, no. 3 (March 1995): 30-34.

**Kurath, Gertrude Prokosch** (1903-1992)

Fenton, William N. *The Iroquois Eagle Dance: An Offshoot of the Calumet Dance*. With an analysis of the Iroquois eagle dance and songs, "The Iroquois and their Neighbors," by Gertrude Prokosch Kurath. Smithsonian Institution, Bureau of American Ethnology, Bulletin 156. Washington, D.C.: U.S. Govt. Print. Off., 1953; reprint Syracuse, N.Y.: Syracuse University Press, 1991.

Kealiinohomoku, Joann W. "The Conviction of Gertrude Prokosch Kurath About the Interconnections of Dance and Music." *UCLA Journal of Dance Ethnology* 19 (1995): 1-5.

———. "In Memoriam: Gertrude Prokosch Kurath, August 19, 1903-August 1, 1992." *DRJ* 24, no. 2 (Fall 1992): 70.

———, and Frank J. Gillis. "Special Bibliography: Gertrude Prokosch Kurath." *Ethnomusicology* 14, no. 1 (January 1970): 114-128.

Kurath, Gertrude Prokosch. *Dance Memoirs*. Cambridge, Mass.: Chimera Press, 1983.

———. *Dance and Song Rituals of Six Nations Reserve, Ontario*. Bulletin 220. Ottawa: National Museum of Canada, 1968.

———. "George Gershwin's Concerto in F at the Yale School of Drama." With an Introduction by Joann W. Kealiinohomoku. *DRJ* 20, no. 1 (Summer 1988): 43-46.

———. *Half A Century of Dance Research*. Flagstaff, Ariz.: Cross-Cultural Dance Resources, 1986.

———. *Iroquois Music and Dance: Ceremonial Arts of Two Seneca Longhouses*. Smithsonian Institution, Bureau of American Ethnology, Bulletin 187. Washington, D.C.: U.S. Govt. Print. Off., 1964.

———. *Michigan Indian Festivals*. Ann Arbor, Mich.: Ann Arbor Publishers, 1966.

———. "Panorama of Dance Ethnology." *Current Anthropology* 1, no. 3 (1960): 233-254.

———. "Research Methods and Background of Gertrude Kurath." *DRA VI* (1972): 35-43.

———. *Tutelo Rituals on Six Nations, Ontario*. Society for Ethnomusicology Special Series #5. Ann Arbor, Mich.: Society for Ethnomusicology, 1981.

———, with the aid of Antonio Garcia. *Music and Dance of the Tewa Pueblos*. Museum of New Mexico Research Records, No. 8. Santa Fe: Museum of New Mexico Press, 1970.

**Kurath, Gertrude Prokosch** *(continued)*

Helm, June, and Nancy Oestreich Lurie. *The Dogrib Hand Game.* With "Dogrib Choreography and Music" by Gertrude P. Kurath. National Museum of Canada Bulletin 205. Ottawa: National Museum of Canada, 1966.

Malm, Joyce R. "Gertrude Kurath Collection, University of Michigan, Ann Arbor." *DRJ* 23, no. 1 (Spring 1991): 61.

Martí, Samuel, and Gertrude Prokosch Kurath. *Dances of Anáhuac: The Choreography and Music of Precortesian Dances.* Viking Fund Publication 38. Chicago: Aldine Publishing Company, 1964.

Wimmer, Shirley. "In Honor of Gertrude Prokosch Kurath." *DRA VI* (1972): 31-34.


**Kyasht, Lydia** (1885-1959)

Kyasht, Lydia. *Romantic Recollections.* Edited by Erica Beale. London & New York: Brentano, 1929; reprint New York: Da Capo Press, 1978.

DAV: 171-174.


**Kylián, Jiří** (1947– )

"Kylián, Jiří." *CBY 1982*: 208-211.

Lanz, Isabelle. *A Garden of Dance.* Amsterdam: Theater Instituut Nederland, in association with Nederlands Dans Theater, 1995. Bilingual: Dutch/English. The Dutch title of this book translates literally *A Garden with a Thousand Flowers.*

L

**Laban, Juana de** (1910-1978)
Laban, Juana de. "Introduction to Dance Notation." *DI* 5, nos. 4-5 (April-May 1946). "A Tribute to Juana de Laban (1910-1978)." *DRJ* 13, no. 2 (Spring 1981). Articles: Robyn Baker Flatt. "Juana de Laban: A Brief Biography" (pp. 4-11). "Photographs from the Dallas Theater Center, Juana de Laban Collection," selected by Robyn Baker Flatt and Gretchen Schneider (pp. 12-15). Suzanne Shelton. "Juana de Laban Collection" (p. 16). Malcolm McCormick. "Recollections" (pp. 16-19). Gretchen Schneider. "Remembering Dr. Laban" (pp. 19-20).

**Laban, Rudolf** (1879-1958)
Foster, John. *The Influences of Rudolph Laban.* London: Lepus Books, 1977.
Green, Martin. "Rudolf Laban." Chapter 3 in his *Mountain of Truth: The Counterculture Begins, Ascona, 1900-1920*, pp. 83-115. Hanover, N.H. & London: Published for Tufts University by University Press of New England, 1986.

**Laban, Rudolf** *(continued)*

Hodgson, John, and Valerie Preston-Dunlop. *Rudolf Laban: An Introduction to his Work & Influence.* Plymouth: Northcote House, 1990.

Hutchinson, Ann. *Labanotation: The System for Recording Movement.* London: Phoenix House, 1954.

———. *Labanotation, or Kinetography Laban: The System of Analyzing and Recording Movement.* rev. and enl. ed. New York: Theatre Arts Books, 1970.

Kozel, Susan. "Essence, Effort and Experience." *DN* 3, no. 1 (Spring 1994): 46-49, 51-53, 55, 57.

Laban, Rudolf. *Choreutics.* Annotated and edited by Lisa Ullmann. London: Macdonald & Evans, 1966.

———. *The Language of Movement: A Guidebook to Choreutics.* Annotated and edited by Lisa Ullmann. Boston: Plays, Inc., 1966. The American edition of Laban's *Choreutics.*

———. *A Life for Dance: Reminiscences.* Translated and annotated by Lisa Ullmann. New York: Theatre Arts Books, 1975.

———. *The Mastery of Movement.* 2d ed., rev. and enl. by Lisa Ullmann. London: Macdonald & Evans, 1960. First published by Macdonald & Evans in 1950 under the title *The Mastery of Movement on the Stage.*

———. *Modern Educational Dance.* London: Macdonald & Evans, 1948.

———. *Principles of Dance and Movement Notation.* London: Macdonald & Evans, 1956.

———, and F.C. Lawrence. *Effort.* London: Macdonald & Evans, 1969. The reprint of a work first published in 1947. The preface contains biographical information on Laban.

Maletic, Vera. "Rudolf Laban's Dance Theory: Its Underlying Paradigms and Debts to the Heritage of Dance." In *Society of Dance History Scholars Proceedings,* pp. 239-252. Sixth Annual Conference, The Ohio State University, 11-13 February 1983.

Newlove, Jean. *Laban for Actors and Dancers: Putting Laban's Movement Theory into Practice, a Step-by-Step Guide.* New York: Routledge, 1993.

Preston-Dunlop, Valerie. "Laban and the Nazis: Towards an Understanding of Rudolf Laban and the Third Reich." *Dance Theatre Journal* 6, no. 2 (Autumn 1988): 4-7.

**L**

**Laban, Rudolf** *(continued)*

———. "The Nature of the Embodiment of Choreutic Units in Contemporary Choreography." Unpublished dissertation, Laban Centre/University of London, Goldsmiths' College, 1981.

———. "Rudolf Laban—The Making of Modern Dance." Part 3: The Nightmare Years, 1914-1919. *Dance Theatre Journal* 10, no. 3 (Spring-Summer 1993): 14-19 and *Dance Theatre Journal* 10, no. 4 (Autumn 1993): 33-35.

———, and Charlotte Purkis. "Rudolf Laban—The Making of Modern Dance." Parts 1 and 2: The Seminal Years in Munich, 1910-1914. *Dance Theatre Journal* 7, no. 3 (Winter 1989): 11-16, 25 and *Dance Theatre Journal* 7, no. 4 (February 1990): 10-13.

Prevots, Naima. "Zurich Dada and Dance: Formative Ferment." *DRJ* 17, no. 1 (Spring/Summer 1985): 3-8.

Ringel, Fred. "EFFORT: A Synthesis of Movement." *DS* 2, no. 1 (Fall 1965): 27-31.

Stephenson, Geraldine. "A Way of Seeing." *DN* 3, no. 2 (Summer 1994): 58-63.

Thornton, Samuel. *Laban's Theory of Movement: A New Perspective.* Boston: Plays, Inc., 1971.

Ullmann, Lisa, comp. *Rudolf Laban: A Vision of Dynamic Space.* [London]: Laban Archives; London & Philadelphia: Falmer Press, 1984.

SOR/1: 145-159.


**Ladré, Illaria Obidenna** (1906– )

Ladré, Illaria Obidenna, with Nancy Whyte. *Illaria Obidenna Ladré: Memoirs of a Child of Theatre Street, An Autobiography.* [Seattle, Wash.]: the author, 1993.

Shapiro, Henry. "For God and the Russian Ballet." *BR* 17, no. 4 (Winter 1990): 73-79.


**Ladré, Marian** (1903-1983)

Shapiro, Henry. "For God and the Russian Ballet." *BR* 17, no. 4 (Winter 1990): 73-79.


**LaFosse, Robert** (1959– )

LaFosse, Robert, with Andrew Mark Wentink. *Nothing to Hide: A Dancer's Life.* New York: Donald I. Fine, 1987.

**Laing, Hugh** (1911-1988)

"Laing, Hugh." *CBY 1946*: 317-318.

Perlmutter, Donna. *Shadowplay: The Life of Antony Tudor*. New York: Viking, 1991.

ATK: 88-91. DAV: 175-176. DEM/2: 191-203.

**Lake, Molly** (1900-1986)

Benari, Naomi. *Vagabonds and Strolling Dancers: The Lives and Times of Molly Lake and Travis Kemp*. London: Imperial Society of Teachers of Dancing, [1990].

**La Meri** (1899-1988)

La Meri. *Dance as an Art-Form: Its History and Development*. New York: A.S. Barnes, 1933.

——. *Dance Composition: The Basic Elements*. Lee, Mass.: Jacob's Pillow Dance Festival, 1965.

—— (Russell Meriwether Hughes). *Dance Out the Answer: An Autobiography*. New York & Basel: Marcel Dekker, 1978.

——. *The Gesture Language of Hindu Dance*. New York: Benjamin Blom, 1964. Reprint of a work originally published in 1941.

——. *Spanish Dancing*. New York: A.S. Barnes, 1948; 2d ed. rev. Pittsfield, Mass.: Eagle Printing Company, 1967.

—— (Russell Meriwether Hughes). *Total Education in Ethnic Dance*. New York & Basel: Marcel Dekker, 1978.

"La Meri." *Dance Magazine* 52, no. 8 (August 1978). A three-part Dance Magazine Portfolio. La Meri. "I Remember" (pp. 55-62). La Meri, edited and with a foreword by Walter Terry. "A Chronology of Learning, Labor, Life" (pp. 62-65). Jane Sherman. "A Lifetime in Ethnic Dance: Two Books by La Meri" (pp. 66-70). The two books reviewed are *Dance Out the Answer: An Autobiography* and *Total Education in Ethnic Dance*, both published in 1978 by Marcel Dekker, New York.

Neal, Josie. "La Meri's *Drishyakava*: A Video Presentation." In *Society of Dance History Scholars Proceedings*, pp. 149-152. Twelfth Annual Conference, Arizona State University, 17-19 February 1989.

**Lamhut, Phyllis** (1933– )

Zupp, Nancy Thornhill. "An Analysis and Comparison of the Choreographic Process of Alwin Nikolais, Murray Louis, and

**Lamhut, Phyllis** *(continued)*

Phyllis Lamhut." Unpublished dissertation, University of North Carolina at Greensboro, 1978. Ann Arbor, Mich.: University Microfilms International, 1978. Order No. 78-24,313. DAI 39-06A, p. 3196.

**Lampert, Rachel** (1948– )

Beck, Jill. "Rachel Lampert's *What's Remembered?*: A Critical Analysis." *DNJ* 3, no. 1, pt. 1 (Spring 1985): 68-119. Look under Leslie Rotman for Labanotation score to part of this work.

Rotman, Leslie. "'Duet' from Rachel Lampert's *What's Remembered?*" *DNJ* 3, no. 1, pt. 2 (Spring 1985): 19-53. Look under Jill Beck for supporting article to this Labanotation score.

**Lander, Toni** (1931-1985)

Lander, Toni. "Fair New World." *DS* 5, no. 2 (Spring 1971): 40-42.

Vaughan, David. "Toni Lander." *BR* 14, no. 1 (Spring 1986): 53-56.

NEW/1: 170-189.

**Lang, Pearl** (1922– )

"Lang, Pearl." *CBY 1970*: 238-239.

"Two Essays for Pearl Lang." *Dance Magazine* 48, no. 9 (September 1974). A two-part Dance Magazine Portfolio. Tobi Tobias. "Lang: A Remembrance" (pp. 47-49). Tobi Tobias. "Lang: Speaking for Herself" (pp. 50-54).

**Lanner, Katti** (1829-1908)

Guest, Ivor. *Ballet in Leicester Square: The Alhambra and the Empire, 1860-1915.* London: Dance Books, 1992.

———. *The Empire Ballet.* London: Society for Theatre Research, 1962.

**Larsen, Gerd** (1921– )

GRU/2: 157-161.

**Larsen, Niels Bjørn** (1913– )

Cunningham, Kitty. "Niels Bjørn Larsen: A Life in Mime." *BR* 10, no. 2 (Summer 1982): 88-94.

NEW/2: 60-76.

## Larson, Bird (1887-1927)

Evan, Blanche. "Tribute to Bird Larson." In *Collected Works By and About Blanche Evan: Dancer, Teacher, Writer, Dance/Movement/Word Therapist*, pp. 35-38. Compiled by Ruth Gordon Benov. San Francisco: Blanche Evan Dance Foundation, 1991. Reprinted from *Dance* 6, no. 5 [i.e. 6] (November 1939): 14, 27.

MAR: 166-169.

## Lavery, Sean (1956– )

Leivick, Laura. "A Dancer's Nightmare." *The New York Times Magazine*, November 8, 1987, pp. 66, 68, 70, 75-78.

GRE/2: 50-58.

## Lavrovsky, Mikhail (1941– )

Helpern, Alice. "Informal Meeting with Mikhail Lavrovsky, Visiting Soviet Choreographer." In *Society of Dance History Scholars Proceedings*, p. 209. Tenth Annual Conference, University of California, Irvine, 13-15 February 1987.

DEM/1: 209-211. ZHD: 108-141.

## LeClercq, Tanaquil (1929– )

"LeClercq, Tanaquil." *CBY 1953*: 349-350.

Le Clercq, Tanaquil. *The Ballet Cook Book*. New York: Stein and Day; Toronto: Saunders of Toronto, 1966.

——, text, with photography by Martha Swope. *Mourka: The Autobiography of a Cat*. New York: Stein and Day, 1964; London: Sidgwick and Jackson, 1965.

Lobenthal, Joel. "Tanaquil Le Clercq." *BR* 12, no. 3 (Fall 1984): 74-86.

Newman, Barbara. "Tanaquil Le Clercq Talks About Dancing." *BR* 10, no. 3 (Fall 1982): 52-75. An extract from Barbara Newman's *Striking a Balance: Dancers Talk About Dancing*. Boston: Houghton Mifflin, 1982.

ATK: 92-95. MON: 50-53. NEW/1: 146-168.

## Lee, Mary Ann (1823-1899)

Moore, Lillian. "Mary Ann Lee: First American Giselle." *DI* 2, no. 5 (May 1943).

**Lee, Mary Ann** *(continued)*

Stern, Madeleine B. "The First American Ballerina to Capture the Nation." Chapter 1 in her *We the Women: Career Firsts of Nineteenth-Century America*, pp. 5-28. New York: Schulte Publishing Company, 1963.

MAG: 102-117. SWI/1: 183-188.

**Legat, Nicolas** (1869-1937)

Gregory, John. *The Legat Saga: Nicolai Gustavovitch Legat, 1869-1937*. On the cover: *The Legat Saga: An Anecdotal Study of the Life and Times of Nicolai Legat*. 2d ed., November 1993. London: Javog Publishing Associates, 1993.

**Dance Research Journal**
Congress on Research in Dance        ISSN 0149 7677        20/2 Winter 1988 $8.50

*RUSSIAN ISSUE*

Е. ЛЕНСКАЯ В. ДРУЦКАЯ Л. ГАЙ.
КОСТЮМЫ Б. ЭРДМАНА.

————, with André Eglevsky, comps. and eds. *Heritage of a Balletmaster: Nicolas Legat*. New York: Dance Horizons, 1977.

Legat, Nicolas. *Ballet Russe: Memoirs of Nicolas Legat*. Translated with a Foreword by Sir Paul Dukes. London: Methuen, 1939.

————. *The Story of the Russian School*. Translated with a Foreword by Sir Paul Dukes. Artists of the Dance. London: British-Continental Press, 1932.

**Leigh, Angela** (1949– )

SID: 105-116.

**Leland, Sara** (1941– )

GRU/2: 353-358.

**Lepeshinskaya, Olga** (1916– )

SLO: 89-92.

**Leslie, Serge** (1903– )
Kovalevsky, Olga. *Studies in Movement of Doris Niles and Serge Leslie*. Los Angeles: [Serge Leslie], 1951.

Leslie, Serge. *A Bibliography of the Dance Collection of Doris Niles & Serge Leslie*. Parts 1-4. Edited by Cyril Beaumont (Parts 1-3). Part 1: A-K. Part 2: L-Z. Part 3: A-Z (Mainly 20th-Century Publications). Part 4: A-Z (Mainly 20th-Century Publications). London: C.W. Beaumont (Parts 1-3), 1966, 1968, 1974. London: Dance Books (Part 4), 1981. Part 4 contains a unique listing of Cyril Beaumont's articles, of which there are approximately 250, published between 1925 and 1975. Serge Leslie is an example of that rare breed, the dancer/scholar. This four-part bibliography, his "monument" (the word is Cyril Beaumont's), is one of the finest annotated bibliographies in the field—an invaluable reference for librarians, scholars, collectors, and students. For a fascinating, two-part article about the Niles-Leslie Collection, see: Francis, Paul V. "The Miracle Library." Part 1: "The Escape" and Part 2: "The Collection Surveyed." *Dance Magazine* 22, no. 10 (October 1948): 26-27, 57 and *Dance Magazine* 22, no. 11 (November 1948): 22-23, 33-36. The Niles-Leslie Collection was sold in 1970 to the city of Stuttgart and is located at the Württembergische Landesbibliothek (Württemberg State Library), adjacent to the Opera House. A notice about the sale and transfer of the collection to Germany appears in *Dance Magazine* 45, no. 6 (June 1971): 84.

——. *A Dancer's Scrapbook: From the Capitol Theatre, New York City, to Carnegie Hall with Doris Niles, a Chronicle 1919-1929*. London: Dance Books, 1987.

——. *The Seven Leagues of a Dancer*. London: C.W. Beaumont, 1958.

**Levi-Tanai, Sara** (1911– )
Ingber, Judith Brin. "The Priestesses." *DC* 18, no. 3 (1995): 453-465.
"Levi-Tanai, Sara." *CBY 1958*: 246-247.

**Lewitzky, Bella** (1916– )
Deny, Sharron Louise Kerr. "Bella Lewitzky: A Description of Her Methods and Views on Performance and Choreography." Unpub-

**Lewitzky, Bella** *(continued)*

lished dissertation, University of Southern California, 1974. Ann
Arbor, Mich.: University Microfilms International, 1974. Order
No. 74-09,064. DAI 34-10A, p. 6430.

Moore, Elvi. "Bella Lewitzky: A Legend Turned Real." *DC* 2, no. 1
(1978): 1-78.

———. "The Performer-Teacher: An Interview with Bella Lewitzky."
*DS* 8, no. 1 (Fall/Winter 1973-74): 7-11.

Rosen, Lillie F. "A Conversation with Bella Lewitzky." *BR* 10, no. 3
(Fall 1982): 81-94.

ROG: 90-101.

**Lichine, David** (1910-1972)

ATK: 96-100. BEL: 46-50. DAV: 177-180. FRA: 68-73. SCH/1: see
Index of Choreographers, p. 135.

**Liepa, Andris** (1962– )

Kokich, Kim. "A Conversation with the Liepas." *BR* 15, no. 2
(Summer 1987): 39-42.

**Liepa, Ilze** (1963– )

Kokich, Kim. "A Conversation with the Liepas." *BR* 15, no. 2
(Summer 1987): 39-42.

**Liepa, Maris** (1936-1990)

Barnes, Patricia, text, with photography by Mira. *Maris Liepa.* Dance
Horizons Spotlight Series. Brooklyn, N.Y.: Dance Horizons, 1975.
DEM/1: 214-218.

**Lifar, Serge** (1905-1986)

Cluzel, Magdeleine E. "Serge Lifar: Ballet Master of the Opera." In
her *Glimpses of the Theatre and Dance*, pp. 53-57. Translated from
the French by Lily and Baird Hastings. New York: Kamin
Publishers, 1953.

Lifar, Serge. *Carlotta Grisi.* Translated by Doris Langley Moore.
London: John Lehmann, 1947.

**Lifar, Serge** *(continued)*

———. *A History of Russian Ballet from its Origins to the Present Day.* Translated by Arnold Haskell. London: Hutchinson 1954.

———. *Ma Vie: From Kiev to Kiev.* An Autobiography. Translated by James Holman Mason. London: Hutchinson, 1970.

———. *Serge Diaghilev: His Life, His Work, His Legend: An Intimate Biography.* New York: Putnam, 1940; reprint New York: Da Capo, 1976.

———. *The Three Graces: The Legends and the Truth.* Translated by Gerard Hopkins. London: Cassell, 1959.

Mayo, Eileen, drawings, with an appreciation by Cyril W. Beaumont. *Serge Lifar.* London: C.W. Beaumont, 1928.

Michaut, Pierre. "The Choreography of Serge Lifar." In *The Ballet Annual 1949: A Record and Year Book of the Ballet*, pp. 81-87. Edited by Arnold L. Haskell. Third Issue. London: Adam & Charles Black, [1948].

Tassart, Maurice. "The Serge Lifar Story." In *The Ballet Annual 1960: A Record and Year Book of the Ballet*, pp. 55-59. Edited by Arnold L. Haskell. Fourteenth Issue. New York: Macmillan, 1959. ATK: 101-104. BLA: 118-121. DAV: 180-186. FRA: 58-67. GRU/2: 3-9. HAL: 176-185. MOO/1: 225-231. NEW/1: 22-27.

**L**

**Lightheart, Kim** (1961– )

Carreiro, Assis. *Kim Lightheart.* Profiles of Canadian Dance, No. 3. Toronto: Press of Terpsichore, 1987.

**Limón, José** (1908-1972)

Becker, Svea. "From Humphrey to Limón: A Modern Dance Tradition." *DNJ* 2, no. 1 (Spring 1984): 37-52.

Cunningham, Katharine S. "A Legacy of José Limón." *DS* 7, no. 2 (Spring/Summer 1973): 6-13.

Friesen, Joanna. "A Comparative Analysis of *Othello* and *The Moor's Pavane*: An Aristotelian Approach to Dances Based on Dramatic Literature." Unpublished dissertation, Florida State University, 1977. Ann Arbor, Mich.: University Microfilms International, 1978. Order No. 780,8949. DAI 38-12A, p. 7026.

Hill, Martha. "José Limón and his Biblical Works." *C&D* 2, pt. 3 (1992): 57-61.

Koner, Pauline. "The Truth About *The Moor's Pavane*." *BR* 8, no. 4 (1980): 386-396.

Lewis, Daniel, in collaboration with Leslie Farlow. *The Illustrated Dance Technique of José Limón*. New York: Harper & Row, c. 1984.

*Limón: A Catalogue of Dances*. Edited by Norton Owen. New York: The Limón Institute, 1994.

"Limón, José." *CBY 1953*: 361-362.

"Limón, José (Arcadio)." *CBY 1968*: 225-228.

Mindlin, Naomi. "José Limón's *The Moor's Pavane*: An Interview with Lucas Hoving." *DRJ* 24, no. 1 (Spring 1992): 13-26.

Pollack, Barbara, and Charles Woodford. *Dance Is A Moment: A Portrait of José Limón in Words and Pictures*. Pennington, N.J.: Princeton Book Company, Publishers, 1993.

Siegel, Marcia B. "José Limón (1908-1972)." *BR* 4, no. 4 (1973): 100-104.

BRO: 97-104. COH/2: 16-27. KON: 191-236. LLO: 198-213. SOR/1: 192-196.

**Lindgren, Robert** (1923– )

MAS: 227-229.

**Linke, Susanne** (1944– )

"An Interview with Susanne Linke." *C&D* 2, pt. 1 (1992): 133-135.

**Lippincott, Gertrude** (1913– )

Ingber, Judith Brin. "Gertrude Lippincott and the Development of Dance in Minneapolis." In *Society of Dance History Scholars*

**Lippincott, Gertrude** *(continued)*

*Proceedings*, pp. 125-132. Joint Conference with The Congress on Research in Dance, New York Public Library for the Performing Arts, New York City, 11-13 June 1993.

**Lisner, Charles** (1928-1988)

Lisner, Charles. *My Journey through Dance*. St. Lucia: University of Queensland Press, 1979.

**Littlefield, Catherine** (1905-1951)

Brooks Schmitz, Nancy. "Catherine Littlefield and Anna Sokolow: Artists Reflecting Society in the 1930s." In *Dance: Current Selected Research*, Volume 1, pp. 115-123. Edited by Lynnette Y. Overby and James H. Humphrey. New York: AMS Press, 1989.

——. "A Profile of Catherine Littlefield, a Pioneer of American Ballet." Unpublished dissertation, Temple University, 1986. Ann Arbor, Mich.: University Microfilms International, 1986. Order No. 862,7509. DAI 47-08A, p. 2773.

SCH/1: see Index of Choreographers, p. 135.

**Littlefield (Carl Edwin** 1915?-1966, **Caroline** 1882?-1957, **Catherine** 1905-1951, and **Dorothie** 1916-1953)

Barzel, Ann. "The Littlefields." Parts One and Two. *Dance Magazine* 19, no. 5 (May 1945): 10-11 and *Dance Magazine* 19, no. 6 (June 1945): 8-9.

Brooks Schmitz, Nancy. "The Contributions of the Littlefields to Concert Dance in Philadelphia." In *Society of Dance History Scholars Proceedings*, pp. 133-147. Ninth Annual Conference, City College, City University of New York, 14-17 February 1986.

Hering, Doris. "The Littlefield Legacy." *Dance Magazine* 67, no. 9 (September 1993): 48-51. Part Two in the series An American Original.

**Litz, Katherine** (1912-1978)

Kendall, Elizabeth. "Katherine Litz: Daughter of Virtue." *BR* 7, nos. 2 & 3 (1978-1979): 1-9.

——. "Talking with Katherine Litz." *DS* 8, no. 2 (Spring/Summer 1974): 6-17.

Maynard, Olga. "Katherine Litz Talks to Olga Maynard." Parts One

**Litz, Katherine** *(continued)*

and Two. *Dance Magazine* 40, no. 1 (January 1967): 52-59 and *Dance Magazine* 40, no. 2 (February 1967): 56-60, 62-64.

SCH/1: see Index of Choreographers, p. 135. SIE: 34-37.


**Livry, Emma** (1842-1863)

Beaumont, Cyril W. "Emma Livry." In his *Three French Dancers of the 19th Century*, pp. 19-28. Essays on Dancing and Dancers, No. 9. London: C.W. Beaumont, 1935.

Guest, Ivor. "The Tragedy of Emma Livry." Chapter 1 in his *The Ballet of the Second Empire 1858-1870*, pp. 1-39. London: Adam & Charles Black, 1953; reprinted in *The Ballet of the Second Empire*, pp. 123-161. London: Pitman Publishing; Middletown, Conn.: Wesleyan University Press, 1974.

———. "Emma Livry, 1842-63." In *The Ballet Annual and Year Book*, pp. 54-60. Edited by Mary Clarke and Arnold L. Haskell. Eighteenth Issue. London: Adam & Charles Black, 1963.

MOO/1: 155-159.


**Lloyd, Gweneth** (1901-1993)

Warner, Mary Jane. "Gweneth Lloyd's *Shadow on the Prairie*: The Computer-assisted Dance History Lesson." In *Society of Dance History Scholars Proceedings*, pp. 261-265. Seventeenth Annual Conference, Brigham Young University, Provo, Utah, 10-13 February 1994. Technical background to and description of the content of the HyperCard project, *Shadow on the Prairie*, at York University, Toronto.


**Lloyd, Maude** (1908– )

Hunt, Marilyn. "A Conversation with Maude Lloyd." *BR* 11, no. 3 (Fall 1983): 5-26.


**Long, Larry** (1936– )

PAG: 75-79.


**Lopez, Lourdes** (1958– )

SWI/3: 163-167.

**Lopokova, Lydia** (1891-1981)

*The Art of Lydia Lopokova.* London: C.W. Beaumont, 1920.

Hill, Polly, and Richard Keynes, eds. *Lydia and Maynard: The Letters of Lydia Lopokova and John Maynard Keynes.* New York: Scribner's, 1990.

Keynes, Milo, ed. *Lydia Lopokova.* London: Weidenfeld and Nicolson, 1983.

*Lydia Lopokova: A Book of Camera Portraits.* London: C.W. Beaumont, 1922.

DAV: 187-191. HAS/1: 126-130.

**Lopukhov, Fedor** (1886-1973)

Souritz, Elizabeth. "Fedor Lopukhov: A Soviet Choreographer in the 1920s." *DRJ* 17, no. 2 & 18, no. 1 (Fall 1985/Spring 1986): 3-20.

———. "Fedor Vasilievich Lopukhov." Chapter 6 in her *Soviet Choreographers in the 1920s,* pp. 255-315. Translated from the Russian by Lynn Visson. Edited, with additional translation, by Sally Banes. Durham, N.C. & London: Duke University Press, 1990.

**Loring, Eugene** (1914-1982)

Guest, Ann Hutchinson. "Selma Jeanne Cohen and Eugene Loring's *Kinesiography.*" *DC* 18, no. 2 (1995): 195-206.

"Loring, Eugene." *CBY 1972*: 288-290.

BEL: 51-53. MAY/1: 227-241. SCH/1: see Index of Choreographers, p. 135.

**Losch, Tilly** (1904-1975)

James, Edward. *Swans Reflecting Elephants: My Early Years.* Edited by George Melly. London: Weidenfeld and Nicolson, 1982.

"Losch, Tilly." *CBY 1944*: 424-426.

**Louis, Murray** (1926– )

"Louis, Murray." *CBY 1968*: 230-232.

Louis, Murray. *Inside Dance*. New York: St. Martin's Press, 1980.

——. *Murray Louis on Dance*. [Pennington, N.J.]: A Cappella Books, 1992.

Zupp, Nancy Thornhill. "An Analysis and Comparison of the Choreographic Process of Alwin Nikolais, Murray Louis, and Phyllis Lamhut." Unpublished dissertation, University of North Carolina at Greensboro, 1978. Ann Arbor, Mich.: University Microfilms International, 1978. Order No. 78-24,313. DAI 39-06A, p. 3196.

GRU/1: 48-51. LYL: 124-135. SIE: 28-33.


**Lowe, Jospeh** (fl. 1852-1860)

Lowe, Joseph. *A New Most Excellent Dancing Master*. The Journal of Joseph Lowe's visits to Balmoral and Windsor (1852-1860) to teach dance to the family of Queen Victoria. Edited by Allan Thomas. Dance and Music Series, No. 5. Stuyvesant, N.Y.: Pendragon Press, 1992.

Thomas, Allan, and J.M. Thomson, eds. "The Lowe Family Collection of Dance Books and Manuscripts." *Stout Centre Review* 3, no. 1 (November 1992).


**Lubovitch, Lar** (1943– )

"Lubovitch, Lar." *CBY 1992*: 365-369.

GRU/1: 79-85. GRU/2: 446-451.


**Lyon, Annabelle** (ca. 1915– )

MAS: 141-143.

**Macdonald, Brian** (1928– )

"Macdonald, Brian." *CBY 1968*: 234-237.

Macdonald, Brian. "The Chance to Dream." In *Visions: Ballet and Its Future*, pp. 153-158. Edited by Michael Crabb. Essays from the International Dance Conference to commemorate the 25th anniversary of the National Ballet of Canada, held at the Town Hall, St. Lawrence Centre for the Arts, Toronto, Nvember 15-16, 1976. Foreword by Sir Frederick Ashton. Introduction by Vincent Tovell. Toronto: Simon & Pierre, c. 1978.

**MacLeary, Donald** (1937– )

NEW/1: 190-203.

**MacMillan, Kenneth** (1929-1992)

Bintley, David. "Sir Kenneth MacMillan 1929-1992." *DN* 1, no. 4 (Winter 1992-93): 42-43, 45.

Kane, Angela. "Kenneth MacMillan: Rebel with a Cause." Dance Study Supplement, pt. 2. *The Dancing Times* 80, no. 950 (November 1989): 8 pp. (i-viii), between pp. 156 & 157.

Thorpe, Edward. *Kenneth MacMillan: The Man and the Ballets.* London: Hamish Hamilton, 1985.

**Magallanes, Nicholas** (1922-1977)

"Magallanes, Nicholas." *CBY 1955*: 402-403.

**Maiorano, Robert** (1946– )

Maiorano, Robert. *Worlds Apart: The Autobiography of a Dancer from Brooklyn*. New York: Coward, McCann & Geoghegan, 1980.

**Makarova, Natalia** (1940– )

Austin, Richard. *Natalia Makarova: Ballerina*. London: Dance Books, 1978.

Makarova, Dina, text and photography. *Natalia Makarova*. Dance Horizons Spotlight Series. Brooklyn, N.Y.: Dance Horizons, 1975.

"Makarova, Natalia." *CBY 1972*: 303-306.

Makarova, Natalia. *A Dance Autobiography*. Introduced and edited by Gennady Smakov. New York: Knopf, 1979.

Maynard, Olga. "Makarova: The Sublime Paradox." *Dance Magazine* 51, no. 4 (April 1977): 59-74. A Dance Magazine Portfolio.

AUS/2: 105-117. GRU/2: 207-215. MON: 72-75. PET: 34-55. SMA: 39-52. SWI/3: 231-236.

**Malakhov, Vladimir** (1968– )

Baier, Nadja, and Jürgen Holwein, with photography by Dieter Blum. *Vladimir Malakhov: Dancer of the Century*. Ostfildern, Germany: Cantz, 1995. Bilingual: German/English.

**Maracci, Carmelita** (1911-1987)

DEM/3: 51-69. PAG: 68-74. SOR/1: 160-169.

**Marchand, Colette** (1925– )

ATK: 105-107.

**Marie-Jeanne** (1920– )

Magriel, Paul, and Don McDonagh. "A Conversation with Marie-Jeanne." *BR* 12, no. 4 (Winter 1985): 59-73.

"Marie-Jeanne." *BR* 12, no. 4 (Winter 1985): 40-58. A portfolio of photographs with a brief introduction by John Taras.

Marie-Jeanne. *Yankee Ballerina: A Story of a Young American Ballet Dancer*. New York: Dodd, Mead & Co., 1941. A novel about a young American ballet dancer who could be Marie-Jeanne.

MAS: 171-176. TRA: 76-83.

**Markova, Alicia** (1910– )

"Alicia Markova." *Dance Magazine* 51, no. 6 (June 1977). A two-part Dance Magazine Portfolio. Anthony Fay. "Alicia Markova: Her Appearances in America" (pp. 48-55). David Vaughan. "Conversations with Markova" (pp. 56-61).

Anthony, Gordon. *Alicia Markova*. London: Phoenix House, 1951.

———. *Markova: A Collection of Photographic Studies*. London: Chatto & Windus, 1935.

Beaumont, Cyril W. *Alicia Markova*. Essays on Dancing and Dancers, No. 8. London: C.W. Beaumont, 1935.

Dolin, Anton. *Alicia Markova: Her Life and Art*. New York: Hermitage House, 1953.

Fisher, Hugh. *Alicia Markova*. Dancers of To-Day, No. 6. New York: Macmillan, 1954.

"Markova, Alicia." *CBY 1943*: 497-500.

Markova, Alicia. *Giselle and I*. New York: The Vanguard Press, 1960.

———. *Markova Remembers*. Boston & Toronto: Little, Brown & Company, 1986.

Nemenschousky, Léon. *A Day with Alicia Markova*. Translated by Margaret McGregor. London: Cassell & Company, 1960.

Williams, Peter. *Alicia Markova and Anton Dolin: A Legend of British Ballet*. London: Hall Publications, n.d.

ATK: 108-114. AUS/1: 152-176. BEL: 55-60. CRO: 65-91. DAV: 191-198. DEM/3: 19-37. GRU/2: 43-51. HUR: 200-204. MAS: 89-92. MCC: 62-75. MON: 30-33. MUI: 101-111. SWI/2: 39-43. VAN: 123-131.

**Marks, Bruce** (1937– )

Mason, Francis. "A Conversation with Bruce Marks." *BR* 22, no. 4 (Winter 1994): 41-59.

COH/1: 24-29. NEW/1: 204-224.

**Marsicano, Merle** (ca. 1920– )
   SOR/2: 238-241.

**Martins, Peter** (1946– )
   Caras, Steven, photography and text. *Peter Martins: Prince of the Dance.* New York: Abrams, 1986.
   "Dance Master." *Manhattan* No. 23 (1989): 20-25. An unsigned interview with Peter Martins.
   "Martins, Peter." *CBY 1978*: 291-294.
   Martins, Peter. "Far from Denmark." *BR* 10, no. 3 (Fall 1982):

24-36. An extract from his *Far from Denmark.* Boston & Toronto: Little, Brown & Company, 1982.
———, with Robert Cornfield. *Far from Denmark.* Boston & Toronto: Little, Brown & Company, 1982.
Paltrow, Scot J. "Peter Martins: Off-Balance." *Los Angeles Times Magazine,* December 6, 1992, pp. 24-26, 28, 30, 68, 70, 72, 74.
Todd, Arthur, text, with photography by Martha Swope. *Peter Martins.* Dance Horizons Spotlight Series. Brooklyn, N.Y.: Dance Horizons, 1975.

   Trustman, Deborah. "Peter Martins: Prince of the Dance." *The New York Times Magazine,* November 9, 1980, pp. 58-64, 66, 68, 70, 72, 74, 76.
   BLA: 160-163. GRE/2: 40-50. GRE/3: 7-8. GRU/1: 170-176. GRU/2: 338-343. MAS: 509-512. NEW/1: 346-362. PET: 132-153. SWI/3: 212-218.

**Maslow, Sophie** (1911– )
   LLO: 183-186, 190-192.

**Mason, Monica** (1941– )
GRU/2: 136-141. NEW/1: 296-311.

**Massine, Leonide** (1895-1979)

Anderson, Jack. *The One and Only: The Ballet Russe de Monte Carlo.* New York: Dance Horizons, 1981.

——. *"The One and Only: The Ballet Russe de Monte Carlo*—The Massine Years." *BR* 8, nos. 2&3 (1980): 141-199. An extract from Anderson's book *The One and Only.* New York: Dance Horizons, 1981.

Anthony, Gordon, with an appreciation by Sacheverell Sitwell. *Massine.* London: George Routledge & Sons, 1939.

Chujoy, Anatole. *The Symphonic Ballet.* New York: Kamin Publishers, 1937.

Clark, Mary Otis. *Leonide Massine: The Prodigal's Return to San Francisco in 1977.* Walnut Creek, Calif.: the author, 1980. [On cover: The Massine Magical Mystique: Informal Memoirs with Photographs].

Daniel, Oliver. *"Rite of Spring,* First Staging in America: Stokowski-Massine-Graham." *BR* 10, no. 2 (Summer 1982): 67-71. An extract, in somewhat different form, from Oliver Daniel's *Stokowski: A Counterpoint of View.* New York: Dodd, Mead, 1982.

Dorris, George. "Massine in 1938: Style and Meaning." In *Society of Dance History Scholars Proceedings*, pp. 200-211. Eleventh Annual Conference, North Carolina School of the Arts, 12-14 February 1988.

Doughty, Heather. "The Choreographer in the Courtroom: Loïe Fuller and Leonide Massine." In *Society of Dance History Scholars Proceedings*, pp. 35-39. Fifth Annual Conference, Harvard University, 13-15 February 1982.

## Massine, Leonide *(continued)*

Fusillo, Lisa Ann. "Leonide Massine: Choreographic Genius with a Collaborative Spirit." Unpublished dissertation, Texas Woman's University, 1982. Ann Arbor, Mich.: University Microfilms International, 1982. Order No. 821,9612. DAI 43-04A, p. 0957.

García-Márquez, Vicente. *Massine: A Biography.* New York: Knopf, 1995.

Gaye, Pamela. "A Conversation with Leonide Massine." *DS* 13, no. 4 (Summer 1979): 18-24.

Gibbon, Monk. *The Red Shoes Ballet.* London: Saturn Press, 1948; reprint New York: Garland Publishing, 1977.

Haskell, Arnold L. "Leonide Massine: An Appreciation." *Dance Magazine* 43, no. 11 (November 1969): 40-55. A Dance Magazine Portfolio.

Hastings, Baird. "Massine's Symphonic Ballets." *BR* 23, no. 1 (Spring 1995): 87-93.

Horwitz, Dawn Lille. "The Hispanic Influence on Leonide Massine." In *Society of Dance History Scholars Proceedings*, pp. 234-249. Fourteenth Annual Conference, New World School of the Arts, Miami, Florida, 8-10 February 1991. This article appears in slightly different form in *C&D* 3, pt. 4 (1994): 61-72.

LoMonaco, Martha Schmoyer. "The Giant Jigsaw Puzzle: Robert Joffrey Reconstructs *Parade.*" *TDR* 28, no. 3/T-103 (Fall 1984): 31-45.

"Massine, Leonide." *CBY 1940*: 566-568.

Massine, Leonide. *Massine on Choreography: Theory and Exercises in Composition.* London: Faber & Faber, 1976.

——. *My Life in Ballet.* Edited by Phyllis Hartnoll and Robert Rubens. London: Macmillan; New York: St. Martin's Press, 1968.

Sorell, Walter. "On Massine and Cocteau, Scandals and Audiences." *DS* 13, no. 4 (Summer 1979): 12-17.

Windreich, Leland. "Massine's *Aleko.*" *DC* 8, nos. 3 & 4 (1985): 153-178.

BLA: 106-109. DAV: 198-205. FRA: 27-43. GRU/2: 15-22. GIB: 55-61. HAL: 126-135. HAS/1: 91-95, 100-105. HAS/2: 114-122. MOO/1: 216-224. SCH/1: see Index of Choreographers, p. 135.

## Maximova, Ekaterina (1939– )

DEM/1: 191-199. SMA: 180-185. ZHD: 60-106.

**May, Pamela** (1917– )
DAV: 205-208.

**Maywood, Augusta** (1825-1876)
Costonis, Maureen Needham. "'The Wild Doe': Augusta Maywood in Philadelphia and Paris, 1837-1840." *DC* 17, no. 2 (1994): 123-148.
Winter, Marian Hannah. "Augusta Maywood." *DI* 2, nos. 1-2 (January-February 1943).
MAG: 118-137. MIG: 179-193. SWI/1: 133-136.

**Mazzo, Kay** (1946– )
"Mazzo, Kay." *CBY 1971*: 264-266.
GRU/2: 332-337. MAS: 523-527. TRA: 160-167.

**McBride, Pat** (fl. 1940-1950)
MAS: 281-285.

**McBride, Patricia** (1942– )
Bivona, Elena. "McBride." *BR* 3, no. 3 (1970): 22-31.
"Celebrating Patricia McBride." *BR* 17, no. 1 (Spring 1989): 35-66. A portfolio of photographs with a brief introduction by Francis Mason.
"McBride, Patricia." *CBY 1966*: 248-251.
Shaw, Alan J. "McBride's Year." *BR* 5, no. 1 (1975-1976): 50-55.
Tobias, Tobi. "Patricia McBride." *Dance Magazine* 51, no. 8 (August 1977): 47-62. A Dance Magazine Portfolio.
Wentink, Andrew Mark, text, with photography by Martha Swope. *Patricia McBride*. Dance Horizons Spotlight Series. Brooklyn, N.Y.: Dance Horizons, 1975.
GRE/2: 34-40. GRE/3: 4-6. GRU/2: 287-294. LYL: 72-80. MAS: 441-448. MON: 76-79. PET: 74-93. SWI/3: 224-230. TRA: 142-147.

**McDonald, Elaine** (1943– )
Dixon, John S., ed. *Elaine McDonald*. [Leeds]: Arno, [1982?].

**McGehee, Helen** (1921– )
McGehee, Helen. *To Be A Dancer*. Edited by A. Umaña. Lynchburg, Va.: Editions Heraclita, 1990.
Umaña, Alfonso. *Helen McGehee: Dancer*. New York: Editions Heraclita, 1974.

**McKayle, Donald** (1930– )
"McKayle, Donald (Cohen)." *CBY 1971*: 251-253.
COH/2: 52-61. SOR/2: 187-192.

**McRae, Edna L.** (ca. 1902-1990)
PAG: 45-54.

**Meehan, Nancy** (1931– )
KRE: 134-147.

**Mejia, Paul** (1947– )
GRU/2: 190-195. MAS: 473-483.

**Menuhin, Diana Gould** (1913– )
Menuhin, Diana. "Dancing for Balanchine: 1933." *BR* 16, no. 3 (Fall 1988): 35-42.
———. *Fiddler's Moll: Life with Yehudi*. New York: St. Martin's Press, 1988.
MAS: 109-112.

**Meri, La** (see **La Meri**)

**Messerer, Asaf** (1903-1992)
SLO: 109-111.

**Mezentseva, Galina** (1952– )
Archer, Kenneth, and Millicent Hodson. "Two Galinas in Glasgow." *DN* 1, no. 3 (Autumn 1992): 56-63.

**Miller, Buffy** (1969– )
Whitaker, Rick. "Buffy Miller: Three Feld Solos." *BR* 21, no. 2 (Summer 1993): 44-51.

**Milloss, Aurel** (1906-1988)
Hastings, Lily, and Geoffrey Handley-Taylor. "Aurel M. Milloss." *Chrysalis* 3, nos. 5-6 (1950): 16-17. Issue title: "Three Choreographers."

**Milloss, Aurel** *(continued)*

Milloss, Aurel M. "The Bases of My Aesthetics." *Chrysalis* 3, nos. 5-6 (1950): 17-[19]. Issue title: "Three Choreographers."

Veroli, Patrizia. "The Choreography of Aurel Milloss." Part One: 1906-1945; Part Two: 1946-1966; Part Three: 1967-1988; and Part Four: Catalogue. *DC* 13, no. 1 (1990): 1-46; *DC* 13, no. 2 (1990): 193-240; *DC* 13, no. 3 (1990-91): 368-392; and *DC* 14, no. 1 (1991): 47-101.

Zoete, Beryl de. "Aurel Milloss." In her *The Thunder and the Freshness*, pp. 83-90. London: Neville Spearman; New York: Theatre Arts Books, 1963.

**Mitchell, Arthur** (1934– )

Latham, Jacqueline Quinn Moore. "A Biographical Study of the Lives and Contributions of Two Selected Contemporary Black Male Dance Artists—Arthur Mitchell and Alvin Ailey—in the Idioms of Ballet and Modern Dance, Respectively." Unpublished dissertation, Texas Woman's University, 1973. Ann Arbor, Mich.: University Microfilms International, 1974. Order No. 74-22,241. DAI 35-04A, p. 2143.

Maynard, Olga. "Arthur Mitchell & The Dance Theater of Harlem." *Dance Magazine* 44, no. 3 (March 1970): 52-64. A Dance Magazine Portfolio.

"Mitchell, Arthur." *CBY 1966*: 278-280.

GRU/1: 41-47. GRU/2: 440-445. HOD: 120-155. LYL: 82-94. MAS: 393-397.

**Moller, Helen** (18– )

Moller, Helen. *Dancing with Helen Moller*. Edited by Curtis Dunham. New York: John Lane Company; London: John Lane, The Bodley Head, 1918.

**Moncion, Francisco** (1922-1995)

MAS: 199-203.

**Monk, Meredith** (1943– )

Baker, Robb. "Landscapes and Telescopes: A Personal Response to the Choreography of Meredith Monk." *Dance Magazine* 50, no. 4 (April 1976): 55-70. A Dance Magazine Portfolio.

**Monk, Meredith** *(continued)*

Banes, Sally. "The Art of Meredith Monk." *PAJ* 3, no. 1 (Spring/ Summer 1978): 3-18.

――. "Meredith Monk and the Making of *Chaco*: Notes from a Journal." *DC* 1, no. 1 (1977): 46-62.

Finkelstein, David. "The Films of Meredith Monk." *BR* 19, no. 2 (Summer 1991): 60-67. Article includes a filmography.

Goldberg, Marianne. "Transformative Aspects of Meredith Monk's *Education of the Girlchild*." *W&P* 1, no. 1/[Issue #1] (Spring-Summer 1983): 19-28.

Koenig, Carole. "Meredith Monk: Performer-Creator." *TDR* 20, no. 3/T-71 (September 1976): 51-66.

Lynch, Joan Driscoll. "*Book of Days*: An Anthology of Monkwork." *Millennium Film Journal* Nos. 23/24 (Winter 1990-91): 38-47.

Marranca, Bonnie. "Meredith Monk's Atlas of Sound: New Opera and the American Performance Tradition." *PAJ* 14, no. 1/Issue #40 (January 1992): 16-29.

――. "Meredith Monk's *Recent Ruins*/The Archeology of Consciousness: Essaying Images." *PAJ* 4, no. 3/Issue #12 [1980]: 39-49.

McNamara, Brooks. "*Vessel*: The Scenography of Meredith Monk." *TDR* 16, no. 1/T-53 (March 1972): 87-103.

"Monk, Meredith." *CBY 1985*: 296-299.

Monk, Meredith. "Ages of the Avant-Garde." *PAJ* 16, no. 1/Issue #46 (January 1994): 12-15.

Poster, Constance H. "Making It New—Meredith Monk and Kenneth King." *BR* 1, no. 6 (1967): 14-21.

BAN: 148-167. FOS: 200-209; 220-227. KRE: 250-265. MCD: 174-189.

**Moore, Jack** (1926-1988)

SIE: 12-17.

**Morales, Hilda** (1948– )

Barton, Peter. "Hilda Morales: American Ballet Theatre." In his *Staying Power: Performing Artists Talk About Their Lives*, pp. 88-105. New York: Dial Press, 1980.

**Mordkin, Mikhail** (1881-1944)

CAF: 180-196. SCH/1: see Index of Choreographers, p. 135. SMA: 292-299. VAN: 95-102.

## Morlacchi, Giuseppina (1843-1886)

Barker, Barbara. "Giuseppina Morlacchi." Part 3 in her *Ballet or Ballyhoo: The American Careers of Maria Bonfanti, Rita Sangalli, and Giuseppina Morlacchi*, pp. 109-167. New York: Dance Horizons, 1984.

——. "Giuseppina Morlacchi: From La Scala to Lowell, Massachusetts." In *Society of Dance History Scholars Proceedings*, pp. 220-232. Sixth Annual Conference, The Ohio State University, 11-13 February 1983.

Logan, Herschel C. *Buckskin and Satin: The Life of Texas Jack and his Wife Mlle Morlacchi*. Harrisburg, Pa.: Stackpole Company, 1954.

MOO/2: 124-130.

## Morris, Margaret (1891-1980)

*Margaret Morris: Drawings and Designs and the Glasgow Years.* Glasgow: Third Eye Centre, 1985.

Morris, Margaret. *Creation in Dance and Life*. London: Peter Owen, 1972.

——, text, with photography by Fred Daniels. *Margaret Morris Dancing*. London: Kegan Paul, Trench, Trubner & Co., 1926.

——. *My Galsworthy Story*. New York: Humanities Press, 1968.

——. *My Life in Movement*. London: Peter Owen, 1969.

——. *The Notation of Movement: Text, Drawings and Diagrams*. London: Kegan Paul, Trench, Trubner & Co., 1928.

## Morris, Mark (1956– )

Acocella, Joan. "*L'Allegro, il Penseroso ed il Moderato*." *BR* 17, no. 2 (Summer 1989): 8-17.

——. *Mark Morris*. New York: Farrar, Straus & Giroux, 1993.

——. "Mark Morris: The Body and What It Means." *DN* 3, no. 2 (Summer 1994): 38-47.

Brazil, Tom. *Dances by Mark Morris*. New York: Dance Research Foundation, 1992.

Croce, Arlene. "An American Ritual." *The New Yorker* 68, no. 45 (December 28, 1992/January 4, 1993): 193-197.

——. "Mark Morris Goes Abroad." *The New Yorker* 64, no. 48 (January 16, 1989): 61-64.

**Morris, Mark** *(continued)*

———. "Multicultural Theatre." *The New Yorker* 66, no. 23 (July 23, 1990): 84-87.

———. *Sight Lines.* New York: Knopf, 1987. See "Mark Morris Comes to Town," pp. 157-160; "Championship Form," pp. 225-228; and "Choreographer of the Year," pp. 313-316.

———. "Wise Guys." *The New Yorker* 65, no. 24 (July 31, 1989): 70-73.

Dupont, Joan. "An American in Brussels." *The New York Times Magazine*, January 22, 1989, pp. 22, 58, 60-62.

Garafola, Lynn. "Mark Morris and the Feminine Mystique." *BR* 16, no. 3 (Fall 1988): 47-53.

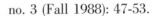

Keefe, Maura, and Marc Woodworth. "An Interview with Mark Morris." *Salmagundi* No. 104-105 (Fall 1994-Winter 1995): 218-240

Lassiter, Laurie. "Mark Morris Dance Group." *TDR* 29, no. 2/T-106 (Summer 1985): 119-125.

Macaulay, Alastair. "Vivamus Atque Amemus." *The New Yorker* 64, no. 18 (June 20, 1988): 86-89.

———. "While the Music Lasts." *The New Yorker* 68, no. 12 (May 11, 1992): 80-84.

Morris, Gay. "Subversive Strategies in *The Hard Nut*." In *Society of Dance History Scholars Proceedings*, pp. 237-244. Seventeenth Annual Conference, Brigham Young University, Provo, Utah, 10-13 February 1994.

"Morris, Mark." *CBY 1988*: 409-413.

Siegel, Marcia B. "Decomposing Sugar Plums & Robot Mice." *BR* 19, no. 1 (Spring 1991): 58-61.

Temin, Christine. "Mark Morris: Brussels and Boston." *BR* 17, no. 3 (Fall 1989): 62-74.

———. "The Triumph of Mark Morris." *The Boston Globe Magazine*, February 19, 1989, pp. 20-21, 38-46, 48.

**Morris, Mark** *(continued)*

Vaughan, David. "A Conversation with Mark Morris." *BR* 14, no. 2 (Summer 1986): 26-36.

——, text, with photography by Tom Brazil. "Mark Morris Here and There." *BR* 18, no. 4 (Winter 1990-1991): 12-22.

——. "Mark Morris: Here and There—II." *BR* 19, no. 1 (Spring 1991): 46-57.

GRU/1: 23-30.

**Moses, Sam** (1944– )

SID: 117-124.

**Moylan, Mary Ellen** (1926– )

"Moylan, Mary Ellen." *CBY 1957*: 386-388.

ATK: 115-118. MAS: 215-222. TRA: 84-91.

**Mukhamedov, Irek** (1960– )

Taylor, Jeffery. *Irek Mukhamedov: The Authorised Biography.* London: Fourth Estate, 1994.

**Mumaw, Barton** (1912– )

Sherman, Jane, and Barton Mumaw. *Barton Mumaw, Dancer: From Denishawn to Jacob's Pillow and Beyond.* New York: Dance Horizons, 1986.

**Mundstock, Ann** (1895?-1971)

*Ann Mundstock: Pioneer in Bay Area Dance and Movement Therapy.* Berkeley: Regional Oral History Office, The Bancroft Library, University of California, 1986. Elizabeth Beckman, Marcelle Chessé Arian, Nina Lathrop et al., interviews by Judith Dunning, 1983-1984.

**Murray, Ruth** (1903?-1991)

Michigan Dance Association. *Dance Education in Michigan, Recollections of Three Pioneers: Grace Ryan, Ruth Murray & Fannie Aronson.* East Lansing: Michigan Dance Association, c. 1979.

## Nagrin, Daniel (1917– )

Bissell, Robyn. "Daniel Nagrin's Path Abroad, 1967." In *Society of Dance History Scholars Proceedings*, pp. 11-20. Fifteenth Annual Conference, University of California, Riverside, 14-15 February 1992.

Nagrin, Daniel. *Dance and the Specific Image: Improvisation.* Pittsburgh, Pa. & London: University of Pittsburgh Press, 1994.

———. *How to Dance Forever: Surviving Against the Odds.* New York: Morrow, 1988.

Schlundt, Christena L. "Daniel Nagrin: A Sketch for a Dance Portrait." In *Society of Dance History Scholars Proceedings*, pp. 253-257. Sixth Annual Conference, The Ohio State University, 11-13 February 1983.

GRU/1: 95-105. SIE: 18-23.

## Nagy, Ivan (1943– )

"Nagy, Ivan." *CBY 1977*: 303-306.

Rosen, Lillie F., text, with photography by Louis Péres. *Ivan Nagy.* Dance Horizons Spotlight Series. Brooklyn, N.Y.: Dance Horizons, 1975.

GRU/2: 227-231. LYL: 36-44.

## Nahat, Dennis (1946– )

Cohen, Barbara Naomi. "Enhancing the Rep: About Dennis Nahat." *DS* 15, no. 3 (August 1981): 55-61.

**Natarova, Anna Petrovna** (1835-1917)
WIL: 135-169.

**Neary, Colleen** (1952– )
GRE/3: 26-27.

**Neary, Patricia** (1942– )
MAS: 469-472.

**Nerina, Nadia** (1927– )
Crisp, Clement, ed. *Ballerina: Portraits and Impressions of Nadia Nerina*. London: Weidenfeld & Nicolson, 1975.
"Nerina, Nadia." *CBY 1957*: 398-399.
Swinson, Cyril. *Nadia Nerina*. Dancers of To-Day, No. 11. London: Adam & Charles Black, 1957.
HUR: 295-296. NEW/1: 128-145.

**Neumeier, John** (1942– )
Jeschke, Claudia. "American Theatricality in Contemporary German Theater Dancing: John Neumeier and William Forsythe." In *Society of Dance History Scholars Proceedings*, pp. 201-206. Fifteenth Annual Conference, University of California, Riverside, 14-15 February 1992.
Loney, Glenn. "Ballet's Freethinker: John Neumeier." *DS* 11, no. 2 (Spring/Summer 1977): 24-33.
"Neumeier, John." *CBY 1991*: 419-423.

**Neville, Phoebe** (1941– )
Kronen, H.B. "Phoebe Neville: Images and Ideas." *DS* 11, no. 1 (Fall/Winter 1976-77): 28-35.

**Newman, Rosalind** (1946– )
KRE: 194-209.

**Newson, Lloyd** (1957– )
Newson, Lloyd. "Lloyd Newson on . . . dance." *DN* 2, no. 2 (Summer 1993): 11-13.

**Nichols, Kyra** (1958– )
GRE/2: 81-84.

**Nielsen, Augusta** (1822-1902)
Veale, Tom G. "Augusta Nielsen: Danish Dancer Who Loved a Prince." Parts One and Two. *Dance Magazine* 31, no. 9 (September 1957): 42-43, 76-78 and *Dance Magazine* 31, no. 10 (October 1957): 40-41, 48-49, 70.

**Nijinska, Bronislava** (1891-1972)
Arkin, Lisa C. "Bronislava Nijinska and the Polish Ballet, 1937-1938: Missing Chapter of the Legacy." *DRJ* 24, no. 2 (Fall 1992): 1-16.

Baer, Nancy Van Norman. *Bronislava Nijinska: A Dancer's Legacy.* San Francisco: Fine Arts Museums of San Francisco, 1986.

"Bronislava Nijinska: Dancers Speak." *BR* 18, no. 1 (Spring 1990): 15-35. A conversation, moderated by Francis Mason, among Alexandra Danilova, Frederic Franklin, Georgina Parkinson, Maria Tallchief, Richard Thomas, and Nina Youshkevitch.

Brown, Tom. "Documenting Bronislava Nijinska's *Les Noces* and Retrieving it for Taiwan's National Institute of the Arts at the National Theater in Taipei." In *Proceedings of the Conference "Dance Reconstructed: Modern Dance Art Past, Present, Future,"* pp. 27-39. Rutgers University, New Brunswick, New Jersey, October 16 and 17, 1992.

Croce, Arlene. "In Memoriam: Bronislava Nijinska." *BR* 4, no. 2 (1972): 74-75.

Garafola, Lynn. "Bronislava Nijinska: A Legacy Uncovered." *W&P* 3, no. 2/Issue #6 (1987/1988): 78-89.

——. "Bronislava Nijinska's *Bolero.*" In *Society of Dance History Scholars Proceedings*, pp. 251-259. Fourteenth Annual Conference, New World School of the Arts, Miami, Florida, 8-10 February 1991.

——. "Choreography by Nijinska." *BR* 20, no. 4 (Winter 1992): 64-71.

Hellman, Eric. "A Conversation with Frank W.D. Ries." *BR* 18, no. 1 (Spring 1990): 40-48. Frank Ries speaks about his approach to reconstructing Bronislava Nijinska's *Le Train Bleu* for Oakland Ballet.

**Nijinska, Bronislava** *(continued)*

——. "Shock of the 'Bleu'?" *BR* 18, no. 1 (Spring 1990): 36-39.

Kaden, Laurie. "Nijinska's Theatre Choréographique Nijinska: The 1925 Tour of English Resort Towns." In *Society of Dance History Scholars Proceedings*, pp. 145-158. Fifteenth Annual Conference, University of California, Riverside, 14-15 February 1992.

Nijinska, Bronislava. *Bronislava Nijinska: Early Memoirs.* Translated and edited by Irina Nijinska and Jean Rawlinson. New York: Holt, Rinehart and Winston, 1981.

——. "Appendix D: The Creation of *Les Noces.*" In *Making a Ballet*, pp. 127-133, by Clement Crisp and Mary Clarke. New York: Macmillan, 1975.

——, with an introduction by Joan Ross Acocella and Lynn Garafola. "On Movement & the School of Movement." *BR* 13, no. 4 (Winter 1986): 75-81.

Ries, Frank W.D. "Acrobats, Burlesque and Cocteau: The Creation of *Le Train Bleu.*" *DS* 11, no. 1 (Fall/Winter 1976-77): 52-67.

Severn, Margaret. "Dancing with Bronislava Nijinska and Ida Rubinstein." *DC* 11, no. 3 (1988): 333-364.

"Stravinsky's *Les Noces.*" Translated and with introductions by Roberta Reeder and Arthur Comegno. *DRJ* 18, no. 2 (Winter 1986-87): 31-61.

Sullivan, Lawrence. "*Les Noces*: The American Premiere." *DRJ* 14, nos. 1 & 2 (Double Issue 1981-82): 3-14.

Weinstock, Stephen Jay. "Independence versus Interdependence in Stravinsky's Theatrical Collaborations: The Evolution of the Original Production of *The Wedding.*" Unpublished dissertation, University of California at Berkeley, 1982. Ann Arbor, Mich.: University Microfilms International, 1983. Order No. 830,0703. DAI 43-08A, p. 2491.

BEL: 61-66. DAV: 208-211. FRA: 25-26. HAL: 138-141; 160-162.

**Nijinska, Irina** (1913-1991)

Huber, Andrea Grodsky. "A Conversation with Irina Nijinska." *BR* 20, no. 1 (Spring 1992): 36-60.

Johnson, Robert. "Irina Nijinska (1913-1991)." *BR* 20, no. 1 (Spring 1992): 28-35.

**Nijinsky, Vaslav** (1889-1950)

Acocella, Joan. "Photo Call with Nijinsky: The Circle and the Center." *BR* 14, no. 4 (Winter 1987): 49-71.

**Nijinsky, Vaslav** *(continued)*

Adler, Alfred. "Preface to *The Diary of Vaslav Nijinsky*." *BR* 9, no. 3 (Fall 1981): 13-16.

Albright, Ann Cooper. "The Long Afternoon of a Faun: Reconstruction and the Discourses of Desire." In *Proceedings of the Conference "Dance Reconstructed: Modern Dance Art Past, Present, Future,"* pp. 219-222. Rutgers University, New Brunswick, New Jersey, October 16 and 17, 1992.

"An Album of Nijinsky Photographs." *DI* 2, no. 3 (March 1943). With notes on the photographs by Edwin Denby.

Aloff, Mindy. "On Death and the Maiden and Diligence: *Sacre* Reconstructed for the Joffrey." *BR* 15, no. 2 (Summer 1987): 68-73.

Anawalt, Sasha. "*Sacre* Reconstructed." *BR* 15, no. 2 (Summer 1987): 72-74.

Ansbacher, Heinz L. "Discussion of Alfred Adler's 'Preface.'" *BR* 9, no. 3 (Fall 1981): 16-27.

Archer, Kenneth. "Roerich's *Sacre* Rediscovered: The Lincoln Center Exhibition." *BR* 15, no. 2 (Summer 1987): 75-81.

——, and Millicent Hodson. "Nijinsky for the 90s—*Till Eulenspiegel* is Coming Back." *Dance Now* 1, no. 1 (Spring 1992): 10-20.

Barbier, George. *Designs on the Dances of Vaslav Nijinsky*. Translated from the French by C. W. Beaumont. London: C.W. Beaumont, 1913.

Barker, Barbara. "Nijinsky's *Jeux* (1913)." *TDR* 26, no. 1/T-93 (Spring 1982): 51-60.

Barrette, Denise. *Nijinsky Dancing*. Boston: Bruce Humphries, 1953. A collection of poems about Nijinsky's dancing.

Beaumont, Cyril. "The Funeral of Vaslav Nijinsky." In *The Ballet Annual 1951: A Record and Year Book of the Ballet*, pp. 106-108. Edited by Arnold L. Haskell. Fifth Issue. London: Adam & Charles Black, [1950].

——. "Garland for Nijinsky—Artist and Dancer." In *The Ballet Annual 1951: A Record and Year Book of the Ballet*, pp. 47-53. Edited by Arnold L. Haskell. Fifth Issue. London: Adam & Charles Black, [1950].

——. *Vaslav Nijinsky*. Essays on Dancing and Dancers, No. 2. 2d ed. London: C.W. Beaumont, 1943.

Berg, Shelley C. *"Le Sacre du printemps": Seven Productions from*

**Nijinsky, Vaslav** *(continued)*

*Nijinsky to Martha Graham*. Theater and Dramatic Studies, No. 48. Ann Arbor, Mich. & London: UMI Research Press, 1988.

Bloch, Alice, "Isadora Duncan and Vaslav Nijinsky: Dancing on the Brink." Unpublished dissertation, Temple University, 1991. Ann Arbor, Mich.: University Microfilms International, 1991. Order No. 91-34,920. DAI 52-07A, p. 2301.

Bourman, Anatole, in collaboration with D. Lyman. *The Tragedy of Nijinsky*. New York & London: Whittlesey House, 1936.

Brighton, Catherine. *Nijinsky: Scenes from the Childhood of the Great Dancer*. New York: Doubleday, 1989.

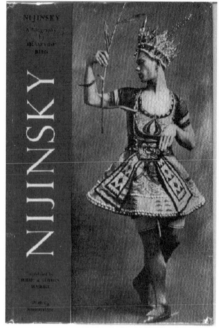

Brunoski, Elizabeth J. "A Psycho-biographical Study of Vaslav Nijinsky." Unpublished dissertation, Adelphi University, Garden City, New York, 1983. Ann Arbor, Mich.: University Microfilms International, 1984. Order No. 840,4462. DAI 44-11B, p. 3519.

Buckle, Richard. *Diaghilev*. London: Weidenfeld & Nicolson, 1979.

———. *Nijinsky*. London: Weidenfeld & Nicolson, 1971.

*Choreography and Dance* 1, pt. 3 (1991). The issue devoted to a revival of Nijinsky's original *L'Après-midi d'un faune*. Jill Beck, Issue Editor. Contents: Jill Beck. Introduction (pp. 1-2). Ann Hutchinson Guest. "Nijinsky's *Faune*" (pp. 3-34). Rebecca Stenn. "A Performer's View: Notes on Learning, Rehearsing and Performing *L'Après-midi d'un faune*" (pp. 35-42). Jill Beck. "Recalled to Life: Techniques and Perspectives on Reviving Nijinsky's *Faune*" (pp. 45-79). Sally Sommer. "Reflections on an Afternoon" (pp. 81-84). Thomas Augustine, with Patrick Daughtry. "*Faune*: Choosing the Fabric" (pp. 85-89). Notes on Contributors (pp. 91-92). Index (pp. 93-94).

Dance Critics Association. *The Rite of Spring at Seventy-Five*. New

**Nijinsky, Vaslav** *(continued)*

York: Dance Critics Association, 1987. A publication of the conference presented by the Dance Critics Association with the Dance Collection, The New York Public Library at Lincoln Center, Bruno Walter Auditorium, Museum and Library of the Performing Arts, New York, November 5-7, 1987. An update, "Rites of Spring," appears in *BR* 20, no. 2 (Summer 1992): 68-100.

de Mayer, Baron Adolf. *"L'Après-midi d'un Faune," Vaslav Nijinsky, 1912.* Thirty-three Photographs by Baron Adolf de Meyer. Essay by Jennifer Dunning and Contributions by Richard Buckle and Ann Hutchinson Guest. New York: Dance Horizons, c. 1983.

Eksteins, Modris. "Paris." Chapter One in his *Rites of Spring: The Great War and the Birth of the Modern Age*, pp. 9-54. Boston: Houghton Mifflin, 1989. An essay about Nijinsky's *Le Sacre du printemps*, set in the social/political context of the period of its premiere.

Fern, Dale Edward. *God Nijinsky: A Realization for the Theatre.* [N.p.]: the author, 1981. The script of a play based on *The Diary of Vaslav Nijinsky.*

Fraser, John. "Nijinsky Photographs and Photographers." *DC* 7, no. 4 (1984-85): 435-474.

——. "The Diaghilev Ballet in Europe: Footnotes to *Nijinsky*." Parts One and Two. *DC* 5, no. 1 (1982): 11-23 and *DC* 5, no. 2 (1982): 156-166.

Gelatt, Roland. *"Nijinsky": The Film.* New York: Ballantine Books, 1980.

Goldschmidt, Hubert. "Millicent Hodson and Kenneth Archer: *Till Eulenspiegel* in Paris." *BR* 23, no. 1 (Spring 1995): 40-47.

Gross, Valentine, drawings, with an Introduction and Notes by Richard Buckle. *Nijinsky on Stage.* London: Studio Vista, 1971.

Guest, Ann Hutchinson, with Claudia Jeschke. "Nijinsky's *Faune* Restored." *BR* 18, no. 2 (Summer 1990): 78-81.

——. *Nijinsky's "Faune" Restored: A Study of Vaslav Nijinsky's 1915 Dance Score "L'Après-midi d'un Faune" and His Dance Notation System.* Language of Dance Series, No. 3. Philadelphia, Pa. & Reading, England: Gordon and Breach, 1991.

Hargrave, Susan Lee. "The Choreographic Innovations of Vaslav Nijinsky: Towards a Dance-Theatre." Unpublished dissertation,

**Nijinsky, Vaslav** *(continued)*

Cornell University, Ithaca, New York, 1980. Ann Arbor Mich.: University Microfilms International, 1980. Order No. 80-15,677. DAI 41-01A, p. 0025.

Hartnoll & Eyre Ltd., London. *Nijinsky, Karsavina and the Diaghilev Ballet 1909-1914*, catalogue of the exhibition of drawings by Valentine Gross, October 16 - November 2, 1973.

Hellman, Eric. "The Scandal of Nijinsky's *Faune.*" *BR* 22, no. 2 (Summer 1994): 10-19. For commentary on this article see Letter to the Editor from Ann Hutchinson Guest. *BR* 23, no. 1 (Spring 1995): 16-17.

Hodson, Millicent. "Nijinsky's Choreographic Method: Visual Sources from Roerich for *Le Sacre du printemps.*" *DRJ* 18, no. 2 (Winter 1986-87): 7-15.

——. *Nijinsky's Crime Against Grace: Reconstruction Score of the Original Choreography for "Le Sacre du Printemps."* Dance & Music Series No. 8. Stuyvesant, N.Y.: Pendragon Press, forthcoming.

——. "Nijinsky's 'New Dance': Rediscovery of Ritual Design in *Sacre du printemps.*" Unpublished dissertation, University of California at Berkeley, 1986. On file, but not available from UMI. Order No. 03-75,358. ADD X1986, p. 299.

——. "*Sacre*: Searching for Nijinsky's Chosen One." *BR* 15, no. 3 (Fall 1987): 53-66.

Horwitz, Dawn Lille. "*Sacre* at the Joffrey." *BR* 15, no. 3 (Fall 1987): 67-69.

Irons, Evelyn. "Looking for Nijinsky." *BR* 10, no. 1 (Spring 1982): 4-6.

Jones, Robert Edmond. "Nijinsky and *Til Eulenspiegel.*" *DI* 4, no. 4 (April 1945).

Kirstein, Lincoln. *Nijinsky Dancing.* New York: Knopf, 1975.

Krasovskaya, Vera. *Nijinsky.* Translated by John E. Bowlt. New York: Schirmer Books, 1979.

Magriel, Paul, ed. *Nijinsky.* New York: Henry Holt, 1946; reprinted in Magriel's *Nijinsky, Pavlova, Duncan.* New York: Da Capo Press, 1977.

Matz, Mary Jane. *The Many Lives of Otto Kahn.* New York: Macmillan, 1963. Chapter 10, "The Amateur Impresario," is

**Nijinsky, Vaslav** *(continued)*

mostly about the visit of the Diaghilev Ballet to the United States in 1916-1917. The tour was largely organized and supported by Otto Kahn, who insisted on Nijinsky's participation as a condition of underwriting the visit.

Montenegro, Robert. *Vaslav Nijinsky: An Artistic Interpretation of his Work in Black, White and Gold.* London: C.W. Beaumont, 1913. With a Note of Introduction by C.W. Beaumont. Plates: 1. *Les Sylphides.* 2. *Le Spectre de la Rose.* 3. *Le Carnival.* 4. *Schéhérazade.* 5. *Daphnis and Chloe.* 6. *Le Dieu Bleu.* 7. *Petrouchka.* 8. *Prélude à l'Après-midi d'un Faune.* 9. *Jeux.* 10. *Danse Orientale.*

Mullock, Dorothy. *Seven Wood-Cuts of Nijinsky the Russian Dancer.*

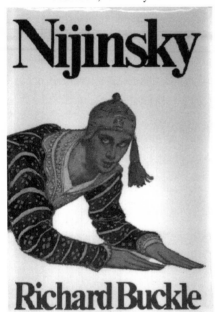

London: Sapphire Press, n.d.

Nectoux, Jean-Michel, ed. *"Afternoon of a Faun": Mallarmé, Debussy, Nijinsky.* New York & Paris: Vendome Press, 1989. Based on the eponymous exhibition at the Musée d'Orsay, Paris, 14 February-21 May 1989.

"Nijinsky." *Dance Magazine* 48, no. 12 (December 1974). A six-part Dance Magazine Portfolio examining Nijinsky in the context of his family. Moira Hodgson. "Nijinsky's Diary" (pp. 37-40). Victoria Huckenpahler. "Conversations with Romola Nijinsky" (pp. 42-45). Pamela Gaye. "Portrait of Kyra Nijinsky" (pp. 46, 48, 52-54). Pamela Gaye. "Tamara Nijinsky" (pp. 56-57). Bronislava Nijinska, translated and introduced by Jean M. Serafetinides and Irina Nijinska. "The Creation of *Les Noces*" (pp. 58-59, 61). John Gruen. "Igor Markevitch" (pp. 62-64).

Nijinsky, Romola. *The Last Years of Nijinsky.* New York: Simon & Schuster, 1952.

———. *Nijinsky.* New York: Simon & Schuster, 1935.

Nijinsky, Tamara. *Nijinsky and Romola: Biography.* London: Bach-

**Nijinsky, Vaslav** *(continued)*

man & Turner, 1991. [On cover: Two Lives from Birth to Death indissolubly linked].

Nijinsky, Vaslav. *The Diary of Vaslav Nijinsky.* Edited by Romola Nijinsky. London: Victor Gollancz, 1937.

"Nijinsky, Waslaw." *CBY 1940*: 616-618.

Nugent, Ann. "*Till* and Twyla: A Myth and a Legend." *DN* 3, no. 1 (Spring 1994): 10-17.

Ostwald, Peter. *Vaslav Nijinsky: A Leap into Madness.* New York: Carol Publishing Group, 1991.

Parker, Derek. *Nijinsky: God of the Dance.* Foreword by Dame Ninette de Valois. Northamptonshire, Wellingborough: Equation, 1988.

Reiss, Françoise. *Nijinsky: A Biography.* Translated by Helen and Stephen Haskell. New York: Pitman, [c. 1960]. First published as *Nijinsky, ou La Grace*, Volume 1: *La Vie de Nijinsky*, Paris: Plon, [c. 1957].

"Rites of Spring." *BR* 20, no. 2 (Summer 1992): 68-100. An update of the Dance Critics Association's *The Rite of Spring at Seventy-Five.*

Sandoz, Maurice. *Diaghilev - Nijinsky and Other Vignettes.* New York: Kamin Publishers, 1956. Originally published in England as *The Crystal Salt Cellar.* London: Guilford Press, 1954.

Strathern, Paul. *Vaslav: An Impersonation of Nijinsky.* London: Quartet Books, 1975. A novel based on the life of Nijinsky.

ARM: 28-30. BLA: 100-105. CLA: 65-94. DAV: 212-221. FRA: 20-25. HAL: 103-116. MCC: 27-35. MOO/1: 193-202. MUI: 73-86. PAL: 116-122. SCH/2: 68-78. SMA: 210-224. VAN: 79-95.

**Nikitina, Alice** (1909-1978)

Nikitina, Alice. *Nikitina.* Translated by Baroness Budberg. London: Allan Wingate, 1959.

**Nikolais, Alwin** (1912-1993)

Byrum, Mary Carolyn. "An Analysis of Three Non-Objective Choreographic Techniques." Unpublished dissertation, University of North Carolina at Greensboro, 1976. Ann Arbor, Mich.: University Microfilms International, 1976. Order No. 76-24,939. DAI 37-05A p. 2716.

Copeland, Roger. "A Conversation with Alwin Nikolais." *DS* 8, no. 1 (Fall/Winter 1973-74): 41-46.

**Nikolais, Alwin** *(continued)*

Hines, Thomas Jensen. "The Sacred and the Profane: *Triad.*" Chapter 7 in his *Collaborative Form: Studies in the Relations of the Arts*, pp. 145-163. Kent, Ohio & London: Kent State University Press, 1991.

Lamhut, Phyllis. "Alwin Nikolais (1912-1993)." *BR* 21, no. 3 (Fall 1993): 8-9.

Nickolich, Barbara Estelle. "Nikolais Dance Theater: A Total Art Work." Unpublished dissertation, New York University, 1979. On file, but not available from UMI. Order No. 801,0385. Available only through the author. ADD X1986, p. 440.

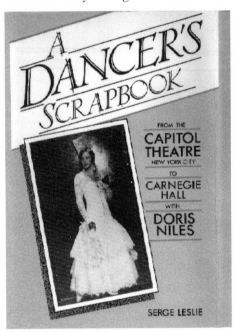

———. "The Nikolais Dance Theatre's Uses of Light." *TDR* 17, no. 2/T-58 (June 1973): 80-91.

"Nikolais, Alwin." *CBY 1968*: 287-289.

Pischl, A.J., and Selma Jeanne Cohen, eds. "Composer/ Choreographer." *DP* 16 (1963): 28, 33-36.

Schonberg, Harold C. "Choreography, Music, Costumes, Sets, Etc., Etc., by Alwin Nikolais." *The New York Times Magazine*, December 6, 1970, pp. 56-57, 169-170, 174, 176-179, 184, 186.

Siegel, Marcia B., ed. "Nik: A Documentary." *DP* 48 (Winter 1971).

Straits, Sue Ann. "The Alwin Nikolais Artist-in-Residence Program at the University of Wisconsin-Madison: An Ethnography of Dance Curriculum-in-Use." Unpublished dissertation, University of Wisconsin-Madison, 1980. Ann Arbor, Mich.: University Microfilms International, 1980. Order No. 802,0583. DAI 41-09A, p. 3868.

Zupp, Nancy Thornhill. "An Analysis and Comparison of the Choreographic Process of Alwin Nikolais, Murray Louis, and Phyllis Lamhut." Unpublished dissertation, University of North

**Nikolais, Alwin** *(continued)*

Carolina at Greensboro, 1978. Ann Arbor, Mich.: University Microfilms International, 1978. Order No. 78-24,313. DAI 39-06A, p. 3196.

BRO: 111-119. COH/2: 62-75. LIV: 188-197. MAZ: 231-243. MCD: 206-223. ROG: 73-89. SOR/2: 231-237.

**Niles, Doris** (1905– )

Conyn, Cornelius. *Doris Niles: Interpreter of the Spanish Dance.* London: C.W. Beaumont, 1937.

Kinney, Troy. *Selected Letters of Troy Kinney to Doris Niles.* Los Angeles: Serge Leslie, 1952.

Kovalevsky, Olga. *Studies in Movement of Doris Niles and Serge Leslie.* Los Angeles: [Serge Leslie], 1951.

Leslie, Serge. *A Dancer's Scrapbook: From the Capitol Theatre, New York City, to Carnegie Hall with Doris Niles, a Chronicle 1919-1929.* London: Dance Books, 1987.

——. *The Seven Leagues of a Dancer.* London: C.W. Beaumont, 1958.

Niles, Doris. "El Duende." *DP* 27 (Autumn 1966).

**Nimura, Yeichi** (1897-1979)

KON: 39-55.

**Nissen, Greta** (1905-1988)

Ryan, Pat M. "'A Dancer Must Be Perfect All Over': Greta Nissen on Stage and Screen." *DC* 12, no. 3 (1989): 285-332; "Greta Nissen: An Addition and Corrections." *DC* 13, no. 2 (1990): 261.

**Novak, Nina** (1927– )

ATK: 119-122.

**Noverre, Jean Georges** (1727-1810)

Caffinière Alexandre, and Katharine Kanter. "Why Noverre is 'Not on the Curriculum.'" *DN* 3, no. 1 (Spring 1994): 58-67.

Carones, Laura. "Noverre and Angiolini: Polemical Letters." *DR* 5, no. 1 (Spring 1987): 42-54.

Hansell, Kathleen Kuzmick. "Opera and Ballet at the Regio Ducal Teatro of Milan, 1771-1776: A Musical and Social History." Unpublished dissertation, University of California at Berkeley,

## Noverre, Jean Georges *(continued)*

1980. Ann Arbor, Mich.: University Microfilms International, 1980. Order No. 802,9419. DAI 41-07A, p. 2821. Noverre, who worked at the Regio Ducal Teatro from 1774 to 1776, rejected the Italian style and the construction of his ballets and pantomimes reveals the extent of his innovations.

Lynham, Deryck. *The Chevalier Noverre: Father of Modern Ballet.* London: Sylvan Press; New York: British Book Centre, 1950.

Noverre, Charles Edwin, ed. *The Life and Works of the Chevalier Noverre.* London: Jarrold and Sons, 1882.

Noverre, Jean Georges. *Letters on Dancing and Ballets [1760].*

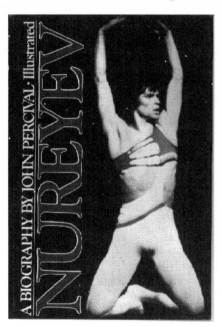

Translated by Cyril W. Beaumont from the rev. and enl. ed. published at St. Petersburg, 1803. London: C.W. Beaumont, 1951.

Storey, Alan. "The Encyclicals of Noverre." Chapter 4 in his *Arabesques*, pp. 38-44. London: Newman Wolsey, 1948.

——. "Noverreana." Chapter 3 in his *Arabesques*, pp. 30-37. London: Newman Wolsey, 1948.

Zagoudakis, Jamie. "Jean-Georges Noverre and the Aesthetic Traditions of His Time." In *Dance Spectrum: Critical and Philosophical Enquiry*, pp. 3-27. Edited by Diana Theodores Taplin. Waterloo, Ontario: Otium Publcations; Dublin: Parsons Press, 1983.

HAS/2: 55-64. MOO/1: 37-50.

## Nureyev, Rudolf (1938-1993)

Anderson, Jack. "Rudolf Nureyev, Charismatic Dancer Who Gave Fire to Ballet's Image, Dies at 54." *The New York Times*, January 7, 1993, p. D19. Obituary.

Barnes, Clive. *Nureyev.* New York: Helene Obolensky Enterprises, 1982.

**Nureyev, Rudolf** *(continued)*

Bland, Alexander. *Fonteyn & Nureyev: The Story of a Partnership.* New York: Times Books, 1979.

——. *The Nureyev Image.* New York: Quadrangle/The New York Times Book Company, 1976.

——. *The Nureyev "Valentino": Portrait of a Film.* New York: Dell Publishing Company, 1977.

Christie's. *Nureyev.* New York: Christie's, 1994. Old Master Paintings, European Furniture and Works of Art, Prints, Musical Instruments, Textiles, Ballet Costumes and Memorabilia from the Collection of Rudolf Nureyev. The catalogue of a public auction held in New York City on Thursday, 12 January 1995, and Friday, 13 January 1995.

Como, William, ed. *Nureyev.* New York: DANAD Publishing Company, 1973. Includes an essay by Olga Maynard: "Nureyev: The Man and the Myth."

Gosling, Maude. "Nureyev in the West." *BR* 22, no. 1 (Spring 1994): 32-40.

Greskovic, Robert. "Nureyev: A Matter of Life and Dance." *Dance Theatre Journal* 10, no. 4 (Autumn 1993): 20-24.

Haubert, Alaine. "In Memoriam: Rudolf Nureyev, March 17, 1938-January 6, 1993." *DRJ* 25, no. 1 (Spring 1993): 69.

Houseal, Joseph. "Dame Ninette de Valois: Remembering Rudolf Nureyev." *BR* 22, no. 2 (Summer 1994): 52-58.

——. "David Wall on Nureyev." *BR* 22, no. 4 (Winter 1994): 96-99.

——. "Peter Brinson: About Nureyev." *BR* 22, no. 2 (Summer 1994): 59-63.

Jennings, Luke. "Nureyev's Coda." *The New Yorker* 68, no. 45 (December 28, 1992/January 4, 1993): 73-80.

[Leonard, David, and Peter Moldon]. *Nureyev.* London: Dance Books, in association with Victor Hochhauser, 1976.

Livingstone, Alistair. "Why I Love Rudolf." *DN* 2, no. 1 (Spring 1993): 6-7, 9-11. An interview with Lynn Seymour about her friendship with Nureyev.

Maynard, Olga. "Nureyev: The Man and the Myth." *Dance Magazine* 47, no. 5 (May 1973): 51-66. A Dance Magazine Portfolio.

Money, Keith. *Fonteyn and Nureyev: The Great Years.* London: Harvill Press, 1994.

*Nureyev.* Edited and designed by Howard Brown. London: Phaidon Press, 1993.

**Nureyev, Rudolf** *(continued)*

"Nureyev, Rudolf (Hametovich)." *CBY 1963*: 299-301.

Nureyev, Rudolf. *Nureyev: An Autobiography*. New York: Dutton, 1963.

Ostlere, Hilary. "Antoinette Sibley on Nureyev." *BR* 22, no. 1 (Spring 1994): 41-42.

Percival, John. *Nureyev: Aspects of the Dancer*. New York: Putnam, 1975.

Pierpont, Claudia Roth. "Nouvelles Cendrillons." *BR* 15, no. 2 (Summer 1987): 93-100.

Radziwill, Lee, with photography by Derry Moore. "Architectural Digest Visits: Rudolf Nureyev." *Architectural Digest* 42, no. 9 (September 1985): 160-167.

Slesin, Suzanne. "The Nutcracker Suite." *The New York Times Magazine*, September 26, 1993, pp. 54-59.

Stuart, Otis. *Perpetual Motion: The Public and Private Lives of Rudolf Nureyev*. New York: Simon & Schuster, 1994.

Tchernichova, Elena, as told to Joel Lobenthal. "Young Nureyev." *BR* 22, no. 1 (Spring 1994): 28-31.

Todd, Arthur, text, with photography by Louis Péres. *Rudolf Nureyev*. Dance Horizons Spotlight Series. Brooklyn, N.Y. Dance Horizons, 1975.

"A Tribute to Rudolf Nureyev." *BR* 21, no. 4 (Winter 1993): 27-37. A symposium presented at the American Film Institute Theater, Kennedy Center, March 22, 1993. Participants: Sonia Arova, Patrice Bart, Joy Brown, Eleanor D'Antuono, Patricia Foy, George Jackson, Sali Ann Kriegsman, Ken Ludden, Roland Petit, Elisabeth Platel, Alla Sizova, and Oleg Vinogradov.

Vaughan, David. "Nureyev's *Raymonda*." *BR* 5, no. 2 (1975-1976): 30-37.

Vollmer, Jurgen, photography, with text by John Devere. *Nureyev in Paris: "Le Jeune homme et la mort."* New York: Modernismo Publications, 1975.

Warfield, Nancy D. "Nureyev: The Valentino Years." *The Little Film Gazette of N.D.W.* 11, no. 1 (January 1985).

Watson, Peter. *Nureyev: A Biography*. London: Hodder & Stoughton, 1994.

BLA: 140-147. GRU/1: 138-144. GRU/2: 109-116. MAS: 489-493. SMA: 225-237.

**Obidenna, Lara** (see **Ladré, Lara Obidenna**)

**O'Donnell, May** (1909– )
   Tobias, Tobi. "A Conversation with May O'Donnell." *BR* 9, no. 1
      (Spring 1981): 64-96.

**Ohno, Kazuo** (1906– )
   Ohno, Kazuo. "Selections from the Prose of Kazuo Ohno." *TDR* 30,
      no. 2/T-110 (Summer 1986): 156-162.
   Schechner, Richard. "Kazuo Ohno Doesn't Commute." *TDR* 30, no.
      2/T-110 (Summer 1986): 163-169.

**Osato, Sono** (1919– )
   "Osato, Sono." *CBY 1945*: 440-442.
   Osato, Sono. *Distant Dances*. New York: Knopf, 1980.
   ———. "Road Pictures." *BR* 8, no. 4 (1980): 397-439. An extract
      from Osato's *Distant Dances*. New York: Knopf, 1980.
   GRU/2: 67-74.

**Osborne, Gregory** (1954-1994)
   Carreiro, Assis. *Gregory Osborne*. Profiles of Canadian Dance, No. 4.
      Toronto: Press of Terpsichore, 1987.

**Osipenko, Alla** (1932– )
   SMA: 200-207.

**Oukrainsky, Serge** (1886-1972)

Barzel, Ann. "Chicago's 'Two Russians': Andreas Pavley and Serge Oukrainsky." *Dance Magazine* 53, no. 6 (June 1979): 63-70, 87-94. A Dance Magazine Portfolio.

Oukrainsky, Serge. *My Two Years with Anna Pavlowa.* Los Angeles, San Francisco, New York: Suttonhouse, 1940.

PRE: 133-151.

**Overlie, Mary** (1946– )

Overlie, Mary, with an introduction by Sally R. Sommer. "Mary Overlie: A Letter." *DS* 14, no. 4 (December 1980): 30-34.

Sommer, Sally R. "Mary Overlie: I Was a Wild Indian Who Happened to Dance." *TDR* 24, no. 4/T-88 (December 1980): 45-58.

**Oxenham, Andrew** (1945– )

SID: 125-132.

P

**Padow, Judy** (1943– )

Paul, Janice. "Judy Padow: An Analysis." *DS* 14, no. 4 (December 1980): 51-61.

**Pagava, Ethéry** (1931– )

DAV: 221-223.

**Page, Ashley** (1956– )

Robertson, Allen. "Ashley Page: Decalogue." *DN* 3, no. 2 (Summer 1994): 24-25, 27-31.

**Page, Ruth** (1900-1991)

Dorris, George. "*Frankie and Johnny* in Chicago and Some Problems of Attribution." *DC* 18, no. 2 (1995): 179-188.

Martin, John. *Ruth Page: An Intimate Biography*. New York & Basel: Marcel Dekker, 1977.

"Page, Ruth." *CBY 1962*: 334-336.

Page, Ruth. *Class: Notes on Dance Classes Around the World, 1915-1980*. Princeton, N.J.: Princeton Book Company, Publishers, 1984.

———. *Page by Page*. Edited and with an Introduction by Andrew Mark Wentink. Brooklyn: Dance Horizons, 1978.

*The Ruth Page Collection*. New York: Sotheby's, 1991. The catalogue of a public auction held in New York City on Thursday, November 7, 1991, for the benefit of The Ruth Page Foundation.

**Page, Ruth** *(continued)*

Turbyfill, Mark. *Ruth Page [and] Kreutzberg.* [Chicago?, 1934].

Wentink, Andrew Mark. "The Ruth Page Collection: An Introduction and Guide to Manuscript Materials through 1970." In *Bulletin of Research in the Humanities* (The New York Public Library) 83, no. 1 (Spring 1980): 67-162.

SCH/1: see Index of Choreographers, p. 135. SOR/1: 223-236.

**Paige, Brydon** (1933– )

Officer, Jill. "Canadian Choreographers: Brydon Paige." In *New Directions in Dance*, pp. 105-111. Edited by Diana Theodores Taplin. Toronto: Pergamon Press, 1979. Collected writings from the Seventh Dance in Canada Conference, University of Waterloo, Canada, June 1979.

**Palmer-Sikelianos, Eva** (1874-1952)

Palmer-Sikelianos, Eva. *Upward Panic: The Autobiography of Eva Palmer-Sikelianos.* Edited by John P. Anton. Choreography and Dance Studies, Vol. 4. Chur, Switzerland: Harwood Academic Publishers, 1994.

**Paltenghi, David** (1919-1961)

DAV: 224-227.

**Palucca, Gret** (1902-1993)

Arnheim, Rudolf. "Visiting Palucca." *DS* 13, no. 1 (Fall 1978): 6-11.

**Panov, Valery** (1938– )

"Panov, Valery (Shulman)." *CBY 1974*: 298-300.

Panov, Valery, with George Feifer. *To Dance.* New York: Knopf, 1978.

**Paredes, Marcos** (1937– )

SID: 133-141.

**Park, Merle** (1937– )

Manchester, P.W., text, with photography by Anthony Crickmay. *Merle Park.* Dance Horizons Spotlight Series. Brooklyn, N.Y.: Dance Horizons, 1976.

"Park, Merle." *CBY 1974*: 301-303.

GRU/2: 125-130. MON: 60-61.

**Parsons, David** (1959– )

Clark, Ina Sorens. "A Conversation with David Parsons." *BR* 22, no. 4 (Winter 1994): 64-75.

**Pavley, Andreas** (1892-1931)

Barzel, Ann. "Chicago's 'Two Russians': Andreas Pavley and Serge Oukrainsky." *Dance Magazine* 53, no. 6 (June 1979): 63-70, 87-94. A Dance Magazine Portfolio.

Corey, Arthur. *Danse Macabre: The Life and Death of Andreas Pavley.* [Dallas]: Southern Methodist University, 1977.

———. "The Life and Death of Andreas Pavley." Parts One, Two, Three, and Four. *The American Dancer* 5, no. 5 (January/February 1932): 8-9, 27; *The American Dancer* 5, no. 6 (March 1932): 18-19; *The American Dancer* 5, no. 7 (April 1932): 14-15; and *The American Dancer* 5, no. 8 (May 1932): 12-13, 28.

**Pavloff, Michel** (1891-1981)

Gale, Joseph. *I Sang for Diaghilev: Michel Pavloff's Merry Life.* Brooklyn: Dance Horizons, 1982.

**Pavlova, Anna** (1881-1931)

"An Album of Pavlova Photographs." *DI* 3, no. 3 (March 1944). With notes on the photographs by Marianne Moore.

Algeranoff, H. *My Years with Pavlova.* London: William Heinemann, 1957.

Almedingen, E.M. *The Young Pavlova.* Famous Childhoods. London: Max Parrish, 1961.

Beaumont, Cyril W. *Anna Pavlova.* Essays on Dancing and Dancers, No. 1. 3d ed. London: C.W. Beaumont, 1945.

Bell, Jasmin Cannon, [comp.]. *Anna Pavlova: A Photographic Essay.* London: Her Majesty's Stationery Office/Museum of London, 1981.

Cull, A. Tulloch. *Poems to Pavlova.* London: Herbert Jenkins, 1913.

*Dance & Dancers* 7, no. 1 (January 1956). A special issue celebrating the art of Anna Pavlova on the twenty-fifth anniversary of her death. Articles: "The Genius of Anna Pavlova" (p. 5). "Pavlova in Russia" (pp. 7 & 9). "Dancing Round the World" (p. 10). "How We Toured with Pavlova" (p. 11). "How She Danced" (pp. 12-14). "What She Meant to Them" (pp. 15-16). "Pavlova's Partners" (pp. 17-18). "A Pavlova Scrapbook" (p. 19).

**Pavlova, Anna** *(continued)*

Dandré, Victor. *Anna Pavlova*. London: Cassell and Company, 1932.

Devine, Maggie Odom. "The Swan Immortalized." *BR* 21, no. 2 (Summer 1993): 67-80. The Pavlova film heritage.

Fonteyn, Margot. *Pavlova: Portrait of a Dancer*. New York: Viking, 1984.

Franks, A.H., ed., in collaboration with members of the Pavlova Commemoration Committee. *Pavlova: A Biography*. London: Burke; New York: Macmillan, 1956; reprint New York: Da Capo Press, 1979.

Hyden, Walford. *Pavlova: The Genius of Dance*. London: Constable & Company; New York: Little, Brown & Co., 1931.

"Images of Pavlova." *Dance Magazine* 55, no. 1 (January 1981). A two-part Dance Magazine Portfolio. John and Roberta Lazzarini. "The Fanciful Photo Legacy" (pp. 59-64). Joan Pikula. "Filling Pavlova's Pointes: DeAngelo and Danias Celebrate the Legendary Ballerina" (pp. 64-66).

Kerensky, Oleg. *Anna Pavlova*. New York: Dutton, 1973.

Lazzarini, John, and Roberta Lazzarini. *Pavlova: Repertoire of a Legend*. New York: Schirmer Books; London: Collier Macmillan 1980.

Levine, Ellen. *Anna Pavlova: Genius of the Dance*. New York: Scholastic, 1995.

Lifar, Serge. "Anna Pavlova." In his *The Three Graces: The Legends and the Truth*, pp. 56-113. Translated by Gerard Hopkins. London: Cassell, 1959.

London Museum and Anna Pavlova Commemoration Committee. *Anna Pavlova 1882-1931*, catalogue of the commemorative exhibition, September 4 - December 31, 1956. London: Her Majesty's Stationery Office, [1956].

Magriel, Paul, ed. *Pavlova*. New York: Henry Holt, 1947; reprinted

**Pavlova, Anna** *(continued)*
  in Magriel's *Nijinsky, Pavlova, Duncan.* New York: Da Capo Press, 1977.

Malvern, Gladys. *Dancing Star: The Story of Anna Pavlova.* New York: Junior Literary Guild and Julian Messner, 1942.

May, Helen. *The Swan: The Story of Anna Pavlova.* Edinburgh: Thomas Nelson and Sons, 1958.

Money, Keith. *Anna Pavlova: Her Life and Art.* New York: Knopf, 1982.

Olivéroff, André, as told to John Gill. *Flight of the Swan: A Memory of Anna Pavlova.* New York: Dutton, 1935; reprint New York: Da Capo Press, 1979.

Oukrainsky, Serge. *My Two Years with Anna Pavlova.* Los Angeles, San Francisco, New York: Suttonhouse, 1940.

"Pavlova." *Dance Magazine* 50, no. 1 (January 1976). A ten-part Dance Magazine Portfolio. Natalia Vladimirovna Trukhanova, translated by Alla Klimov and Alison Hilton. "Anna Pavlova: A Remembrance" (pp. 44-46, 48-50). Andrew Wentink. "Pavlova, Humphrey, and Page" (pp. 50, 52-55). Victoria Huckenpahler. "Pavlova and Diaghilev" (pp. 55-58, 60-61). Victoria Huckenpahler. "Pavlova and Hurok" (pp. 62-63). Marian Horosko. "Pavlova and Muriel Stuart" (pp. 63-64). Vera Caspary. "Pavlova's Words" (pp. 64-65). Anna Pavlova. "An Answer to the Critics of Ballet" (p. 65). Anna Pavlova. "A Russian Ballet Girl's Education" (p. 66). John Gruen. "Pavlova's Music" (pp. 67-68). Tobi Tobias. "Pavlova on Film" (pp. 68, 70). K.R.N. Swamy. "Pavlova's Museum" (pp. 70-71, 73).

"Pavlova: Legend and Fact." *Dance Magazine* 30, no. 1 (January 1956). A special section commemorating the 25th anniversary of Pavlova's death. Articles: Lydia Joel. "Pavlova: Legend and Fact" (p. 17). Muriel Stuart. "Pavlova Was Real" (pp. 18-19). Frank I. Odell. "Indiana Interview/October 26, 1910" (pp. 20-22, 84-85). Eugene K. Ilyin. "The Garden at Ivy House" (p. 27). Lillian Moore. "Fedorova's Favorite Senior Student" (pp. 28, 58). Diana P. Daniels. "A Childhood Memory" (pp. 28, 58). Michel Fokine. "A Choreographer Remembers" (pp. 29, 70-71). Nina Kirsanova. "The Night That Pavlova Died" (pp. 31-33).

Ries, Frank W.D. "Rediscovering Pavlova's Dances." *BR* 11, no. 4 (Winter 1984): 71-85.

**Pavlova, Anna** *(continued)*

——, assisted by Sandra Hammond. "Rediscovered Dances of Anna Pavlova 1913-1916." In *Society of Dance History Scholars Proceedings*, p. 189. Sixth Annual Conference, The Ohio State University, 11-13 February 1983.

Stier, Theodore. *With Pavlova Round the World*. London: Hurst & Blackett, [1927].

Svetloff, V[alerian]. *Anna Pavlova*. Translated from the Russian by A. Grey. New York: Dover Publications, 1974. An unabridged republication of the work originally published in a limited edition by M. de Brunoff, Paris, 1922.

——. *Anna Pavlova*. Artists of the Dance. London: British- Continental Press, 1931.

Vaughan, David. "Further Annals of *The Sleeping Beauty*: Anna Pavlova, 1916." *BR* 3, no. 2 (1969): 3-18.

ARM: 35-37. AUS/1: 38-65. AUS/2: 55-66. CAF: 197-213. CLA: 42-64. DAV: 227-234. DEM/2: 42-50, 72-79. DRU: 114-137. HAL: 279-281. HAS/1: 53-64. HUR: 17-27. MCC: 36-48. MON: 14-17. MOO/1: 210-215. MUI: 43-53. PAL: 106-108. SMA: 2-18. VAN: 95-104.


**Paxton, Steve** (1939– )

Banes, Sally. "Steve Paxton: Physical Things." *DS* 13, nos. 2&3 (Winter/Spring 1979): 11-25.

——. "Vital Signs: Steve Paxton's *Flat* in Perspective." *DRA XVI* (1987): 120-134.

Rainer, Yvonne. "Backwater: Twosome/Paxton and Moss." *DS* 13, nos. 2&3 (Winter/Spring 1979): 8-10.

Wynne, Peter. *Judson Dance: An Annotated Bibliography of the Judson Dance Theater and of Five Major Choreographers—Trisha Brown, Lucinda Childs, Deborah Hay, Steve Paxton, and Yvonne Rainer*. Englewood, N.J.: author, May 1978.

BAN: 56-74. MCD: 119-133.


**Pecour, Guillaume-Louis** (1651 or 1653-1729)

La Gorce, Jérôme de. "Guillaume-Louis Pecour: A Biographical Essay." *DR* 8, no. 2 (Autumn 1990): 3-26.

**Pecour, Guillaume-Louis** *(continued)*

Witherell, Anne L. *Louis Pécour's 1700 "Recueil de dances."* Studies in Musicology, No. 60. Ann Arbor, Mich.: UMI Research Press, 1983.

**Pemberton, Edmund** (fl. 1711-1733; d. 1733)

Goff, Moira. "Edmund Pemberton, Dancing-Master and Publisher." *DR* 11, no. 1 (Spring 1993): 52-81.

**Pendleton, Moses** (1949– )

"Pendleton, Moses." *CBY 1989*: 434-438.

**Penney, Jennifer** (1946– )

GRU/2: 147-152.

**Pereyaslavec, Valentina** (1907– )

GAL: 29-38.

**Perez, Rudy** (1929– )

MCD: 259-269.

**Perreault, Jean-Pierre** (1947– )

Gélinas, Aline, comp. and ed. *Jean-Pierre Perreault Choreographer.* Translated from the French by Lynne Carson. Toronto: Dance Collection Danse, 1992.

Neels, Sandra. *"Vue Parallèle*—A Collaboration with Jean-Pierre Perreault." *YDR* Issue #6 (Spring 1977): 15-19.

**Perron, Wendy** (1947– )

Perron, Wendy. "Containing Differences in Time." *TDR* 29, no. 2/T-106 (Summer 1985): 20-28.

**Perrot, Jules** (1810-1892)

Beaumont, Cyril W. "Jules Perrot." Chapter 3 in his *The Ballet Called "Giselle,"* pp. 28-38. rev. ed. London: C.W. Beaumont, 1945.

Guest, Ivor. *Jules Perrot: Master of the Romantic Ballet.* London: Dance Books, 1984.

**Perrot, Jules** *(continued)*
Slonimsky, Yury. "Jules Perrot." Translated by Anatole Chujoy. *DI* 4, no. 12 (December 1945).
HAS/2: 82-86. MOO/1: 111-118.


**Petipa, Marius** (1818-1910)
*Ballet* (Special Issue of the Journal *Ballet*, formerly *Soviet Ballet*, published in Moscow in 1993, to Celebrate the 175th Anniversary of the Birth of Marius Petipa). Articles: Victor Vanslov, Boris Lvov-Ano[k]hin, Evgenia Grigoryeva, Natalia Sadovskaya, Vio-

letta Mainietse, and Valeria Ural-skaya. "Roundtable Discussion at the Journal *Ballet*: Marius Petipa—Still Current (pp. 3-6). Natalia Dudinskaya. "We Must Preserve the Heritage of Petipa's Genius" (pp. 7-8). Vyacheslav Gordeyev. "The Mozart of Chore-ography" (p. 9). Marina Semyo-nova. "The Inexhaustible Joy of Creation" (pp. 9-10). Vadim Gayevsky. "Petipa's Choreo-graphic Style" (pp. 11-12). Ni-kolai Elyash. "There Is No Better School than Petipa's" (pp. 13-17). Elena Derevtshikova. "Petipa's Dancers: Carlotta Brianza, Pavel Gerdt, Pierina Legnani, and Eka-terina Vazem" (pp. 18-20). Olga Fedorchenko. "Divertissements in the Ballet *Camargo*: An At-tempt at Descriptive Reconstruction" (pp. 21-23). Olga Vede-khina. "*Les Caprices du Papillon*" (pp. 24-26). Jadviga Ostrovskaya-Albrecht. "Forgotten Episode: On the History of the Ballet *Bluebeard*" (pp. 27-28). Natalia Zozulina. "Petipa's Ballets Set in Seville, Granada, Madrid" (pp. 29-30). Irina Skvortsova. "Thoughts on *The Nutcracker*" (pp. 31-33). Natalia Chernova. "Choreographer for All Seasons" (pp. 33-36). Chronology of Petipa's Productions in Russia (pp. 37-40). Valerian Svetlov. "The

**Petipa, Marius** *(continued*

Pride of Russian Ballet" (p. 41). Serge Lifar. "The Petipa Era" (pp. 43-45). Mikhail Yakovlev. "A Warning" (pp. 43-45).

Koegler, Horst. "Marius Petipa: A New Perspective." *Dance Magazine* 52, no. 9 (September 1978): 63-78. A Dance Magazine Portfolio.

Krasovskaya, Vera. "Marius Petipa and *The Sleeping Beauty.*" *DP* 49 (Spring 1972).

Leshkov, D.I. *Marius Petipa.* Adapted from the Russian and edited by Cyril Beaumont. London: C.W. Beaumont, 1971.

Moore, Lillian. "The Petipa Family in Europe and America." *DI* 1, no. 5 (May 1942).

Petipa, Marius. "The Diaries of Marius Petipa." *SDH* 3, no. 1 (Spring 1992). Edited, translated, and introduced by Lynn Garafola.

——. *Russian Ballet Master: The Memoirs of Marius Petipa.* Translated by Helen Whittaker. Edited by Lillian Moore. London: Adam & Charles Black, 1958.

Slonimsky, Yury. "Marius Petipa." Translated by Anatole Chujoy. *DI* 6, nos. 5-6 (May-June 1947).

Souritz, Elizabeth. "Marius Petipa's *Don Quixote.*" Précis prepared by Selma Jeanne Cohen. In *Society of Dance History Scholars Proceedings*, p. 250. Fourteenth Annual Conference, New World School of the Arts, Miami, Florida, 8-10 February 1991.

Waren, Florence. "Petipa and Bournonville: Ballet Seminar at Varna." *PAJ* 2, no. 3 (Winter 1978): 85-93.

Wiley, Roland John. *Tchaikovsky's Ballets: "Swan Lake," "Sleeping Beauty," "Nutcracker."* Oxford: Clarendon Press, 1985.

HAS/2: 96-104. MOO/1: 163-175. ROS: 85-123. SCH/2: 21-45. WIL: 350-356.

**Petipa Family**

Moore, Lillian. "The Petipa Family in Europe and America." *DI* 1, no. 5 (May 1942).

Petipa, Marius. "The Diaries of Marius Petipa." *SDH* 3, no. 1 (Spring 1992). Edited, translated, and introduced by Lynn Garafola.

MOO/2: 82-102. SWI/1: 175-181.

**Petit, Roland** (1924– )

Craig-Raymond, Peter. *Roland Petit.* Surbiton, Surrey: Losely Hurst Publishing, 1953.

**Petit, Roland** *(continued)*
Moss, Howard. "Petit Proust." *BR* 8, no. 4 (1980): 373-385.
"Petit, Roland." *CBY 1952*: 467-470.
ATK: 123-126. DAV: 235-239. FRA: 182-198. HAL: 246-252.

**Petronio, Stephen** (1956– )
Petronio, Stephen, with David Allan Harris. "The Stephen Petronio
File." *TDR* 29, no. 2/T-106 (Summer 1985): 29-40.

**Pilarre, Susan** (1947– )
GRE/3: 20-21.

**Pilobolus** (1971– )
Matson, Tim. *Pilobolus*. New York: Random House, 1978.
Moore, Elvi. "Talking with Pilobolus." *DS* 10, no. 2 (Spring/ Summer
1976): 56-66. Reprinted in Jean Morrison Brown's *The Vision of
Modern Dance*, pp. 151-161. Princeton, N.J.: Princeton Book
Company Publishers, 1979.

**Pinska, Klarna** (1904-1994)
Sticklor, Susan Reimer. "The Spirit of Denishawn: Klarna Pinska."
*DS* 11, no. 2 (Spring/Summer 1977): 43-46.

**Plisetskaya, Maya** (1925– )
Feifer, George. *Our Motherland and Other Ventures in Russian
Reportage*. New York: Viking, 1973.
Messerer, Azary. "Maya Plisetskaya: Childhood, Youth, and First
Triumphs, 1925-59." *DC* 12, no. 1 (1989): 1-47.
"Plisetskaya, Maya (Mikhailovna)." *CBY 1963*: 331-333.
Roslavleva, Natalia. *Maya Plisetskaya*. Moscow: Foreign Languages
Publishing House, 1956.
Voznesensky, Andrei, Andrei Vavra, Vadim Gayevsky, Viktor Komis-
sarzhevsky, Boris Lvov-Anokhin, Yuri Tyurin, and Georgi Shu-
valov. *Maya Plisetskaya*. Moscow: Progress Publishers, 1976.
Zhdanov, Leonid. *Maya Plisetskaya*. Moscow: Izdatelstvo Iskusstvo,
1965. An album of photographs of Plisetskaya in her major roles,
with a Preface by Victor Komissarzhevsky in Russian, English
and French.
DEM/1: 167-177. MON: 46-49. SMA: 129-143.

**Porter, Marguerite** (1950– )
  Porter, Marguerite, with Anne Dunhill. *Ballerina: A Dancer's Life.*
  London: Michael O'Mara Books, 1989.

**Posokhov, Yuri** (1964– )
  Kaplan, Larry. "The Bolshoi: Klevtsov and Posokhov." *BR* 18, no. 4
  (Winter 1990-1991): 26-37.
  ——. "Yuri Posokhov." *BR* 20, no. 4 (Winter 1992): 12-17.

**Poulsen, Ulla** (1905– )
  MAS: 93-95.

**Praagh, Peggy van** (see **van Praagh, Peggy**)

**Preobrazhenskaya, Olga** (1870-1962)
  Roné, Elvira. *Olga Preobrazhenskaya: A Portrait.* Translated, adapted,
  and introduced by Fernau Hall. New York & Basel: Marcel Dekker,
  1978.
  SMA: 64-71.

**Prévost, Françoise** (ca. 1680-1741)
  MIG: 11-12.

**Price Family** (**Amalie** 1831-1892, **Ellen** 1878-1968, **James** 1801-
  1865, **Juliette** 1831-1906, **Sophie** b. 1832, and **Valdemar** 1836-
  1908)
  Veale, Tom G. "The Dancing Prices of Denmark." *DP* 11 (Summer
  1961).

**Priest, Joanna** (1910?– )
  Denton, Margaret Abbie. *Joanna Priest: Her Place in Adelaide's
  Dance History.* Adelaide, Australia: the author, 1993.

**Priest, Josias** (165?-1734)
  Cohen, Selma Jeanne. "Josias Priest." In *Famed for Dance: Essays
  on the Theory and Practice of Theatrical Dancing in England,
  1660-1740*, pp. 22-33, by Ifan Kyrle Fletcher, Selma Jeanne
  Cohen, and Roger Lonsdale. New York: The New York Public

**Priest, Josias** *(continued)*

Library, 1960; reprinted from the *Bulletin of The New York Public Library*, June, November 1959; January, February, May 1960.

Martin, Jennifer Kaye Lowe. "The English Dancing Master, 1660–1728: His Role at Court, in Society, and on the Public Stage." Unpublished dissertation, University of Michigan, 1977. Ann Arbor, Mich.: University Microfilms International, 1977. Order No. 77-18,074. DAI 38-03A p. 1127.

**Primus, Pearl** (1919-1994)

Barber, Beverly Anne Hillsman. "Pearl Primus: In Search of Her Roots, 1943–1970." Unpublished dissertation, Florida State University, 1984. Ann Arbor, Mich.: University Microfilms International, 1984. Order No. 842,7288. DAI 45-09A, p. 2678.

Foulkes, Julia. "In Memorian: Pearl Primus—Pearl in Our Midst (November 29, 1919–October 29, 1994)." *DRJ* 27, no. 1 (Spring 1995): 80-82.

Green, Richard C. "Pearl Primus and 'The Negro Problem' in American Modern Dance." *UCLA Journal of Dance Ethnology* 19 (1995): 68-76.

"Primus, Pearl." *CBY 1944*: 551-553.

Wenig, Adele R. *Pearl Primus: An Annotated Bibliography of Sources from 1943 to 1975*. Oakland, Calif.: Wenadance Unlimited, 1983. LLO: 265-276. SOR/1: 255-258.

**Prinz, John** (1946– )

GRU/2: 254-257.

**Prokhorova, Violetta** (see **Elvin, Violetta**)

**Rabovsky, Istvan** (1930– )

Kovach, Nora, and Istvan Rabovsky, with George Mikes. *Leap Through the Curtain: The Story of Nora Kovach and Istvan Rabovsky*. New York: Dutton, 1955.

Walther, Suzanne K. "From Behind the Iron Curtain." *Dance Research Monograph One 1971–1972*, pp. 153-161. Co-edited by Patricia A. Rowe and Ernestine Stodelle. New York: Committee on Research in Dance (CORD), 1973.

**Radchenko, Sergei** (1944– )

ZHD: 300-309.

**Rainer, Yvonne** (1934– )

Anderson, Jack. "Yvonne Rainer: The Puritan as Hedonist." *BR* 2, no. 5 (1969): 31-37.

Goldberg, Marianne. "The Body, Discourse, and *The Man Who Envied Women*." *W&P* 3, no. 2/Issue #6 (1987/1988): 97-102.

Hecht, Robin Silver. "Reflections on the Career of Yvonne Rainer and the Values of Minimal Dance." *DS* 8, no. 1 (Fall/Winter 1973-74); 12-25.

"The Performer as a Persona: An Interview with Yvonne Rainer." *Avalanche* No. 5 (Summer 1972): 46-59.

Rainer, Yvonne. "Ages of the Avant-Garde." *PAJ* 16, no. 1/Issue #46 (January 1994): 33-35.

**Rainer, Yvonne** *(continued)*

––––. *"The Man Who Envied Women*—A Filmscript." *W&P* 3, no. 2/Issue #6 (1987/1988): 103-160.

––––. "Retrospective Notes." *TDR* 10, no. 2 (Winter 1965): 168-178. Some retrospective notes on a dance for ten people and twelve matresses called *Parts of Some Sextets*, performed at the Wadsworth Atheneum, Hartford, Connecticut, and Judson Memorial Church, New York, in March, 1965.

––––. *Work 1961-73*. Halifax: The Press of the Nova Scotia College of Art and Design; New York: New York University Press, 1974.

Sargent-Wooster, Ann. "Yvonne Rainer's *Journeys from Berlin/1971.*" *TDR* 24, no. 2/T-86 (June 1980): 101-118.

Wynne, Peter. *Judson Dance: An Annotated Bibliography of the Judson Dance Theater and of Five Major Choreographers*—*Trisha Brown, Lucinda Childs, Deborah Hay, Steve Paxton, and Yvonne Rainer*. Englewood, N.J.: author, 1978.

BAN: 40-55. BRO: 141-150. MCD: 148-161. SOR/2: 245.


**Rambert, Marie** (1888-1982)

Bland, Alexander. "Marie Rambert." In *The Ballet Annual 1955: A Record and Year Book of the Ballet*, pp. 58-63. Edited by Arnold L. Haskell. Ninth Issue. New York: Macmillan, 1954.

Bradley, Lionel. *Sixteen Years of Ballet Rambert*. London: Hinrichsen Edition Limited, 1946.

Clarke, Mary. *Dancers of Mercury: The Story of Ballet Rambert*. London: Adam & Charles Black, 1962.

Crisp, Clement, Anya Sainsbury, and Peter Williams. *Ballet Rambert: 50 Years and On*. rev. and enl. ed. N.p., 1981.

*Dance & Dancers* 6, no. 10 (October 1955). A special issue that looks at Marie Rambert's thirty-five years of activity in British ballet. Articles: "Mid-wife of British Ballet" (p. 5). "This is Rambert" (pp. 7, 9-10). "Why We Applaud Her" (pp. 11-12). "Perpetual Phoenix" (pp. 13-17). "Rambert's Guests and What They Danced" (p. 18). "Rambertiana" (p. 19).

Haskell, Arnold L. *The Marie Rambert Ballet*. Artists of the Dance. London: British-Continental Press, 1930.

"Rambert, Marie." *CBY 1981*: 324-328.

Rambert, Marie. *Quicksilver*. London: Macmillan, 1972.

**Rambert, Marie** *(continued)*
Setterfield, Valda. "A Passion for Dance." *BR* 11, no. 2 (Summer 1983): 30-34.
Tudor, Antony, Noël Goodwin, and P.W. Manchester. "Rambert Remembered." *BR* 11, no. 1 (Spring 1983): 62-67.
DAV: 240-247. DEM/2: 181-190. NOB: 202-232.

**Rambova, Natacha** (1897-1966)
Morris, Michael. *Madam Valentino: The Many Lives of Natacha Rambova.* New York, London, Paris: Abbeville Press, [1991].

**Rapp, Richard** (1933- )
MAS: 409-412.

**Rasch, Albertina** (1896-1967)
Miller, Raphael Francis. "The Contributions of Selected Broadway Musical Theatre Choreographers: Connolly, Rasch, Balanchine, Holm, and Alton." Unpublished dissertation, University of Oregon, 1984. Ann Arbor, Mich.: University Microfilms International, 1984. Order No. 842,2855. DAI 45-07A, p. 1922.
Ries, Frank W.D. "Albertina Rasch." Part 1: "The Broadway Career"; Part 2: "The Hollywood Career"; and Part 3: "The Concert Career and the Concept of the American Ballet." *DC* 6, no. 2 (1983): 95-137; *DC* 6, no. 4 (1983): 281-362; and *DC* 7, no. 2 (1984): 159-197.

**Rassine, Alexis** (1919-1992)
DAV: 247-249.

**Rawe, Tom** (1947- )
Barton, Peter. "Tom Rawe: Twyla Tharp Company." In his *Staying Power: Performing Artists Talk About Their Lives*, pp. 73-87. New York: Dial Press, 1980.

**Reagan, Ron** (1958- )
"Reagan, Ron." *CBY 1992*: 467-470.

**Redlich, Don** (1933- )
SIE: 24-27.

**Redpath, Christine** (1951– )
GRE/3: 28.

**Reed, Janet** (1920– )
ATK: 127-130. MAS: 339-345.

**Reiman, Elise** (1914-1993)
TRA: 70-75.

**Reiser, Wendy** (1953– )
SID: 143-151.

**Reitz, Dana** (1948– )
Jowitt, Deborah. "Dana Reitz." *TDR* 24, no. 4/T-88 (December 1980): 27-36.

**Renaud, Jeanne** (1928– )
Ellenwood, Ray. *Egregore: The Montreal Automatist Movement.* Toronto: Exile Editions, 1992.

**Reynolds, Nancy** (1938– )
SID: 153-163.

**Riabouchinska, Tatiana** (1917– )
ATK: 131-134. BEL: 67-69. DAV: 250-254.

**Rice, Marion** (1904-1995)
Laakso, Wendy. "Nurtured on the Denishawn Tradition." *YDR* Issue #6 (Spring 1977): 28-34.

**Robbins, Jerome** (1918– )
Bivona, Elena. "The World of *Goldberg Variations*." *BR* 3, no. 6 (1971): 39-45.
Challender, James Winston. "The Function of the Choreographer in the Development of the Conceptual Musical: An Examination of the Work of Jerome Robbins, Bob Fosse, and Michael Bennett on Broadway Between 1944 and 1981." Unpublished dissertation, Florida State University, 1986. Ann Arbor, Mich.: University

**Robbins, Jerome** *(continued)*
Microfilms International, 1986. Order No. 862,6788. DAI 47-08A, p. 2803.
"A Fanfare for Jerome Robbins." *BR* 16, no. 2 (Summer 1988): 12-30. A selection of tributes by Francis Mason, Dorothy Bird, Janet Reed, Todd Bolender, Yuriko, and Kay Mazzo.
"A Festival for Jerome Robbins." *BR* 18, no. 1 (Spring 1990): 67-73. A pictorial overview of A Festival of Jerome Robbins' Ballets, presented by New York City Ballet during its 1990 spring season.
Kotlowitz, Robert. "Corsets, Corned Beef and Choreography: The north, south, east and west side story of Jerome Robbins." *Show* 4, no. 11 (December 1964): 38-40, 90-92.
Moore, Lillian. "Jerome Robbins." *Chrysalis* 3, nos. 5-6 (1950): [3-10]. Issue title: "Three Choreographers."
"Robbins, Jerome." *CBY 1947*: 542-544.
"Robbins, Jerome." *CBY 1969*: 365-368.
FRA: 167-178. HAL: 241-246. MAY/1: 263-276. SCH/1: see Index of Choreographers, p. 135 and Index of Directors, p. 176.

**Rodgers, Rod** (1938– )
BRO: 172-175.


**Romanoff, Boris** (1891-1957)
MOO/1: 254-257.


**Ronaldson, James** (1930?-1987)
SID: 165-171.


**Roper, June** (1906-1991)
Windreich, Leland. "June Roper." *DC* 10, no. 1 (1987): 105-141.


**Rubinstein, Ida** (1885-1960)
de Cossart, Michael. *Ida Rubinstein (1885-1960): A Theatrical Life.* Liverpool Historical Studies, No. 2. Liverpool: Liverpool University Press, 1987.
———. "Ida Rubinstein and Diaghilev: A One-Sided Rivalry." *DR* 1, no. 2 (Autumn 1983): 3-20.
Garafola, Lynn. "Circles of Meaning: The Cultural Contexts of Ida Rubinstein's *Le Martyre de Saint Sébastien*." In *Society of Dance*

**Rubinstein, Ida** *(continued)*

*History Scholars Proceedings*, pp. 27-47. Seventeenth Annual Conference, Brigham Young University, Provo, Utah, 10-13 February 1994.

Lester, Keith. "Rubinstein Revisited." *DR* 1, no. 2 (Autumn 1983): 21-31.

Mayer, Charles S. "Ida Rubinstein: A Twentieth-Century Cleopatra." *DRJ* 20, no. 2 (Winter 1988): 33-51.

Severn, Margaret. "Dancing with Bronislava Nijinska and Ida Rubinstein." *DC* 11, no. 3 (1988): 333-364.

**Russell, Francia** (1938– )

MAS: 449-453.

**Ryan, Grace** (fl. 1920-1945)

Michigan Dance Association. *Dance Education in Michigan, Recollections of Three Pioneers: Grace Ryan, Ruth Murray & Fannie Aronson*. East Lansing: Michigan Dance Association, c. 1979.

**Ryberg, Flemming** (1940– )

Kanter, Katharine. "Flemming Ryberg." *DN* 3, no. 4 (Winter 1994): 58-62.

**Sacchetto, Rita** (1879-1968)
  CAF: 214-228.

**Saddler, Donald** (1920– )
  "Saddler, Donald (Edward)." *CBY 1963*: 367-369.
  SCH/1: see Index of Choreographers, p. 135

**St. Denis, Ruth** (1879-1968)
  Beiswanger, Barbara Page. "The Ideational Source of the Modern
    Dance in America as Expressed in the Works of Two Leading
    Exponents, Isadora Duncan and Ruth St. Denis." Unpublished
    dissertation, New York University, 1944. Ann Arbor, Mich.:
    University Microfilms International, 1973. Order No. 73-08,423.
    No DAI abstract available.
  Cohen, Barbara Naomi. *The Franchising of Denishawn*. Dance Data
    No. 4. Brooklyn, N.Y.: Dance Horizons, n.d.
  Coorlawala, Uttara Asha. "Ruth St. Denis and India's Dance
    Renaissance." *DC* 15, no. 2 (1992): 123-152.
  Hastings, Baird. "The Denishawn Era (1914-1931)." *DI* 1, no. 6
    (June 1942).
  Kendall, Elizabeth. "Salomé Where She Danced." *BR* 6, no. 2
    (1977-1978): 57-70. Reprinted in slightly different form in
    Kendall's *Where She Danced*. New York: Knopf, 1979.
  ——. *Where She Danced*. New York: Knopf, 1979.
  "Ruth St. Denis." *Dance Magazine* 50, no. 2 (February 1976). A

**St. Denis, Ruth** *(continued)*
three-part Dance Magazine Portfolio. Andrew Wentink. "Being an Idealist: Doris Humphrey's Letters Regarding Her Break with Ruth St. Denis and Ted Shawn, January-September 1928" (pp. 48-50). Iris M. Fanger. "Ruth St. Denis and Ted Shawn: The Breakup" (pp. 51-58). Eleanor King. "Other Ruths" (pp. 58-61).
Ruyter, Nancy Lee Chalfa. "The American Way: Ruth St. Denis and Ted Shawn." Chapter 4 in her *Reformers and Visionaries: The Americanization of the Art of Dance*, pp. 57-73. New York: Dance Horizons, 1979.

"St. Denis, Ruth." *CBY 1949*: 545-547.
St. Denis, Ruth. *Lotus Light: Poems by Ruth St. Denis*. Boston & New York: Houghton Mifflin, 1932.
————. *Ruth St. Denis: An Unfinished Life*. New York: Harper & Brothers Publishers. 1939.
Schlundt, Christena Lindborg. "The Choreographer of *Soaring*: The Documentary Evidence." *DC 6*, no. 4 (1983): 363-373.
————. "Into the Mystic with Miss Ruth." *DP 46* (Summer 1971).
————. *The Professional Appearances of Ruth St. Denis & Ted Shawn: A Chronology and an Index of Dances 1906-1932*. New York: The New York Public Library, 1962.
————. "The Role of Ruth St. Denis in the History of American Dance: 1906–1922." Unpublished dissertation, Claremont Graduate School, Claremont, California, 1959. Ann Arbor Mich.: University Microfilms International, 1959. Order No. 59-04,428. DAI 20-07, p. 2778.
————. "The Still Point of Perfection." In *Society of Dance History Scholars Proceedings*, pp. 103-110. Fifth Annual Conference, Harvard University, 13-15 February 1982.
Shawn, Ted. *Ruth St. Denis: Pioneer and Prophet*. Being a History of

**St. Denis, Ruth** *(continued)*

her Cycle of Oriental Dances. Volume One: The Text; Volume Two: The Plates. San Francisco: Printed for John Howell by John Henry Nash, 1920.

Shelton, Suzanne. *Divine Dancer: A Biography of Ruth St. Denis.* Garden City, N.Y.: Doubleday, 1981.

——. "The Influence of Genevieve Stebbins on the Early Career of Ruth St. Denis." *DRA IX* (1978): 33-49.

Sherman, Jane. *Denishawn: The Enduring Influence.* Boston: Twayne Publishers, 1983.

——. "Denishawn Oriental Dances." *DS* 13, nos. 2&3 (Winter/ Spring 1979): 33-43.

——. "Denishawn Revisited." *BR* 9, no. 1 (Spring 1981): 97-108.

——. *The Drama of Denishawn Dance.* Middletown, Conn.: Wesleyan University Press, 1979.

——. *Soaring: The Diary and Letters of a Denishawn Dancer in the Far East 1925-1926.* Middletown, Conn.: Wesleyan University Press, 1976.

——, with Christena L. Schlundt. "Who's St. Denis? What Is She?" *DC* 10, no. 3 (1987): 305-329.

Terry, Walter. *Miss Ruth: The "More Living Life" of Ruth St. Denis.* New York: Dodd, Mead & Company, 1969.

ARM: 38-41. BRO: 20-25. CAF: 82-97. HAL: 275-278. LLO: 22-34. MAG: 224-237. MAR: 149-160. MAY/2: 72-85. MAZ: 61-83. MOO/1: 281-286. PAL: 34-42. SOR: 13-19. TER: 48-66.


**Saint-Léon, Arthur** (1821-1870)

Guest, Ann Hutchinson, text and Labanotation score. *"La Vivandière Pas de Six."* Language of Dance Series, No. 6. Music by Cesare Pugni and Jean-Baptiste Naduad. Lausanne, Switzerland: Gordon and Breach, 1994.

Hammond, Sandra Noll. *"La Sténochorégraphie* by Saint-Léon: A Link in Ballet's Technical History." In *Society of Dance History Scholars Proceedings,* pp. 148-154. Fifth Annual Conference, Harvard University, 13-15 February 1982.

Saint-Léon, Arthur. *Letters from a Ballet-Master: The Correspondence of Arthur Saint-Léon.* Edited by Ivor Guest. New York: Dance Horizons, 1981.

MOO/1: 136-146.

**Saint-Léon, Michel** (b. 1767 or 1777; fl. 1800-1826)
Hammond, Sandra Noll. "Early Nineteenth-Century Ballet Technique from Léon Michel [i.e., Michel Saint-Léon]." In *Society of Dance History Scholars Proceedings*, pp. 202-208. Tenth Annual Conference, University of California, Irvine, 13-15 February 1987.
——. "A Nineteenth-Century Dancing Master at the Court of Württemberg: The Dance Notebooks of Michel Saint Léon." *DC* 15, no. 3 (1992): 291-315.

**Saint-Point, Valentine de** (1875-1953; also known as **Valentine de Glans de Cessiat-Vercell**)
Berghaus, Günter. "Dance and the Futurist Woman: The Work of Valentine de Saint-Point (1875-1953)." *DR* 11, no. 2 (Autumn 1993): 27-42.
Satin, Leslie. "Valentine de Saint-Point." *DRJ* 22, no. 1 (Spring 1990): 1-12.

**Saland, Stephanie** (1954– )
Daniels, Don, Marvin Hoshino, Francis Mason, and Shields Remine. "A Conversation with Stephanie Saland: 'The One with the Dark Eyes.'" *BR* 22, no. 4 (Winter 1994): 18-40.
GRE/3: 28-29.

**Sallé, Marie** (1707-1756)
Beaumont, Cyril W. "Marie Sallé." In his *Three French Dancers of the 18th Century*, pp. 18-25. Essays on Dancing and Dancers, No. 6. London: C.W. Beaumont, 1934.
Migel, Parmenia. "Marie Sallé 1707-1756." *BR* 4, no. 2 (1972): 3-14.
Vince, Stanley W.E. "Marie Sallé, 1707-56." *Theatre Notebook* 12, no. 1 (Autumn 1957): 7-14.
DRU: 29-46. MIG: 15-30. MOO/1: 30-36.

**Samsova, Galina** (1937– ; sometimes **Samtsova**)
Archer, Kenneth, and Millicent Hodson. "Two Galinas in Glasgow." *DN* 1, no. 3 (Autumn 1992): 56-63.
Conyers, Claude. "I Shall Remember Her Running." *BR* 1, no. 5 (1966): 13-23.

**Sangalli, Rita** (1850-1909)

Barker, Barbara. "Rita Sangalli." Part 2 in her *Ballet or Ballyhoo: The American Careers of Maria Bonfanti, Rita Sangalli, and Guiseppina Morlacchi*, pp. 35-107. New York: Dance Horizons, 1984.

**Sansom, Bruce** (1963– )

Rigby, Cormac. "Bruce Sansom." *DN* 2, no. 2 (Summer 1993): 58-62.

**Santlow, Hester** (ca. 1690-1773)

Cohen, Selma Jeanne. "Hester Santlow." In *Famed for Dance: Essays on the Theory and Practice of Theatrical Dancing in England, 1660-1740*, pp. 35-48, by Ifan Kyrle Fletcher, Selma Jeanne Cohen, and Roger Lonsdale. New York: The New York Public Library, 1960; reprinted from the *Bulletin of The New York Public Library*, June, November 1959; January, February, May 1960.

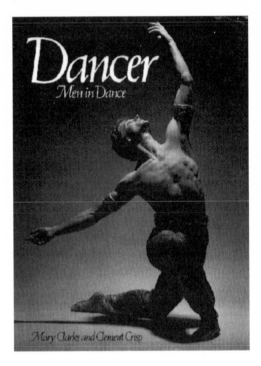

**Sarry, Christine** (1947– )

NEW/2: 348-364.

**Schaufuss, Peter** (1949– )

Kaplan, Larry. "Peter Schaufuss." *BR* 22, no. 4 (Winter 1994): 15-17.

"Schaufuss, Peter." *CBY 1982*: 385-388.

BLA: 173-175.

**Schlemmer, Oskar** (1888-1943)

Akademie der Künste, Berlin. *Oskar Schlemmer—"The Triadic Ballet."* Text and editing, Dirk Scheper; text of the music section, Hans-Joachim Hespos; translation into English, Leanore Ickstadt. Documentation 5. Berlin: Druckhaus Hentich, 1985.

**Schlemmer, Oskar** *(continued)*

Gropius, Walter, ed. *The Theater of the Bauhaus.* Translated by Arthur S. Wensinger. Middletown, Conn.: Wesleyan University Press, 1961.

Lahusen, Susanne. "Oskar Schlemmer: Mechanical Ballets?" *DR* 4, no. 2 (Autumn 1986): 65-77.

Lehman, Arnold L., and Brenda Richardson, eds. *Oskar Schlemmer.* Baltimore: Baltimore Museum of Art, 1986.

Moynihan, D.S., with Leigh George Odom. "Oskar Schlemmer's *Bauhaus Dances*: Debra McCall's Reconstructions." *TDR* 28, no. 3/T-103 (Fall 1984): 46-58.

Scheyer, Ernst. "The Shapes of Space: The Art of Mary Wigman and Oskar Schlemmer." *DP* 41 (Spring 1970).

Schlemmer, Oskar. *The Letters and Diaries of Oskar Schlemmer.* Selected and edited by Tut Schlemmer. Translated by Krishna Winston. Middletown, Conn.: Wesleyan University Press, 1972.


**Schönberg, Bessie** (1906– )

Jowitt, Deborah. "A Conversation with Bessie Schönberg." *BR* 9, no. 1 (Spring 1981): 31-63.

Schoenberg, Bessie. "A Lifetime of Dance." *PAJ* 4, nos. 1-2 (Issue #10-11) [c. 1979]: 106-117.


**Schorer, Suki** (1939– )

MAS: 455-463.


**Schwezoff, Igor** (1904-1982)

Schwezoff, Igor. *Russian Somersault.* New York & London: Harper & Brothers Publishers, 1936. Originally published in England as *Borzoi.* London: Hodder and Stoughton, 1935.


**Semenyaka, Ludmila** (1952– )

Terry, Walter, text, with photography by Mira. *Ludmila Semenyaka.* Dance Horizons Spotlight Series. Brooklyn, N.Y.: Dance Horizons, 1975.

GRE/1: 23-26.


**Semyonova, Marina** (1908– )

SLO: 75-77. SMA: 98-107.

**Sergeyev, Konstantin** (1910-1992)
SLO: 115-118. SMA: 266-274.

**Sergeyev, Nicolai** (1876-1951)
DAV: 254-257.

**Sergievsky, Orest** (1911-1984)
Gruen, John. "Character Dancer with Russian Roots: Orest Sergievsky." *Dance Magazine* 53, no. 2 (February 1979): 63-78. A Dance Magazine Portfolio.
Sergievsky, Orest. *Memoirs of a Dancer: Shadows, Dreams, Memories.* New York: Dance Horizons, 1979.

**Setterfield, Valda** (1934– )
Croce, Arlene. "Making Work." *The New Yorker* 58, no. 41 (November 29, 1982): 51-52, 55-56, 59-60, 63-64, 67-68, 73-74, 76, 78-86, 88, 93-94, 96, 98-103, 105-107.

**Severn, Margaret** (1901– )
Severn, Margaret. "Dancing with Bronislava Nijinska and Ida Rubinstein." *DC* 11, no. 3 (1988): 333-364.
——. "Scenes from a Dancer's Life." Part One: 1910-1919; Part Two: 1919-1921. *DC* 15, no. 3 (1992): 253-290 and *DC* 16, no. 1 (1993): 73-114.

**Seymour, Lynn** (1939– )
Austin, Richard. *Lynn Seymour: An Authorised Biography.* London: Angus and Robertson Publishers, 1980.
Crickmay, Anthony. *Lynn Seymour.* London: Studio Vista, 1980.
"Seymour, Lynn." *CBY 1979*: 344-348.
Seymour, Lynn, with Paul Gardner. *Lynn: The Autobiography of Lynn Seymour.* London: Granada, 1984.
Vaughan, David, text, with photography by Anthony Crickmay. *Lynn Seymour.* Dance Horizons Spotlight Series. Brooklyn, N.Y.: Dance Horizons, 1976.
GRU/2: 131-135. MON: 66-67. NEW/1: 226-242.

**Shawn, Ted** (1891-1972)
Cohen, Barbara Naomi. *The Franchising of Denishawn.* Dance Data No. 4. Brooklyn, N.Y.: Dance Horizons, n.d.

**Shawn, Ted** *(continued)*

Dixon-Stowell, Brenda. "Ethnic and Exotic Aspects in the Choreography of Selected Works by Ted Shawn and Martha Graham." In *Society of Dance History Scholars Proceedings*, pp. 21-28. Seventh Annual Conference, Goucher College, Towson, Maryland, 17-19 February 1984.

Dreier, Katherine S. *Shawn the Dancer.* New York: A.S. Barnes & Company, 1933.

Guest, Ann Hutchinson, ed. *Shawn's Fundamentals of Dance.* Recorded in Labanotation by Ann Hutchinson Guest. Language of Dance Series, No. 2. New York & London: Gordon and Breach, 1988.

Hastings, Baird. "The Denishawn Era (1914-1931)." *DI* 1, no. 6 (June 1942).

Jordan, Stephanie. "Ted Shawn's Music Visualizations." *DC* 7, no. 1 (1984): 33-49.

Kendall, Elizabeth. *Where She Danced.* New York: Knopf, 1979.

McDonagh, Don. "In Memoriam: Ted Shawn." *BR* 4, no. 2 (1972): 68-73.

Mumaw, Barton, with Jane Sherman. "Ted Shawn, Teacher and Choreographer." *DC* 4, no. 2 (1981): 91-112.

Ruyter, Nancy Lee Chalfa. "The American Way: Ruth St. Denis and Ted Shawn." Chapter 4 in her *Reformers and Visionaries: The Americanization of the Art of Dance*, pp. 57-73. New York: Dance Horizons, 1979.

Schlundt, Christena L. *The Professional Appearances of Ruth St. Denis & Ted Shawn: A Chronology and an Index of Dances 1906-1932.* New York: The New York Public Library, 1962.

——. *The Professional Appearances of Ted Shawn & his Men Dancers: A Chronology and an Index of Dances 1933-1940.* New York: The New York Public Library, 1967.

——. "The Still Point of Perfection." In *Society of Dance History*

**Shawn, Ted** (*continued*)

 *Scholars Proceedings*, pp. 103-110. Fifth Annual Conference, Harvard University, 13-15 February 1982.

"Shawn, Ted." *CBY 1949*: 563-565.

Shawn, Ted. *Dance We Must*. [New illustrated ed.] [Pittsfield, Mass.: Eagle Printing and Binding Company, pref. 1963, c. 1950]. Lectures delivered by Shawn at George Peabody College for Teachers, Nashville, Tenn., from June 13th to July 2nd, 1938.

——. *Fundamentals of Dance Education*. Girard, Kansas: Haldeman-Julius Publications, 1937.

——. *Gods Who Dance*. New York: Dutton, 1929.

——. *Ruth St. Denis: Pioneer and Prophet*. Being a History of her Cycle of Oriental Dances. Volume One: The Text; Volume Two: The Plates. San Francisco: Printed for John Howell by John Henry Nash, 1920.

——, with Gray Poole. *One Thousand and One Night Stands*. Garden City, N.Y.: Doubleday, 1960.

Sherman, Jane. "The American Indian Imagery of Ted Shawn." *DC* 12 (1989): 366-382.

——. *Denishawn: The Enduring Influence*. Boston: Twayne Publishers, 1983.

——. "Denishawn Oriental Dances." *DS* 13, nos. 2&3 (Winter/Spring 1979): 33-43.

——. *The Drama of Denishawn Dance*. Middletown, Conn.: Wesleyan University Press, 1979.

——. *Soaring: The Diary and Letters of a Denishawn Dancer in the Far East 1925-1926*. Middletown, Conn.: Wesleyan University Press, 1976.

——, and Barton Mumaw. *Barton Mumaw, Dancer: From Denishawn to Jacob's Pillow and Beyond*. New York: Dance Horizons, 1986.

Terry, Walter. *Ted Shawn: Father of American Dance*. New York: Dial Press, 1976.

BRO: 26-32. DRU: 156-174. LLO: 22-34. MAG: 224-237. MAR: 149-160. MAY/2: 85-97. MAZ: 85-116. MOO/1: 281-286. PAL: 26-33. ROG: 1-9. TER: 67-82.

**Shearer, Moira** (1926– )

Crowle, Pigeon. *Moira Shearer: Portrait of a Dancer*. New York: Pitman, c. 1950.

Fisher, Hugh. *Moira Shearer*. Dancers of To-Day, No. 2. London: Adam & Charles Black, 1952.

**Shearer, Moira** *(continued)*
Gibbon, Monk. *The Red Shoes Ballet*. London: Saturn Press, 1948; reprint New York: Garland Publishing, 1977.
McLean, Adrienne L. "*The Red Shoes* Revisited." *DC* 11, no. 1 (1988): 31-83.
"Shearer, Moira." *CBY 1950*: 530-531.
Shearer, Moira. *Balletmaster: A Dancer's View of George Balanchine*. London: Sidgwick & Jackson, 1986.
Tenent, Rose. *Moira Shearer*. Ballet Album No. 1. Edinburgh: Albyn Press, 1947.
ATK: 135-139. DAV: 257-264. GIB: 62-67. GRU/1: 164-169. HUR: 289-292. MAS: 335-337. MCC: 76-85. NEW/1: 88-111.

**Shearer, Sybil** (1918– )
Martin, John, text, with photography by Helen Morrison. *Sybil Shearer*. Folio I. [Palatine, Ill.: Distributed by M. Yoshimasu, 1965].
Shearer, Sybil, Dawn Lille Horwitz, and Stuart Hodes. "A Sybil Shearer Sampler." *BR* 12, no. 3 (Fall 1984): 22-40.
LLO: 232-243.

**Sherman, Jane** (1908– )
Sherman, Jane. *Denishawn: The Enduring Influence*. Boston: Twayne Publishers, 1983.
——. *The Drama of Denishawn Dance*. Middletown, Conn.: Wesleyan University Press, 1979.
——. *Soaring: The Diary and Letters of a Denishawn Dancer in the Far East 1925-1926*. Middletown, Conn.: Wesleyan University Press, 1976.
——, and Barton Mumaw. *Barton Mumaw, Dancer: From Denishawn to Jacob's Pillow and Beyond*. New York: Dance Horizons, 1986.

**Shire, Ellen** (1941– )
SID: 173-181.

**Shook, Karel** (1920-1985)
Shook, Karel. *Elements of Classical Ballet Technique as Practiced in the School of the Dance Theatre of Harlem*. New York: Dance Horizons, 1977.
GAL: 39-48.

**Shuler, Arlene** (1947– )
SID: 183-192.

**Shurr, Gertrude** (1905-1992)
Mason, Francis. "Gertrude Shurr (1905-1992)." *BR* 20, no. 1 (Summer 1992): 4-6.
McDonagh, Don. "A Conversation with Gertrude Shurr." *BR* 4, no. 5 (1973): 3-20.

**Sibley, Antoinette** (1939– )
Harris, Dale, text, with photography by Anthony Crickmay. *Antoinette Sibley*. Dance Horizons Spotlight Series. Brooklyn, N.Y.: Dance Horizons, 1976.
Newman, Barbara. *Antoinette Sibley: Reflections of a Ballerina*. London: Hutchinson, 1986.
——. "Sibley Talks About Dancing." *BR* 9, no. 2 (Summer 1981): 8-28. An extract from Barbara Newman's *Striking a Balance: Dancers Talk About Dancing*. Boston: Houghton Mifflin, 1982.
"Sibley, Antoinette." *CBY 1970*: 392-394.
Spatt, Leslie E., photography, with text by Mary Clarke. *Antoinette Sibley*. London: Dance Books, 1981.
——, photography, with text by Nicholas Dromgoole. *Sibley & Dowell*. London: Collins, 1976.
GRU/2: 117-124. MON: 62-65. NEW/1: 244-265.

**Silvers, Sally** (ca. 1953– )
Silvers, Sally. "Methods (*No Best Better Way*)." *TDR* 29, no. 2/T-106 (Summer 1985): 3-19.

**Simon, Victoria** (1939– )
MAS: 405-407.

**Siris, P.** (fl. 1708-1725)
Thorp, Jennifer. "P. Siris: An Early Eighteenth-Century Dancing-Master." *DR* 10, no. 2 (Autumn 1992): 71-92.

**Skeaping, Mary** (1902-1984)
Anastos, Peter. "A Conversation with Mary Skeaping." *BR* 6, no. 1 (1977-1978): 17-28.

**Skibine, George** (1920-1981)

Anastos, Peter. "A Conversation with George Skibine." *BR* 10, no. 1 (Spring 1982): 68-97.

Nemenschousky, Léon. *A Day with Marjorie Tallchief and Georges Skibine.* London: Cassell & Company, 1960.

ATK: 140-143. DAV: 264-267. SWI/2: 57-60.

**Skorik, Irène** (1928– )

SWI/2: 44-48.

**Skura, Stephanie** (1948– )

Skura, Stephanie. "Truncated Initiations and Other Approaches." *TDR* 29, no. 2/T-106 (Summer 1985): 41-52.

**Slavenska, Mia** (1914– )

"Slavenska, Mia." *CBY 1954*: 577-579.

Swisher, Viola Hegyi. "Mia Slavenska: A Study in Contrasts." *Dance Magazine* 47, no. 3 (March 1973): 55-70. A Dance Magazine Portfolio.

ATK: 144-146.

**Sleep, Wayne** (1948– )

Search, Gay, text, with photography by Chris Nash. *Variations on Wayne Sleep.* London: Heinemann, 1983.

**Smith, George Washington** (1820-1899)

Moore, Lillian. "George Washington Smith." *DI* 4, nos. 6-8 (June-August 1945).

MAG: 138-188.

**Smuin, Michael** (1938– )

"Smuin, Michael." *CBY 1984*: 383-386.

**Sobotka, Ruth** (1925-1967)

[Sobotka, Walter and Gisela]. *Ruth.* New York: the authors, 1968.

**Sokolova, Lydia** (1896-1974)

Sokolova, Lydia. *Dancing for Diaghilev: The Memoirs of Lydia*

**Sokolova, Lydia** *(continued)*

   *Sokolova.* New York: Macmillan, 1961; reprint San Francisco: Mercury House, 1989.

   HAS/1: 118-126, 130.

**Sokolow, Anna** (1912– )

   Beck, Jill. "Anna Sokolow's *Scenes From the Music of Charles Ives*: A Critical Analysis." *DNJ* 3, no. 1, pt. 1 (Spring 1985): 9-67. Look under Ilene Fox for Labanotation score to part of this work.

   Bissell, Robyn. "*Rooms*: An Analysis." *DNJ* 1, no. 1 (January 1983): 18-34.

   Brooks Schmitz, Nancy. "Catherine Littlefield and Anna Sokolow: Artists Reflecting Society in the 1930s." In *Dance: Current Selected Research*, Volume 1, pp. 115-123. Edited by Lynnette Y. Overby and James H. Humphrey. New York: AMS Press, 1989.

   Cook, Ray, and Ann Hutchinson Guest, eds. *"Ballade."* Language of Dance Series, No. 5. Yverdon, Switzerland: Gordon and Breach, 1993.

   Driver, Senta. "Passion Is Also Important: Anna Sokolow at Ohio State." *DS* 3, no. 1 (Fall 1966): 25-29.

   Fox, Ilene. "'The Unanswered Question' from Anna Sokolow's *Scenes From the Music of Charles Ives*." *DNJ* 3, no. 1, pt. 2 (Spring 1985): 1-17. Look under Jill Beck for supporting article to this Labanotation score.

   Morris, Kelly, and Leslie Morris. "An Interview with Anna Sokolow." *TDR* 14, no. 1/T-45 (Fall 1969): 98-102.

   "Sokolow, Anna." *CBY 1969*: 407-410.

   Stodelle, Ernestine. "Anna Sokolow, Spokesman for the Psyche." *BR* 23, no. 1 (Spring 1995): 33-39.

**Sokolow, Anna** *(continued)*
Warren, Larry. *Anna Sokolow: The Rebellious Spirit.* Princeton, N.J.: Princeton Book Company, Publishers, 1991.
BRO: 105-110. COH/2: 28-37. LIV: 198-209. LLO: 214-223. LYL: 138-147. SCH/1: see Index of Choreographers, p. 135.

**Solomons, Gus, Jr.** (1940– )
Sorell, Walter. *The Dance Has Many Faces.* 3d rev. ed. Pennington, N.J.: A Cappella Books, 1992.
Zalk, Mark. "An Elegance Is Implied: An Interview with Gus Solomons, Jr." *DS* 3, no. 2 (Spring 1967): 11-16.
KRE: 176-193. MCD: 162-173.

**Soloviev, Yuri** (1940-1977)
SMA: 282-289.

**Somes, Michael** (1917-1994)
Fisher, Hugh. *Michael Somes.* Dancers of To-Day, No. 7. London: Adam & Charles Black, 1955.
"Somes, Michael (George)." *CBY 1955:* 568-569.
DAV: 267-271. GRU/2: 162-168.

**Sorokina, Nina** (1942– )
ZHD: 218-241.

**Sparling, Peter** (1951– )
GRU/1: 131-137.

**Spencer, Penelope** (1901-1993)
Haskell, Arnold L. *Penelope Spencer and Other Studies.* Artists of the Dance. London: British-Continental Press, 1930.

**Spencer, Sybil** (1899–1992)
Spencer, Sybil. *Love for Ballet.* Liss, Hants, England: Triplegate Ltd., 1985.

**Spessivtzeva, Olga** (1895-1991)
Dolin, Anton. *The Sleeping Ballerina.* London: Frederick Muller, 1966.

**Spessivtzeva, Olga** *(continued)*

Fern, Dale Edward. "Spessivtzeva." Parts One, Two and Three. *Dance Magazine* 34, no. 4 (April 1960): 39-43; *Dance Magazine* 34, no. 5 (May 1960): 43-45; and *Dance Magazine* 34, no. 7 (July 1960): 32-33, 67. Part Three is a selection of tributes, introduced by Dale Edward Fern, from Spessivtseva's colleagues: Nathalie Branitzka, Anton Dolin, Felia Doubrovska, Serge Grigoriev, Tamara Karsavina, Serge Lifar, Vera Nemtchinova, Romola Nijinsky, Anatole Oboukhoff, Michel Pavloff, Lubov Tchernicheva, and Pierre Vladimiroff.

Kniaseff, Boris. "The Reminiscences of Boris Kniaseff: In the Footsteps of Olga Spessivtseva." Parts One, Two and Three. *Ballet Today* 10, no. 6 (July 1957): 14-16; *Ballet Today* 10, no. 7 (August-September 1957): 8; and *Ballet Today* 10, no. 8 (October 1957): 21.

Lifar, Serge. "Olga Spessivtseva." In his *The Three Graces: The Legends and the Truth*, pp. 159-239. Translated by Gerard Hopkins. London: Cassell, 1959.

Spessivtzeva, Olga. *Technique for the Ballet Artiste*. London: Frederick Muller, 1967.

AUS/1: 124-150. AUS/2: 67-78. MON: 22-23. SMA: 146-157.

**Spink, Ian** (1947– )

Rubidge, Sarah. "The Spink-Gough Collaboration." *C&D* 1, pt. 4 (1992): 23-55.

JOR: 182-206, 233-238.

**Spohr, Arnold** (1927– )

Wyman, Max. *The Royal Winnipeg Ballet: The First Forty Years.* Toronto: Doubleday Canada; Garden City, N.Y.: Doubleday, 1978.

**Spurgeon, Jack** (1908-1994)

DAV: 271-272.

**Staff, Frank** (1918-1971)

DAV: 273-276. HAL: 239-241.

**Stebbins, Genevieve** (1857-1914)

Ruyter, Nancy Lee Chalfa. "The Intellectual World of Genevieve Stebbins." *DC* 11, no. 3 (1988): 381-397.

**Stebbins, Genevieve** *(continued)*

Shelton, Suzanne. "The Influence of Genevieve Stebbins on the Early Career of Ruth St. Denis." *DRA IX* (1978): 33-49.

Stebbins, Genevieve. *Delsarte System of Expression.* 6th ed., rev. and enl. New York: Dance Horizons, 1977. Originally published by Edgar S. Werner Publishing & Supply Co., New York, 1902.

——. *Dynamic Breathing and Harmonic Gymnastics.* 2d ed. New York: Edgar S. Werner & Company, c. 1913.

——. *The Genevieve Stebbins System of Physical Training.* Enl. ed. New York: Edgar S. Werner & Company, c. 1913.

——. *Society Gymnastics and Voice Culture.* 6th ed. New York: Edgar S. Werner Publishing & Supply Co., c. 1888.

**Steele, Michael** (1941– )

GRE/3: 27-28.

**Stepanov, Vladimir Ivanovich** (1866-1896)

Gorsky, Alexander. *Two Essays on Stepanov Dance Notation.* Translated from the Russian by Roland John Wiley. New York: Congress on Research in Dance (CORD), 1978.

Stepanov, V.I. *Alphabet of Movements of the Human Body.* A Study in Recording the Movements of the Human Body by Means of Musical Signs. Translated by Raymond Lister from the French edition of 1892. Cambridge, England: The Golden Head Press, 1958; reprint Brooklyn, N.Y.: Dance Horizons, [1969].

**Stiefel, Ethan** (1973– )

Stuart, Otis. "Ciao Ethan: A Conversation with Ethan Stiefel." *BR* 20, no. 3 (Fall 1992): 41-46.

**Stierle, Edward** (1968-1991)

Driver, Senta. "Edward Stierle (1968-1991)." *BR* 19, no. 3 (Fall 1991): 47-48.

Solway, Diane. *A Dance Against Time.* New York, London, Toronto: Pocket Books, 1994.

**Stone, Bentley** (1908-1984)

Dorris, George. "*Frankie and Johnny* in Chicago and Some Problems of Attribution." *DC* 18, no. 2 (1995): 179-188.

PAG: 55-59.

**Stowell, Kent** (1939– )
MAS: 465-468.

**Streb, Elizabeth** (1950– )
Burns, Judy. "Wild Bodies/Wilder Minds: Streb/Ringside and Spectacle." *W&P* 7, no. 1/Issue #13 (1994): 97-121.

**Stroganova, Nina** (1916?-1994)
BEL: 71-73.

**Struchkova, Raisa** (1925– )
Fradkin, Herman. *Raisa Struchkova*. Moscow: Foreign Languages Publishing House, 1956.

**Stuart, Muriel** (1903-1991)
Kirstein, Lincoln, and Muriel Stuart. *The Classic Ballet: Basic Technique and Terminology*. Illustrations by Carlus Dyer. Preface by George Balanchine. Foreword by Moira Shearer. London, New York, Toronto: Longmans, Green, and Co., 1953.
Lerner, Davie, and David Vaughan. "Muriel Stuart (1900-1991)." *BR* 19, no. 2 (Summer 1991): 51-59.
GAL: 49-57. GRU/2: 36-42.

**Stukolkin, Timofei Alexeyevich** (1829–1894)
WIL: 107-134.

**Stukolkina, Nina** (fl. 1922-1958)
MAS: 79-80.

**Subligny, Marie-Thérèse Perdou de** (1666-ca. 1735)
MIG: 9-10.

**Sullivan, Françoise** (1925– )
Ellenwood, Ray. *Egregore: The Montreal Automatist Movement*. Toronto: Exile Editions, 1992.

**Summers, Elaine** (1925– )
Sargent-Wooster, Ann. "Elaine Summers: Moving to Dance." *TDR*
24, no. 4/T-88 (December 1980): 59-70.

**Sumner, Carol** (1940– )
GRU/2: 365-370. MAS: 403-404.

**Taglioni, Marie** (1804-1884)

Aschengreen, Erik. "The Beautiful Danger: Facets of the Romantic Ballet." *DP* 58 (Summer 1974). "*La Sylphide*, Marie Taglioni, and the Romantic Ballet," pp. 7-15.

Binney, Edwin, 3rd. *Longing for the Ideal: Images of Marie Taglioni in the Romantic Ballet*. A Centenary Exhibition. Cambridge: Harvard Theatre Collection, 1984.

Heiberg, Johanne Luise. "Memories of Taglioni and Elssler." Translated by Patricia McAndrew. *DC* 4, no. 1 (1981): 14-18.

Hill, Lorna. *La Sylphide: The Life of Marie Taglioni*. London: Evans Brothers, 1967.

Levinson, André. *Marie Taglioni (1804-1884)*. Translated by Cyril W. Beaumont, 1930. Imperial Society of Teachers of Dancing; Publisher to the Society: C.W. Beaumont, 1930; reprint London: Dance Books, 1977. First published in French by Librairie Félix Alcan, Paris, 1929, in the series Acteurs et Actrices d'Autrefois.

Mayne, Ethel Colburn. "Marie Taglioni." In her *Enchanters of Men*,

**Taglioni, Marie** *(continued)*

pp. 252-262. London: Methuen & Co., 1909; reprinted New York: Putnam, 1925.

Migel, Parmenia. "Marie Taglioni, 1804-1884." *Dance Magazine* 46, no. 9 (September 1972): 43-58. An extract from her *The Ballerinas: From the Court of Louis XIV to Pavlova.* New York: Macmillan, 1972. A Dance Magazine Portfolio.

"Le Quatuor dansè [i.e., dansé] à Londres par Taglioni, Charlotte Grisi, Cerrito et Fanny Elsler [sic]." *DI* 3, nos. 7-8 (July- August 1944). Portion on Taglioni, pp. 118-120.

*Six Sketches of Mademoiselle Taglioni in the Characters in which she Appeared during the Present Season.* Drawn from the life by A.E. Chalon, R.A. Drawn on stone by R.J. Lane, A.R.A. London: J. Dickinson, 1831. Six numbered lithographs printed in black; 1) Flore; 2) La Tyrolienne; 3) La Napolitaine; 4) La Bayadère; 5) La Naiade; and 6) Marie Taglioni, with facsimile signature. Followed by six leaves, on each of which is a poem by F.W.N. Bayley corresponding to the plate numbers of the lithographs, except that poem no. 3 should be no. 5 and poem no. 5 should be no. 3.

Woodcock, Sarah C. "Margaret Rolfe's Memoirs of Marie Taglioni." Part One and Part Two. *DR* 7, no. 1 (Spring 1989): 3-19 and *DR* 7, no. 2 (Autumn 1989): 55-69.

AUS/1: 12-37. CLA: 11-41. DRU: 47-66. MCC: 1-13. MIG: 115-144. MOO/1: 77-90. MUI: 19-27.

**Taglioni, Paul** (1808-1884) and **Amelie** (**Galster**) (1808-1881)
MOO/2: 70-81. SWI/1: 163-173.

**Takei, Kei** (1946– )

Pierce, Robert J. "Kei Takei's Moving Earth." *DS* 9, no. 2 (Spring/ Summer 1975): 18-27.

Sommers, Pamela. "Kei Takei's Moving Earth: *Light.*" *TDR* 25, no. 2/T-90 (Summer 1981): 101-110.

KRE: 12-23. LYL: 150-160.

**Taliaferro, Clay** (1940– )

Beck, Jill. "Clay Taliaferro's *Falling Off the Back Porch*: A Critical Analysis." *DNJ* 3, no. 1, pt. 1 (Spring 1985): 120-172. Look under Mary Corey for Labanotation score to part of this work.

**Taliaferro, Clay** *(continued)*
  Corey, Mary. "'Fourth Movement' from Clay Taliaferro's *Falling Off the Back Porch.*" *DNJ* 3, no. 1, pt. 2 (Spring 1985): 55-69. Look under Jill Beck for supporting article to this Labanotation score.

**Tallchief, Maria** (1925– )
  DeLeeuw, Adèle, text, with illustrations by Russell Hoover. *Maria Tallchief: American Ballerina.* Champaign, Ill.: Garrard Publishing Company, 1971.
  Gruen, John, text, with photography by Tony Soluri. "On Point: Choreographing Interiors for Maria Tallchief." *Architectural Digest* 41, no. 10 (October 1984): 102-109, 204, 206.
  Maynard, Olga. *Bird of Fire: The Story of Maria Tallchief.* New York: Dodd, Mead & Company, 1961.
  Myers, Elizabeth P. *Maria Tallchief: America's Prima Ballerina.* New York: Grosset & Dunlap, 1966.
  "Tallchief, Maria." *CBY 1951*: 618-620.
  Tobias, Tobi. *Maria Tallchief.* New York: Thomas Y. Crowell Company, 1970.
  ATK: 147-151. CRO: 137-150. DAV: 277-279. DRU: 193-212. MAS: 231-243. MCC: 157-164. MON: 42-45. MUI: 149-156. SWI/2: 27-32. TRA: 102-109.

**Tallchief, Marjorie** (1927– )
  Nemenschousky, Léon. *A Day with Marjorie Tallchief and Georges Skibine.* London: Cassell & Company, 1960.
  ATK: 152-154. DAV: 279-281.

**Tamiris, Helen** (1905-1966)
  "In Memoriam: Helen Tamiris 1902-1966." *DS* 3, no. 1 (Fall 1966): 8-9.

**Tamiris, Helen** *(continued)*

Nagrin, Daniel. "Appendix A: Helen Tamiris." In his *Dance and the Specific Image: Improvisation*, p. 193. Pittsburgh, Pa. & London: University of Pittsburgh Press, 1994.

——. "Helen Tamiris and the Dance Historians." In *Society of Dance History Scholars Proceedings*, pp. 15-43. Twelfth Annual Conference, Arizona State University, 17-19 February 1989.

Schlundt, Christena L. *Tamiris: A Chronicle of Her Dance Career 1927-1955*. New York: The New York Public Library, 1972; reprinted in *SDH* 1, no. 1 (Fall-Winter 1989-90): 65-154.

Tamiris, Helen. "Tamiris in Her Own Voice: Draft of an Autobiography." Transcribed, edited, and annotated by Daniel Nagrin. *SDH* 1, no. 1 (Fall/Winter 1989-90): 1-64.

Tish, Pauline. "Remembering Helen Tamiris." *DC* 17, no. 3 (1994): 327-360.

LLO: 132-155. MAY/2: 156-163. SCH/1: see Index of Choreographers, p. 135. SOR/1: 267-270. TER: 129-138.


**Tanaka, Min** (1945– )

Stein, Bonnie Sue. "Min Tanaka: Farmer/Dancer or Dancer/Farmer." *TDR* 30, no. 2/T-110 (Summer 1986): 142-151.


**Tanner, Richard** (1948– )

MAS: 563-569.


**Taras, John** (1919– )

FRA: 179-181. GRU/1: 58-72. MAS: 195-198.


**Taubert, Gottfried** (b. 1679)

Gerbes, Angelika R. "Gottfried Taubert on Social and Theatrical Dance of the Early Eighteenth-Century." Unpublished dissertation, The Ohio State University, 1972. Ann Arbor, Mich.: University Microfilms International, 1973. Order No. 73-02,001. DAI 33-08A, p. 4578.

——. "Eighteenth Century Dance Instruction: The Course of Study Advocated by Gottfried Taubert." *DR* 10, no. 1 (Spring 1992): 40-52.

## Taylor, Paul (1930– )

Anderson, Jack. "Paul Taylor: Surface and Substance." *BR* 6, no. 1 (1977-1978): 39-44.

Barnes, Clive. "Paul Taylor." *BR* 2, no. 1 (1967): 20-25.

Bivona, Elena. "Paul Taylor: Two Works." *BR* 2, no. 5 (1969): 37-39.

Daniels, Don. "Paul Taylor and the Post-Moderns." *BR* 9, no. 2 (Summer 1981): 66-82.

Jacobson, Daniel. "Private Domains in Public Spaces." *BR* 17, no. 1 (Spring 1989): 67-75.

Kagan, Elizabeth. "Towards the Analysis of a Score: A Comparative Study of *Three Epitaphs* by Paul Taylor and *Water Study* by Doris Humphrey." *DRA IX* (1978): 75-92.

Lobenthal, Joel. "Christopher Gillis: Dancing for Paul Taylor." *BR* 13, no. 2 (Summer 1985): 10-22.

Macaulay, Alastair. "The Music Man." *The New Yorker* 64, no. 11 (May 2, 1988): 100, 113-115.

McDonagh, Don. "Paul Taylor in Orbit." *DS* 3, no. 1 (Fall 1966): 10-18.

Reiter, Susan. "Baroque and Beyond with Paul Taylor." *BR* 14, no. 3 (Fall 1986): 65-71.

Rosen, Lillie F. "Talking with Paul Taylor." *DS* 13, nos. 2&3 (Winter/Spring 1979): 82-92.

Sorens, Ina. "Taylor Reconstructs Balanchine." *BR* 14, no. 2 (Summer 1986): 54-65.

"Taylor, Paul." *CBY 1964*: 443-445.

**Taylor, Paul** *(continued)*
Taylor, Paul. *Private Domain.* New York: Knopf, 1987.
COE: 192-204. COH/2: 90-102. HOD: 12-47. LYL: 108-121. MAZ: 256-270. MCD: 224-240.

**Tcherina, Ludmilla** (1924– )
GIB: 78-84.

**Tcherkassky, Marianna** (1955– )
"Tcherkassky, Marianna." *CBY 1985*: 411-414.

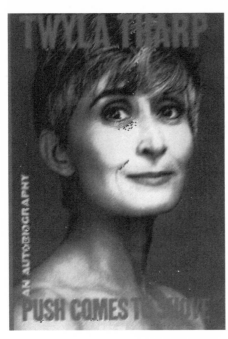

**Tchernicheva, Lubov** (1890-1976)
*The Art of Lubov Tchernicheva.*
London: C.W. Beaumont. 1921.

**Tetley, Glen** (1926– )
"Tetley, Glen." *CBY 1973*: 406-409.
GRU/2: 424-432. ROG: 118-131.

**Tharp, Twyla** (1941– )
Albert, Steven. "Utopia Lost—and Found? A Look at Tharp's Way." *BR* 14, no. 1 (Spring 1986): 17-35.
Buirge, Susan, Marcia B. Siegel, and Bill Kosmas. "Twyla Tharp: Questions and Answers." *BR* 4, no. 1 (1971): 41-49.
Jowitt, Deborah. "Twyla Tharp's New Kick." *The New York Times Magazine*, January 4, 1976, pp. 10-12, 18-21.
Nugent, Ann. *"Till* and Twyla: A Myth and a Legend." *DN* 3, no. 1 (Spring 1994): 10-17.
"Tharp, Twyla." *CBY 1975*: 401-404.
Tharp, Twyla. *"Group Activities." BR* 2, no. 5 (1969): 19-24.
——. *Push Comes to Shove: An Autobiography.* New York: Bantam Books, 1992.
Tobias, Tobi. "Twyla Tharp." *DS* 4, no. 2 (Spring 1970): 6-17.
COE: 205-228. FOS: 209-220; 220-227. FOW: 76-97. LIV: 210-223. MCD: 105-118. ROG: 132-148.

**Théleur, E.A.** (fl. ca. 1817-ca. 1844)
Théleur, E.A. "Letters on Dancing (1831)." *SDH* 2, no. 1 (Fall-Winter 1990). With an introduction by Sandra N. Hammond, pp. 1-6.

**Theodore, Lee** (1933-1987)
GRU/1: 111-120.

**Théodore, Mlle** (see **Crespé, Marie-Madeleine**)

**Thesmar, Ghislaine** (1943– )
GRU/1: 86-94. PET: 114-131.

**Thomas, Richard** (1926– )
MAS: 271-275.

**Tikhomirov, Vasily** (1876-1956)
SMA: 260-265.

**Timofeyeva, Nina** (1935– )
DEM/1: 178-182. GRE/1: 22-23.

**Tomasson, Helgi** (1942– )
Kisselgoff, Anna, text, with photography by Martha Swope. *Helgi Tomasson.* Dance Horizons Spotlight Series. Brooklyn, N.Y.: Dance Horizons, 1975.
"Tomasson, Helgi." *CBY 1982*: 420-423.
COH/1: 30-33. GRE/2: 58-62. GRE/3: 12-14. GRU/2: 312-318. MAS: 537-548.

**Tomlinson, Kellom** (b. early 1690s; fl. 1715-1744)
Shennan, Jennifer. "Discovery of New Kellom Tomlinson Manuscript." *DRJ* 22, no. 1 (Spring 1990): 58-61.
Tomlinson, Kellom. *A Work Book by Kellom Tomlinson.* Commonplace Book of an Eighteenth-Century English Dancing Master, A Facsimile Edition. Edited by Jennifer Shennan. Dance & Music Series, No. 6. Stuyvesant, N.Y.: Pendragon Press, 1992.

**Toscanini, Cia Fornaroli** (1888-1954)
PAG: 64-67.

**Toumanova, Tamara** (1919– )
Anastos, Peter. "A Conversation with Tamara Toumanova." *BR* 11, no. 4 (Winter 1984): 33-57.
Swisher, Viola Hegyi. "Tamara Toumanova: A Unique Career." *Dance Magazine* 44, no. 9 (September 1970): 44-63. A Dance Magazine Portfolio.
ATK: 155-158. DAV: 281-285. MAS: 97-107. MOO/1: 236-238. SWI/2: 71-75. TRA: 46-55.

**Toye, Wendy** (1917– )
Dodd, Craig. "The Golden Toye." *DN* 1, no. 2 (Summer 1992): 66-69.

**Trefilova, Vera** (1875-1943)
Haskell, Arnold L. *Vera Trefilova: A Study in Classicism.* Artists of the Dance. London: British-Continental Press, 1928.
SMA: 166-171.

**Tudor, Antony** (1908-1987)
Anderson, Jack. "The View From the House Opposite: Some Aspects of Tudor." *BR* 4, no. 6 (1974): 14-23.
"Antony Tudor: The American Years." *C&D* 1, pt. 2 (1989). Muriel Topaz, Issue Editor. Contents: Linda Szmyd. "Antony Tudor: Ballet Theatre Years" (pp. 3-26). Sally Brayley Bliss. "Antony Tudor: Personal Reminiscences, 1950-66" (pp. 27-37). Martha Hill. "Antony Tudor: The Juilliard Years" (pp. 38-58). Mary Farkas. "Antony Tudor: The First Zen Institute" (pp. 59-67). Judith Chazin-Bennahum. "After *Pillar of Fire*" (pp. 69-96). Tudor Ballets: Alphabetized List (pp. 97-105). Tudor Ballets: Chronological List (pp. 106-107). Notes on Contributors (pp. 109-110). Index (pp. 111-113).
Chazin-Bennahum, Judith. *The Ballets of Antony Tudor: Studies in Psyche and Satire.* New York: Oxford University Press, 1994.
——. "Scandinavian Memories of Antony Tudor." *BR* 20, no. 4 (Winter 1992): 46-51.

**Tudor, Antony** *(continued)*

——. "Shedding Light on *Dark Elegies.*" In *Society of Dance History Scholars Proceedings*, pp. 131-144. Eleventh Annual Conference, North Carolina School of the Arts, 12-14 February 1988.

Cohen, Selma Jeanne. "Antony Tudor, Part Two: The Years in America and After." *DP* 18 (1963).

Guest, Ann Hutchinson, ed. *"Soirée Musicale."* Language of Dance Series, No. 4. Yverdon, Switzerland: Gordon and Breach, 1993.

Huxley, Michael. "A History of Dance: An Analysis of *Dark Elegies* from Written Criticism." Chapter 8 in *Dance Analysis: Theory and Practice*, pp. 141-160. Edited by Janet Adshead. London: Dance Books, 1988.

Kaye, Nora, moderated by Selma Jeanne Cohen. "Nora Kaye Talks About Working with Antony Tudor." In *Society of Dance History Scholars Proceedings*, pp. 84-90. Eighth Annual Conference, University of New Mexico, 15-17 February 1985.

Manchester, P.W. "Reflections After Reading *Shadowplay.*" *BR* 20, no. 1 (Spring 1992): 74-77.

Percival, John. "Antony Tudor, Part One: The Years in England." *DP* 17 (1963).

Perlmutter, Donna. *Shadowplay: The Life of Antony Tudor*. New York: Viking, 1991.

Rosen, Lillie F. "Talking with Antony Tudor: A Choreographer for All Seasons." *DS* 9, no. 1 (Fall/Winter 1974-75): 14-23.

"Toasting Tudor: The Capezio Awards." *BR* 14, no. 3 (Fall 1986): 31-37. Transcript of tributes given by Oliver Smith, Dame Alicia Markova, Eliot Feld, Paul Taylor, Jerome Robbins, Mikhail Baryshnikov, Agnes de Mille, William Schuman, and Donald Saddler.

Topaz, Muriel. "Notating and Reconstructing for Antony Tudor." In *Society of Dance History Scholars Proceedings*, pp. 91-97. Eighth

**Tudor, Antony** *(continued)*
Annual Conference, University of New Mexico, 15-17 February 1985.

"Tudor, Antony." *CBY 1945*: 630-633.

van Praagh, Peggy. "Working with Antony Tudor." *DR* 2, no. 2 (Summer 1984): 56-67.

Vaughan, David. "Antony Tudor's Early Ballets." In *Society of Dance History Scholars Proceedings*, pp. 72-83. Eighth Annual Conference, University of New Mexico, 15-17 February 1985.

"What Constitutes a Dance?: Investigating the Constitutive Properties of Antony Tudor's *Dark Elegies*." *DRJ* 24, no. 2 (Fall 1992): 17-30. Ann Dils. Preface (pp. 17-18). John Giffin. "A Dance Director's Investigation into Selected Constitutive Properties of Antony Tudor's *Dark Elegies*" (pp. 19-24). Vera Maletic. "The Identity of Tudor's *Dark Elegies* as Mediated by Two Dance Companies and Two Technologies" (pp. 25-27). Ann Dils. "*Dark Elegies* and Gender" (pp. 28-30).

BEL: 75-77. DAV: 285-292. DEM/2: 191-203. FRA: 112-121. GRU/1: 52-57. GRU/2: 258-267. HAL: 200-219. HAS/2: 166-171. NOB: 166-180. SCH/1: see Index of Choreographers, p. 135.


**Tupine, Oleg** (1920– )
ATK: 159-162.


**Turbyfill, Mark** (1896?-1990)
Turbyfill, Mark. "Memoirs of a Poet-Dancer." Edited by Ann Barzel. *BR* 13, no. 1 (Spring 1985): 22-36.

———. *Ruth Page [and] Kreutzberg*. [Chicago?, 1934].


**Turner, Harold** (1909-1962)
DAV: 292-296.

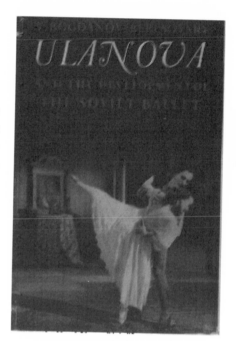

**Ulanova, Galina** (1910– )

Bogdanov-Beresovsky, V. *Ulanova and the Development of the Soviet Ballet*. Translated by Stephen Garry and Joan Lawson. Foreword by Cyril Beaumont. London: MacGibbon & Kee, 1952.

Brinson, Peter, ed. *Ulanova, Moiseyev & Zakharov on Soviet Ballet*. Translations by E. Fox and D. Fry. London: Society for Cultural Relations with the U.S.S.R., 1954.

Gould, Susan. "Talking with Galina Ulanova." *DS* 14, no. 3 (September 1980): 8-15.

Ilupina, Anna. *Ballerina: The Life and Work of Galina Ulanova*. Philadelphia: Provident Publishing Company, 1965.

Kahn, Albert E. *Days with Ulanova*. New York: Simon & Schuster, 1962.

Lvov-Anokhin, B. *Galina Ulanova*. Moscow: Foreign Languages Publishing House, 1956.

Nemenschousky, Léon. *A Day with Galina Ulanova*. Translated by Margaret McGregor. London: Cassell & Company, 1960.

Sizòva, M.I. *Ulanova: Her Childhood and Schooldays*. Translated by Marie Rambert. London: Adam & Charles Black, 1962.

**Ulanova, Galina** *(continued)*

"Ulanova, Galina (Sergeyevna)." *CBY 1958*: 443-445.

Ulanova, Galina. *Autobiographical Notes and Commentary on Soviet Ballet*. London: Soviet News, 1956. Includes an Appreciation of Ulanova by B. Lvov-Anokhin.

——. "Creating the Role of Juliet." *Harper's Magazine* 219, no. 1310 (July 1959): 40-41.

——. *The Making of a Ballerina*. Translated from the Russian by S. Rosenberg. Moscow: Foreign Languages Publishing House, 1956. CLA: 127-157. MON: 26-29. SLO: 81-85. SMA: 26-38.

**Uris, Victoria** (1949– )

Lobenthal, Joel. "Victoria Uris: Dancing for Paul Taylor." *BR* 15, no. 1 (Spring 1987): 26-37.

## Vaganova, Agrippina (1879-1951)

Vaganova, Agrippina. *Basic Principles of Classical Ballet: Russian Ballet Technique.* Translated from the Russian by Anatole Chujoy. New York: Dover Publications, [1969]. This Dover edition is an unabridged and unaltered republication of the second English edition published in 1953 by Adam & Charles Black, London. Incorporates all the material from the fourth Russian edition. Includes Vaganova's Sample Lesson with musical accompaniment, translated by John Barker. An Index has been added based on entries from the first edition, *Fundamentals of the Classic Dance: Russian Ballet Technique*, published in 1946 by Kamin Dance Publishers, New York. New York: Dover Publications, [1969].
SLO: 45-47.

## Valberkh, Ivan (1766-1819)
ROS: 34-38.

## van Dantzig, Rudi (1933– )

Utrecht, Luuk. *Rudi van Dantzig: A Controversial Idealist in Ballet.* Zutphen, The Netherlands: Walburg Pers, 1992.

van Dantzig, Rudi. "A Question of Values." In *Visions: Ballet and Its Future*, pp. 150-153. Edited by Michael Crabb. Essays from the International Dance Conference to commemorate the 25th anni-

**van Dantzig, Rudi** *(continued)*
versary of the National Ballet of Canada, held at the Town Hall,
St. Lawrence Centre for the Arts, Toronto, November 15-16, 1976.
Foreword by Sir Frederick Ashton. Introduction by Vincent
Tovell. Toronto: Simon & Pierre, c. 1978.

**van Hamel, Martine** (1945– )
"van Hamel, Martine." *CBY 1979*: 415-418.
LYL: 10-20. MON: 84-87. PET: 198-213.

**van Praagh, Peggy** (1910-1990)
Sexton, Christopher. *Peggy van Praagh: A Life of Dance*. Melbourne:
Macmillan, 1985.
van Praagh, Peggy. *How I Became a Ballet Dancer*. London: Thomas
Nelson and Sons, 1954.
———, and Peter Brinson. *The Choreographic Art: An Outline of its
Principles and Craft*. London: Adam & Charles Black, 1963.

**Van Tuyl, Marian** (1907-1987)
Morgan, Barbara. "Testimony to Marian Van Tuyl Campbell." *DRA
VI* (1972): 169-172.

**Vasiliev, Vladimir** (1940– )
Kisselgoff, Anna, text, with photography by Mira. *Vladimir Vasiliev*.
Dance Horizons Spotlight Series. Brooklyn, N.Y.: Dance Hori-
zons, 1975.
BLA: 148-151. DEM/1: 203-209. GRE/1: 12-13. SMA: 322-331.
ZHD: 12-59.

**Vazem, Yekaterina** (1848-1937)
Vazem, Yekaterina. "Memoirs of a Ballerina of the St. Petersburg
Bolshoi Theatre." Translated by Nina Dimitrievitch, with a
preliminary note by Clement Crisp. Part One; Part Two; Part
Three; and Part Four. *DR* 3, no. 2 (Autumn 1985): 3-22; *DR* 4, no.
1 (Spring 1986): 3-28; *DR* 5, no. 1 (Spring 1987): 21-41; and *DR*
6, no. 2 (Autumn 1988): 30-47.
WIL: 279-290.

**Vazquez, Roland** (1927– )
SID: 193-199.

**Verdy, Violette** (1933– )
Haggin, B.H., text, with photography by Martha Swope. *Violette Verdy*. Dance Horizons Spotlight Series. Brooklyn, N.Y.: Dance Horizons, 1975.
Huckenpahler, Victoria. *Ballerina: A Biography of Violette Verdy*. New York & Basel: Marcel Dekker, 1978.
Marks, Marcia. "Violette: 'Because She Is So Modest.'" *Dance Magazine* 46, no. 2 (February 1972): 47-62. A Dance Magazine Portfolio.
"The Paris Opéra: A Conversation with Violette Verdy." *BR* 14, no. 3 (Fall 1986): 23-30. Violette Verdy was interviewed by Francis Mason on 2 October 1986.
Rudin, Seymour. "Conversation with Violette Verdy." *YDR* Issue #6 (Spring 1977): 9-15.
"Verdy, Violette." *CBY 1969*: 437-439.
"Verdy, Violette." *CBY 1980*: 414-417.
GRE/3: 18-19. GRU/2: 304-311. LYL: 60-70. MAS: 423-430. TRA: 134-141.

**Vernon, Barbara** (1918– ; called **"Brangwen"**)
Gregory, John, comp. and ed. *Brangwen: The Poet and the Dancer*. A story based on letters from the Poet Laureate John Masefield to a young ballerina during World War II. Buffalo, N.Y.: Prometheus Books, 1989. First published in England by the Book Guild, 1988.

**Vestris, Auguste** (1760-1842)
Chapman, John V. "Auguste Vestris and the Expansion of Technique." *DRJ* 19, no. 1 (Summer 1987): 11-18.
BLA: 98-99.

**Vestris, Gaetano** (1728-1808)
BLA: 97. MOO/1: 57-64.

**Vestris, Thérèse** (1726-1808)
MIG: 46-49.

**Viganò, Salvatore** (1769-1821)
Terzian, Elizabeth. "Salvatore Viganò: His Ballets at the Teatro La Scala (1811-1821), The Attitudes of His Contemporaries." In *Society of Dance History Scholars Proceedings*, pp. 38-44. Tenth Annual Conference, University of California, Irvine, 13-15 February 1987.
MOO/1: 65-73.

**Villella, Edward** (1936– )
The Cadet Fine Arts Forum, U.S. Military Academy, West Point, New York. *Edward Villella: American Dancer*, catalogue of the exhibition, Class of 1929 Gallery, Eisenhower Hall, May 2-28, 1982. Includes an essay, "Edward Villella: A Man and His Roles," by Arlene Croce, which also appears in her collection of writings, *Sight Lines*, pp. 325-329. New York: Knopf, 1987.

Croce, Arlene. [Edward Villella, two-part profile]. "Slower is Faster." *The New Yorker* 64, no. 40 (November 21, 1988): 59-60, 62-70, 72, 74-78, 82-93; "The Prodigal." *The New Yorker* 64, no. 41 (November 28, 1988): 42-46, 49-60, 64-66.

Kotlowitz, Robert. "1962: The Year of Edward Villella." *Show* 2, no. 1 (January 1962): 54-55.

Shapiro, Brett. "One Ballet Dancer: Edward Villella." *DS* 15, no. 1 (March 1981): 52-57.

"Villella, Edward." *CBY 1965*: 434-436.

Villella, Edward, with Larry Kaplan. *Prodigal Son: Dancing for*

**Villella, Edward** *(continued)*
*Balanchine in a World of Pain and Magic.* New York: Simon & Schuster, 1992.
BLA: 137-139. COH/1: 38-48. GRE/3: 14-15. GRU/2: 295-303. MAS: 249-254.

**Vilzak, Anatole** (1898– )
NEW/1: 12-21.

**Vladimiroff, Pierre** (1893-1970)
SMA: 300-305.

**Vladimirov, Yuri** (1942– )
DEM/1: 210-214. ZHD: 186-217.

**Volinine, Alexander** (1882-1955)
Volinine, Alexandre, in collaboration with A.R. Pirie. "My Dance of Life." Part One; Part Two; and Part Three. *The Dance Magazine* 13, no. 3 (January 1930): 20-21, 56-57; *The Dance Magazine* 13, no. 4 (February 1930): 16-17, 58; and *The Dance Magazine* 13, no. 5 (March 1930): 34-35, 55.
PAG: 40-44.

**Volkoff, Boris** (1902-1974)
Collier, Cliff. "Years of Achievement: Time for Respect." *YDR* Issue #3 (Winter 1974): 22-25.
Mitchell, Lillian Leonora. "Boris Volkoff: Dancer, Teacher, Choreographer." Unpublished dissertation, Texas Woman's University, 1982. Ann Arbor, Mich.: University Microfilms International, 1983. Order No. 831,2285. DAI 44-01A, p. 0257.
Tatarnic, Joseph. "Boris Volkoff Memorial Exhibition." *YDR* Issue #4 (Spring 1975): 33-38.

**Volkova, Vera** (1904-1975)
Arkell, David. "Going Back." In his *Ententes Cordiales: The French in London & Other Adventures*, pp. 79-81. Manchester, England: Carcanet Press, 1989.

**Vollmar, Jocelyn** (1925– )
ATK: 163-165.

**von Aroldingen, Karin** (1941– )
"Aroldingen, Karin von." *CBY 1983*: 19-21.
GRE/3: 15-16. GRU/2: 344-348. MAS: 495-503. TRA: 168-175.

**Vyroubova, Nina** (1921– )
SWI/2: 61-66.

**Wagoner, Dan** (1932– )
KRE: 24-39.

**Walczak, Barbara** (1940– )
MAS: 255-262.

**Wall, David** (1946– )
Todd, Arthur, text, with photography
by Anthony Crickmay. *David Wall.*
Dance Horizons Spotlight Series.
Brooklyn, N.Y.: Dance Horizons,
1976.
NEW/1: 364-379.

**Waring, James** (1922-1975)
Chin, Daryl. "Remembering James Waring." *DS* 10, no. 2 (Spring/
Summer 1976): 10-18.
Vaughan, David. "James Waring: A Remembrance." *PAJ* 5, no. 2/
Issue #14 [c. 1981]: 108-111.
——. "Remembering James Waring." *BR* 5, no. 4 (1975-1976):
102-107.
Waring, James. "Five Essays on Dancing." *BR* 2, no. 1 (1967):
65-77. The essays are (1) Alexandra Danilova and Other Unself-
ish Dancers. (2) Gracie Allen and the Wheel of Life. (3) Why I

**Waring, James** *(continued)*
Like the Rockettes, or, *Coppélia* Revisited. (4) Dance Journal. (5)
Meaning in Dance, or Dance vs. Drama.
———. "My Work." *BR* 5, no. 4 (1975-1976): 108-113.
———. *"Nights at the Tango Palace." PAJ* 5, no. 2/Issue #14 [c.
1981]: 112-122. The text of a play.
MCD: 241-258.

**Waters, Elizabeth** (1910?-1993)
Adler-Friess, Aanya. "Three Grand Ladies of Modern Dance: Eve
Gentry, Eleanor King and Elizabeth Waters." In *Society of Dance
History Scholars Proceedings*, pp. 147-155. Eighth Annual Con-
ference, University of New Mexico, 15-17 February 1985.

**Waters, Flavia** (1902?-1992)
Champe, Flavia Waters. *Innocents on Broadway*. Lincoln, Neb.:
Media Publishing & Marketing, 1987.

**Watts, Heather** (1953– )
Croce, Arlene. "Dimming the Lights." *The New Yorker* 64, no. 3
(March 7, 1988): 119-122. Portion on Watts, pp. 121-122.
Swift, Edward. "A Conversation with Heather Watts." *BR* 13, no. 1
(Spring 1985): 37-43.
"Watts, Heather." *CBY 1983*: 430-433.
GRU/1: 31-40.

**Wayne, Dennis** (1945– )
GRU/2: 394-398.

**Weaver, John** (1673-1760)
Chatwin, Amina, and Philip J.S. Richardson. "The Father of English
Ballet: John Weaver (1673-1760)." In *The Ballet Annual 1961: A
Record and Year Book of the Ballet*, pp. 60-64. Edited by Arnold
L. Haskell and Mary Clarke. Fifteenth Issue. New York: Mac-
millan, 1960.
Cohen, Selma Jeanne. "John Weaver." In *Famed for Dance: Essays
on the Theory and Practice of Theatrical Dancing in England,
1660-1740*, pp. 49-58, by Ifan Kyrle Fletcher, Selma Jeanne

**Weaver, John** *(continued)*

Cohen, and Roger Lonsdale. New York: The New York Public Library, 1969; reprinted from the *Bulletin of The New York Public Library*, June, November 1959; January, February, May 1960.

Martin, Jennifer Kaye Lowe. "The English Dancing Master, 1660-1728: His Role at Court, in Society, and on the Public Stage." Unpublished dissertation, University of Michigan, 1977. Ann Arbor, Mich.: University Microfilms International, 1977. Order No. 77-18,074. DAI 38-03A, p. 1127.

Ralph, Richard. *The Life and Works of John Weaver*. New York: Dance Horizons, 1985. An account of his life, writings, and theatrical productions, with an annotated reprint of his complete publications.

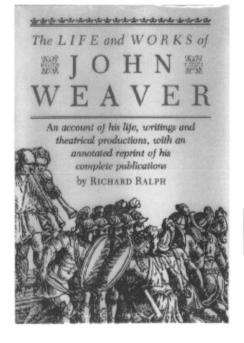

**Webster, Clara** (1821-1844)

Guest, Ivor. *Victorian Ballet-Girl: The Tragic Story of Clara Webster*. London: Adam & Charles Black, 1957; reprint New York: Da Capo Press, 1980.
GUE: 29-31.

**Weidman, Charles** (1901-1975)

Becker, Svea, and Joenine Roberts. "A Reaffirmation of the Humphrey-Weidman Quality." *DNJ* 1, no. 1 (January 1983): 3-17.

King, Eleanor. *Transformations: The Humphrey-Weidman Era*. New York: Dance Horizons, 1978.

Kriegsman, Sali Ann. *Modern Dance in America: The Bennington Years*. Boston: G.K. Hall & Co., 1981.

Manasevit, Shirley D. "A Last Interview with Charles Weidman." *DS* 10, no. 1 (Fall/Winter 1975-76): 32-40, 45-50.

Martin, John, with photography by Thomas Bouchard. "Days of Divine Indiscipline." *DP* 12 (Autumn 1961).

Richards, Sylvia Pelt. "A Biography of Charles Weidman with

**Weidman, Charles** *(continued)*
Emphasis Upon His Professional Career and His Contributions to the Field of Dance." Unpublished dissertation, Texas Woman's University, 1972. On file, but not available from UMI. Order No. 02-33,463. ADD X1972, p. 0213.

Sherman, Jane. "Charles Weidman at Denishawn." *BR* 13, no. 3 (Fall 1985): 73-82.

Smith, A. William. "*Flickers*: A Fifty-Year Old 'Flicker' of the Weidman Tradition." In *Proceedings of the Conference "Dance Reconstructed: Modern Dance Art Past, Present, Future,"* pp. 245-261. Rutgers University, New Brunswick, New Jersey, October 16 and 17, 1992.

"Weidman, Charles." *CBY 1942*: 398-400.

Wynne, David W. "Three Years with Charles Weidman." *DP* 60 (Winter 1974).

BRO: 65-69. LLO: 76-131. MAR: 227-240. MOO/1: 287-297. PAL: 75-84. ROG: 10-24. SCH/1: see Index of Choreographers, p. 135. SOR/1: 264-267. TER: 114-120.

**Weiss, Robert** (1949– )
MAS: 513-521.

**Weller, Dawn** (1947– )
Allyn, Jane. *Dawn Weller: Portrait of a Ballerina.* Johannesburg: Macmillan South Africa, 1984.

**Wells, Bruce** (1950– )
GRE/3: 22-23.

**Weslow, William** (1925– )
MAS: 315-324. SID: 201-208.

**West, Elizabeth** (1927-1962)
Massie, Annette. "Elizabeth West and Western Theatre Ballet." *DR* 6, no. 1 (Spring 1988): 45-58.

**Wheeldon, Christopher** (1973– )
Whitaker, Rick. "A Conversation with Christopher Wheeldon." *BR* 23, no. 1 (Spring 1995): 75-86.

**Whitman, Sylvia** (195?– )
Whitman, Sylvia, and Susan Weil. *Two Notebooks: Sylvia Whitman/ Dancer [&] Susan Weil/Painter.* Captiva Island, Fla.: Untitled Press, n.d.

**Wiener, Nina** (1948– )
Daniels, Don. "Boutique Items and Risky Business: Cunningham, Wiener, Peters, Tomasson." *BR* 13, no. 2 (Summer 1985): 39-56.

**Wiesenthal, Grete** (1885-1970)
CAF: 244-254.

**Wigman, Mary** (1886-1973)
Howe, Dianne Shelden. "Manifestations of the German Expressionist Aesthetic as Presented in Drama and Art in the Dance and Writings of Mary Wigman." Unpublished dissertation, University of Wisconsin-Madison, 1985. Ann Arbor, Mich.: University Microfilms International, 1985. Order No. 851,2305. DAI 46-07A, p. 1762.

——. "The Notion of Mysticism in the Philosophy and Choreography of Mary Wigman 1914-1931." *DRJ* 19, no. 1 (Summer 1987): 19-24.

——. "Parallel Visions: Mary Wigman and the German Expressionists." In *Dance: Current Selected Research*, Volume 1, pp. 77-88. Edited by Lynnette Y. Overby and James H. Humphrey. New York: AMS Press, 1989.

Maletic, Vera. "Wigman and Laban: The Interplay of Theory and Practice." *BR* 14, no. 3 (Fall 1986): 86-95.

Manning, Susan Allene. "Body Politic: The Dances of Mary Wigman." Unpublished dissertation, Columbia University, New York, New York, 1987. Ann Arbor, Mich.: University Microfilms International, 1988. Order No. 880-9388. DAI 49-07A, p. 1623.

——. *Ecstasy and the Demon: Feminism and Nationalism in the Dances of Mary Wigman.* Berkeley, Los Angeles, London: University of California Press, 1993.

——. "From Modernism to Fascism: The Evolution of Wigman's Choreography." *BR* 14, no. 4 (Winter 1987): 87-98.

**Wigman, Mary** *(continued)*

Müller, Hedwig. "Wigman and National Socialism." *BR* 15, no. 1 (Spring 1987): 65-73.

Odom, Maggie. "Mary Wigman: The Early Years, 1913-1925." *TDR* 24, no. 4/T-88 (December 1980): 81-92.

Odom, Selma Landen. "Wigman at Hellerau." *BR* 14, no. 2 (Summer 1986): 41-53.

Scheyer, Ernst. "The Shapes of Space: The Art of Mary Wigman and Oskar Schlemmer." *DP* 41 (Spring 1970).

Toepfer, Karl. "Speech and Sexual Difference in Mary Wigman's Dance Aesthetic." In Laurence Senelick's *Gender in Performance: The Presentation of Difference in the Performing Arts*, pp. 260-278. Hanover, N.H. & London: University Press of New England for Tufts University, 1992.

"Wigman, Mary." *CBY 1969*: 448-451.

Wigman, Mary. *The Language of Dance*. Translated by Walter Sorell. Middletown, Conn.: Wesleyan University Press, 1966.

————. *The Mary Wigman Book*. Edited and translated by Walter Sorell. Middletown, Conn.: Wesleyan University Press, 1975.

BRO: 33-40. HUR: 39-46. LLO: 11-21. MAY/2: 25-30. PAG: 84-95. SOR/1: 182-191.

**Wilde, Patricia** (1928– )

"Wilde, Patricia." *CBY 1968*: 432-435.

GRU/2: 91-98. MAS: 325-333.

**Wilder, Valerie** (1947– )

SID: 209-220.

**Williams, Stanley** (1925– )
MAS: 399-401.

**Wilson, Edward** (1929– )
MAS: 311-313.

**Wilson, Sallie** (1932– )
GRU/2: 244-253.

**Woetzel, Damian** (1967– )
Kornbluth, Jesse. "Damian Woetzel." *The New York Times Magazine*
June 11, 1995, pp. 32-35.

**Wong, Mel** (1938– )
KRE: 72-93.

**Wright, Rebecca** (1947– )
GRU/2: 390-393.

**Wyman, Anna** (1928– )
Price, Kenneth. "Anna Wyman's Star Rises in the West." *YDR* Issue
#3 (Winter 1974): 10-15.

**Yermolayev, Alexei** (1910-1975)
SLO: 101-103, 105-106. SMA: 306-312.

**Youskevitch, Igor** (1912-1994)
Barker, Barbara. "Celebrating Youskevitch." *BR* 11, no. 3 (Fall 1983): 27-29.

Gruen, John. "The Dancer as Legend: Igor Youskevitch." Parts One and Two. *Dance Magazine* 56, no. 3 (March 1982): 52-59 and *Dance Magazine* 56, no. 5 (May 1982): 52-54, 56-58.

Hunt, Marilyn. "Igor Youskevitch Dancing." *BR* 11, no. 3 (Fall 1983): 32-63. A portfolio of photographs with a brief introduction by Marilyn Hunt.

Quiros, Rod. *Igor Youskevitch*. Chicago: Dance Press, 1956.

University of Texas at Austin, College of Fine Arts, Department of Drama. *Golden Gala: A Tribute to Igor Youskevitch*, March 28, 1982. Souvenir program.

"Youskevitch, Igor." *CBY 1956*: 661-663.

Youskevitch, Igor. "Masculinity in Dance." *BR* 9, no. 3 (Fall 1981): 90-91.

ATK: 166-169. COH/1: 12-23. MAS: 297-302. MUI: 127-132. NEW/1: 44-59.

# Z

**Zalewski, Jan** (1880?– )
PAG: 4-11.

**Zambelli, Carlotta** (1875-1968)
Guest, Ivor. "Carlotta Zambelli." Part One and Part Two. *Dance Magazine* 48, no. 2 (February 1974): 51-66 and *Dance Magazine* 48, no. 3 (March 1974): 43-58. Originally published in French by the Société d'Histoire du Théâtre, Paris, 1969. Both parts are Dance Magazine Portfolios.
———. "Carlotta Zambelli: La Grande Mademoiselle de la Danse Française." In *The Ballet Annual 1958: A Record and Year Book of the Ballet*, pp. 68-77. Edited by Arnold L. Haskell. Twelfth Issue. New York: Macmillan, 1957.

**Zamir, Batya** (194?– )
Carroll, Noël. "Air Dancing." *TDR* 19, no. 1/T-65 (March 1975): 5-12.

**Zane, Arnie** (1940-1988)
Zimmer, Elizabeth, and Susan Quasha, eds. *Body Against Body: The Dance and Other Collaborations of Bill T. Jones & Arnie Zane.* Barrytown, N.Y.: Station Hill Press, 1989.
KRE: 110-111, 113-115, 130, 133.

**Zaraspe, Hector** (1931– )
GAL: 59-67.

**Zeglovsky, Valentin** (1908– )
Zeglovsky, Valentin. *Ballet Crusade*. Melbourne & Adeline: Reed & Harris, 1945.

**Zelensky, Igor** (1969– )
Mason, Francis. "Igor Zelensky." *BR* 20, no. 1 (Spring 1992): 16-18.

**Zemach, Benjamin** (1901– )
Prevots, Naima. "Benjamin Zemach: Social Content." In *Society of Dance History Scholars Proceedings*, pp. 166-175. Eighth Annual Conference, University of New Mexico, 15-17 February 1985. PRE: 197-218.

**Zide, Rochelle** (1938– )
Zide-Booth, Rochelle. "Dancing for Joffrey." *DC* 12, no. 1 (1989): 48-104.

**Zorina, Vera** (1917– )
"Zorina, Vera." *CBY 1941*: 946-947.
Zorina, Vera. *Zorina*. New York: Farrar Straus & Giroux, 1986.
GRU/2: 59-66.

**Zoritch, George** (1919– )
ATK: 170-172.

**Zucchi, Virginia** (1849-1930)
Benois, Alexandre. "The Divine Zucchi." Chapter 7 in his *Reminiscences of the Russian Ballet*, pp. 73-98. Translated by Mary Britnieva. London: Putnam, 1941; reprint New York: Da Capo Press, 1977.
Guest, Ivor. *The Divine Virginia: A Biography of Virginia Zucchi*. New York & Basel: Marcel Dekker, 1977.
GUE: 100-103.

# SELECTED REFERENCE WORKS

**DICTIONARIES**

Bremser, Martha, ed. *International Dictionary of Ballet*. Larraine Nicholas, asst. ed. Leanda Shrimpton, picture ed. 2 Volumes. Vol. 1: A-K. Vol. 2: L-Z. Detroit, London, Washington, D.C.: St. James Press, 1993.

Chujoy, Anatole, comp. and ed. *The Dance Encyclopedia*. New York: A.S. Barnes and Company, 1949.

——, and P. W. Manchester, comps. and eds. *The Dance Encyclopedia*. rev. and enl. ed. New York: Simon & Schuster, 1967.

Clarke, Mary, and David Vaughan, eds. *The Encyclopedia of Dance & Ballet*. London: Pitman Publishing, 1977.

Cohen-Stratyner, Barbara Naomi. *Biographical Dictionary of Dance*. New York: Schirmer Books, 1982.

Crosland, Margaret. *Ballet Lovers' Dictionary*. London: Arco Publications, 1962.

Gadan, Francis, and Robert Maillard, general eds.; Selma Jeanne Cohen, American ed. *Dictionary of Modern Ballet*. Translated from the French by John Montague and Peggie Cochrane. New York: Tudor Publishing Company, 1959.

Koegler, Horst. *The Concise Oxford Dictionary of Ballet*. London & New York: Oxford University Press, 1977; 2d ed., [corrected], 1982; 2d ed., updated, 1987.

Officer, Jill. *The Encyclopedia of Theatre Dance in Canada.* Toronto: Dance Collection Danse, 1989. Published on nine floppy diskettes (5 ¼" or 3.5") which will run on the IBM PC or compatible computers with minimum 256K RAM, MS DOS 3.0 or higher. For the Macintosh Plus or higher the Encyclopedia is published on five 3.5" floppy diskettes. Length equivalent to 670 printed pages.

Raffé, W.G., assisted by M.E. Purdon. *Dictionary of the Dance.* New York: A.S. Barnes and Company; London: Thomas Yoseloff, 1964.

Wilson, G.B.L. *A Dictionary of Ballet.* Harmondsworth, Middlesex & Baltimore, Md.: Penguin Books, 1957; completely rev. ed. London: Cassell & Company, 1961; 3d ed. rev. and enl. New York: Theatre Arts Books, 1974.

## INDEXES

*Attitudes & Arabesques.* Leslie Getz, comp. and ed. Producer: Mid-Peninsula Dance Guild/A CAPA Affiliate, Cultural Center, 1313 Newell Road, Palo Alto, CA 94303. Vol. 1, no. 1- ; May 1980- .

Belknap, S. Yancey, comp. and ed. *Guide to Dance Periodicals, 1931-1962.* 10 vols. Gainesville, [Fla.]: University of Florida Press, 1955 (vol. 5, 1951-1952), 1956 (vol. 6, 1953-1954), 1958 (vol. 7, 1955-1956), 1959 (vol. 1, 1931-1935); New York: Dance and Music Archives, c. 1950 (vol. 2, 1936-1940, c. 1951 (vol. 4, 1946-1950); Ashville, N.C.: The Stephens Press, 1948 (vol. 3, 1941-1945); New York: Scarecrow Press, 1960 (vol. 8, 1957-1958), 1962 (vol. 9, 1959-1960), 1963 (vol. 10, 1961-1962).

*Dance Abstracts and Index 1989: English-Language Publications in the United States.* Elsie Ivancich Dunin, senior comp. and ed. Producer: Dance Database Project, Dance Department, University of California at Los Angeles, Los Angeles, CA 90024. Continued as *Dance Abstracts and Index 1990: English-Language Publications in the United States and Canada.* Elsie Ivancich Dunin, senior comp. and ed. Producer: Dance Database Project, Dance Department, University of California at Los Angeles, Los Angeles, CA 90024.

*Dance: Current Awareness Bulletin.* Producer: National Resource Centre for Dance, University of Surrey, Guildford, Surrey GU2 5XH,
England. 1983- .

*Index to Dance Periodicals.* Producer: 866 Third Avenue, New York,
NY 10022. 1991- .

*Readers' Guide to Periodical Literature.* New York: The H.W. Wilson
Company, 1905- . Has indexed *Dance Magazine* from Vol. 27, no.
1 (January 1953).

Sharp, Harold S., and Marjorie Z. Sharp. *Index to Characters in the
Performing Arts.* Part III - Ballet. A - Z and Symbols. Metuchen,
N.J.: Scarecrow Press, 1972.

Studwell, William E., and David A. Hamilton. *Ballet Plot Index: A
Guide to Locating Plots and Descriptions of Ballets and Associated
Material.* New York & London: Garland Publishing, 1987.

NOTE: In addition to these specialized dance indexes, there are a
number of standard indexes which incorporate dance material:
*Humanities Index, Music Index,* and *British Humanities Index.*
On-line bibliographic data bases which should not be overlooked
as sources of dance material are RLIN, OCLC, and DIALOG's
RILM and RILA. For an overview of dance-related data bases see
Tricia Henry's article, "The Joy of Modem: Computer Access to
Resources in Dance" (*DRJ* 26, no. 1, Spring 1994: 56-58).

## BIBLIOGRAPHIES

Adamczyk, Alice J. *Black Dance: An Annotated Bibliography.* New
York & London: Garland Publishing, 1989.

*Arts in America: A Bibliography.* Bernard Karpel, ed. Vol. 3, Chapter
17, Section Q on "Dance" by Genevieve Oswald. Washington,
D.C.: Smithsonian Institution Press, 1979.

Beaumont, Cyril W. *A Bibliography of Dancing.* London: Dancing
Times, 1929; reprint New York: Benjamin Blom/Holland Press,
1963.

Benson-Talley, Lois. "Annual International Bibliography of Dance
History: The Western Tradition. Works Published in 1979." Part

III. *Dance Research Journal* 17, no. 1 (Spring-Summer 1985): 43-51.

Derra de Moroda, Friderica. *The Dance Library: A Catalogue*. Edited from the Manuscript left by the Author by Sibylle Dahms and Lotte Rothe-Wölfle. Munich: Robert Wölfle, 1982.

Fleshman, Bob, ed. *Theatrical Movement: A Bibliographical Anthology*. Metuchen, N.J. & London: Scarecrow Press, 1986.

Forbes, Fred R., Jr. *Dance: An Annotated Bibliography 1965-1982*. New York & London: Garland Publishing, 1986.

Forrester, F.S. *Ballet in England: A Bibliography and Survey, c. 1700 - June 1966*. Foreword by Ivor Guest. Library Association Bibliographies, No. 9. London: Library Association, 1968.

Hodgens, Pauline. *Dance: A Selected and Annotated Bibliography of Philosophical Readings in Art, Aesthetics and Criticism*. Surrey, England: National Resource Centre for Dance, 1985.

Kahn, Marion-Clare, comp., and Susan Au, ed. "Balanchine: A Selected Bibliography." Parts One and Two. *Ballet Review* 11, no. 2 (Summer 1983): 9-11 and *Ballet Review* 11, no. 3 (Fall 1983): 97-99.

Kaprelian, Mary H. *Aesthetics for Dancers: A Selected Annotated Bibliography*. Washington, D.C.: National Dance Association, 1976.

Leslie, Serge. *A Bibliography of the Dance Collection of Doris Niles & Serge Leslie*. Parts 1-4. Edited by Cyril Beaumont (Parts 1-3). Part 1: A-K. Part 2: L-Z. Part 3: A-Z (Mainly 20th-Century Publications). Part 4: A-Z (Mainly 20th-Century Publications). London: C.W. Beaumont (Parts 1-3), 1966, 1968, 1974. London: Dance Books (Part 4), 1981. Part 4 contains a valuable listing of Cyril Beaumont's articles, of which there are approximately 250, published between 1925 and 1975.

Magriel, Paul David. *A Bibliography of Dancing*. A List of Books and Articles on the Dance and Related Subjects. New York: H.W.

Wilson Company, 1936; Fourth Cumulated Supplement 1936-1940, New York: H.W. Wilson Company, 1941.

——. "Bibliography of Isadora Duncan: A List of References in American Libraries." *Bulletin of Bibliography* 16, no. 9 (May-August 1939): 173-175.

National Diet Library. *Catalog of the Ashihara Collection in the National Diet Library. Books in European Languages,* Vol. 1. Tokyo: National Diet Library, 1982.

Oswald, Genevieve. "Dance." Vol. 3, Chapter 17, Section Q in *Arts in America: A Bibliography.* Bernard Karpel, ed. Washington, D.C.: Smithsonian Institution Press, 1979.

Palfy, Barbara. "The Published Writings of Selma Jeanne Cohen." *DC* 18, no. 2 (1995): 319-332.

Russo, W. "Sergei Diaghilev and the Ballets Russes: A Bibliography." *Bulletin of Bibliography* 35, no. 2 (April-June 1978): 88-91.

Ruyter, Nancy Chalfa, comp. "Annual International Bibliography of Dance History: The Western Tradition. Works Published in 1978." Parts I and II. *Dance Research Journal* 12, no. 2 (Spring-Summer 1980): 23-30 and *Dance Research Journal* 16, no. 1 (Spring 1984): 41-49.

Wenig, Adele R. *Pearl Primus: An Annotated Bibliography of Sources from 1943 to 1975.* Oakland, Calif.: Wenadance Unlimited, 1983.

Wynne, Peter. *Judson Dance: An Annotated Bibliography of the Judson Dance Theater and of Five Major Choreographers—Trisha Brown, Lucinda Childs, Deborah Hay, Steve Paxton, and Yvonne Rainer.* Englewood, N.J.: author, May 1978.

## DANCE COLLECTION, THE NEW YORK PUBLIC LIBRARY, REFERENCES

*Bibliographic Guide to Dance.* 1975- Boston: G.K. Hall, 1975- 28 cm. Annual. "*Bibliographic Guide to Dance* serves as an annual supplement to the *Dictionary Catalog of the Dance Collection,* Performing Arts Research Center, The Research Libraries of The

New York Public Library . . .". –cf. Introd., 1975. Includes works in many languages and various forms (e.g., motion pictures, videotapes, photographs, etc.) cataloged by the Dance Collection of The New York Public Library.

*Dance on Disc* [computer file]: the complete catalog of the Dance Collection of The New York Public Library on CD ROM. [Boston]: G.K. Hall & Co., c1992- 1 computer laser optical disk; 4-3/4 in. + 1 user's manual. Annual. System requirements: IBM PC or compatible; 640K; MS DOS CD ROM Extensions (MSCDEX) Version 2.0 or higher; 1 compact disk drive. Represents a cumulation of the ten-volume *Dictionary Catalog of the Dance Collection* (G.K. Hall, 1974) with the seventeen supplements that have been published as the annual *Bibliographic Guide to Dance* (G.K. Hall, 1975- ). The bibliographic file contains approximately 189,000 records representing the entire Dance Collection holdings covering all aspects of dance, in various languages and in all media. Also includes the Dance Collection authority file of 153,000 names, dance titles, and subjects, with cross- references and first performance history notes. Indexed by author, title, subjects, names, material type, item number, LC card number, ISBN, NYPL local call number, language, country and date of publication, publisher, physical description, series, source (host item for indexed articles), and keyword.

*Dictionary Catalog of the Dance Collection.* 10 v. A list of authors, titles, and subjects of multi-media materials in the Dance Collection of the Performing Arts Research Center of The New York Public Library. [New York] The New York Public Library, Astor, Lenox and Tilden Foundations & G.K. Hall & Co., Boston, 1974. 10 v. col. front. 29 cm. "This catalog . . . consists of bibliographic data for materials cataloged prior to October 1, 1973. It contains approximately 300,000 entries representing 96,000 cataloged items."

*Index to Dance Periodicals.* Dance Collection, The New York Public Library for the Performing Arts. Boston: G.K. Hall & Co., c1992- v. ; 29 cm. Annual. Taken from: New York Public Library. Dance Collection. *Dictionary Catalog of the Dance Collection*, and: New York Public Library. Dance Collection. *Bibliographic Guide to Dance.*

## CHRONOLOGIES & LISTS OF WORKS

*Choreography by George Balanchine: A Catalogue of Works.* Project directors: Leslie George Katz, Nancy Lassalle, and Harvey Simmonds. New York: Eakins Press Foundation, 1983; trade edition, with addenda, New York: Viking, 1984.

Cohen, Selma Jeanne, and A.J. Pischl. "The American Ballet Theatre: 1940-1960." *Dance Perspectives* 6 (1960).

*George Balanchine: A Reference Guide, 1987.* New York: Ballet Society, July 1987. This reference guide is intended to supplement *Choreography by George Balanchine: A Catalogue of Works* by updating the bibliography and the listings of stagings and telecasts, and to broaden its scope by including information on photographers and addresses of sources.

Reynolds, Nancy. *Repertory in Review: 40 Years of the New York City Ballet.* Introduction by Lincoln Kirstein. New York: Dial Press, 1977.

Schlundt, Christena L. *Dance in the Musical Theatre: Jerome Robbins and His Peers, 1934-1965.* New York & London: Garland Publishing, 1989. A joint publication with The New York Public Library. Error on cover: read 1934 for 1943.

———. *The Professional Appearances of Ruth St. Denis & Ted Shawn: A Chronology and an Index of Dances 1906-1932.* New York: The New York Public Library, 1962.

———. *The Professional Appearances of Ted Shawn and His Men Dancers: A Chronology and an Index of Dances 1933-1940.* New York: The New York Public Library, 1967.

———. *Tamiris: A Chronicle of Her Dance Career 1927-1955.* New York: The New York Public Library, 1972; reprinted in *Studies in Dance History* 1, no. 1 (Fall-Winter 1989-90): 65-154.

## RESOURCES FOR DANCE RESEARCH

Adshead-Lansdale, Janet, and June Layson, eds. *Dance History: An Introduction.* 2d ed., rev. and updated. London & New York:

Routledge, 1994. First published as *Dance History: A Methodology for Study* by Dance Books, London, 1983.

*The Art of Terpsichore: From Renaissance Festivals to Romantic Ballets.* Catalogue of an Exhibition Held at Brigham Young University, February 10-13, 1994. Books and Prints Selected and Described by Madison U. Sowell. Introduction by Debra H. Sowell. Provo, Utah: Friends of the Brigham Young University Library, 1994. *Friends of the Brigham Young University Library Newsletter*, No. 44 (1994).

Bellingham, Susan, comp. *A Catalogue of the Dance Collection in the Doris Lewis Rare Book Room, University of Waterloo Library.* 2d ed., rev. and enl. University of Waterloo Bibliographies, No. 10. Waterloo, Ontario: University of Waterloo, 1983.

Bopp, Mary S. *Research in Dance: A Guide to Resources.* Foreword by Genevieve Oswald. New York & Toronto: G.K. Hall & Co., 1993.

Brennan, Mary Alice, ed. *Research in Dance III.* Reston, Va.: National Dance Association; American Alliance for Health, Physical Education, Recreation and Dance, 1982.

Brinson, Peter. *Background to European Ballet: A Notebook from its Archives.* European Aspects. Foreword by Mary Skeaping. Leyden: A.W. Sijthoff, 1966.

Bryan, George B., comp. *Stage Lives: A Bibliography and Index to Theatrical Biographies in English.* Westport, Conn.: Greenwood Press, 1985.

Cohen-Stratyner, Naomi, ed. *Performing Arts Resources.* [No. 1- ]. New York: Theatre Library Association, 1975- .

Collier, Clifford, and Pierre Guilmette. *Dance Resources in Canadian Libraries.* Research Collections in Canadian Libraries, Special Studies 8. Ottawa: Resources Survey Division, Collections Development Branch, 1982. Bilingual: English/French.

Committee on Research in Dance. *Dance International: A Directory of Dance Research Scholars and Affiliates.* Compiled by Marilyn

Basler, Romanie Kramoris, and Mary Sandy. New York: CORD, 1978.

*Completed Research in Health, Physical Education, Recreation and Dance.* [No. 1- ]. Reston, Va.: American Alliance for Health, Physical Education, Recreation and Dance, 1981- . Annual.

Congress on Research in Dance. *Scholars Directory 1993.* [Brockport, N.Y.: CORD, 1993].

Dienes, Gedeon P. *European Dance Research Information Network (EDRIN): A Directory.* Budapest: Aesculart Publisher, 1992.

*Directory of Performing Arts Collections in Greater Los Angeles.* Los Angeles: Performing Arts Libraries Network of Greater Los Angeles, 1990.

Eames, Marian. *When All the World Was Dancing: Rare and Curious Books from the Cia Fornaroli Toscanini Collection.* 2d ed. New York: New York Public Library, 1958.

Fletcher, Ifan Kyrle, comp. *A Bibliographical Description of Forty Rare Books Relating to the Art of Dancing in the Collection of P.J.S. Richardson, O.B.E.* London: Dancing Times, 1954; reprint London: Dance Books, 1977.

*George Balanchine: A Reference Guide, 1987.* New York: Ballet Society, July 1987. This reference guide is intended to supplement *Choreography by George Balanchine: A Catalogue of Works* by updating the bibliography and the listings of stagings and telecasts, and to broaden its scope by including information on photographers and addresses of sources.

Gray, Judith A., ed. *Research in Dance IV: 1900-1990.* Reston, Va.: National Dance Association/American Alliance for Health, Physical Education, Recreation and Dance, [1992]. A compilation of over 500 dissertations in dance from 1900 to 1990, with brief descriptions, this volume reflects the considerable growth of doctoral-level research in dance. For background about this book, see Judith A. Gray's "Creating and Navigating a Dance Research Database." *The Journal of Physical Education, Recreation & Dance* 63, no. 9 (November-December 1992): 29-31, 57.

Haskell, Arnold Lionel. *Ballet: A Reader's Guide.* London: National Book League, 1947.

———, and P.J.S. Richardson, eds. *Who's Who in Dancing, 1932: Being a List of Alphabetically Arranged Biographies of the Leading Men and Women in the World of Dancing.* London: Dancing Times, 1932.

Henry, Tricia. "The Joy of Modem: Computer Access to Resources in Dance." *Dance Research Journal* 26, no. 1 (Spring 1994): 56-58.

Highfill, Philip H., Jr., Kalman A. Burnim, and Edward A. Langhaus. *A Biographical Dictionary of Actors, Actresses, Musicians, Dancers, Managers, and Other Stage Personnel in London, 1660-1800.* 14 vols. Carbondale: Southern Illinois University Press, 1973.

Hollinshed, Marjorie (Mrs. K.M. Lucas). *Some Professional Dancers of, or from, Queensland and Some Teachers of the Past and Present.* Brisbane: W.R. Smith & Paterson, 1963. [On cover: Dancers of Queensland].

Ingber, Judith Brin, and Judith Mirus, comps. *A Reader's Guide to the Dance Book Collection of the St. Paul Public Library.* St. Paul, Minn.: St. Paul Public Library, November 1988.

Irey, Charlotte, and Fannie H. Melcer. *Research in Dance II.* Washington, D.C.: American Association for Health, Physical Education and Recreation, 1973.

Karpel, Bernard, ed. *Photography, Film, Theatre, Dance, Music.* Arts in America, Vol. 3. Washington, D.C.: Smithsonian Institution, 1979.

McNeil, Barbara. *Performing Arts Biographies Master Index: A Consolidated Index to Over 270,000 Biographical Sketches of Persons Living and Dead, as They Appear in over 100 of the Principal Biographical Dictionaries Devoted to the Performing Arts.* Detroit: Gale Research, 1982.

Moomaw, Virginia. *Dance Research: Reference Materials with Suggestions for Future Research.* Washington, D.C.: American Alliance for Health, Physical Education and Recreation, 1958.

The National Book League. *Ballet: An Exhibition of Books, MSS, Playbills, Prints &c., illustrating the development of the art from its origins until modern times.* Organised by Ivor Guest. 7 November 1957 to 4 January 1958. London: National Book League, n.d.

Pease, Edward J. *Researching the Music of Dance: A Guide to the Methodology, a Bibliography, a Discography, and Other Basic Information.* ERIC Document 184546. Bowling Green: Western Kentucky University Press, 1980.

———. *Researching Theatrical Dance: A Guide to Basic Collections, Bibliographies, Reference Books, Serials, Historical Surveys, Manuals, Special Studies, Films, Addresses, and Other Essentials; Primarily as Related to Theatrical Dance.* ERIC Document 225572. Bowling Green: Western Kentucky University Press, 1982.

Pease, Esther. *Compilation of Dance Research, 1901-1964.* Washington, D.C.: American Alliance for Health, Physical Education, Recreation and Dance, 1964.

Pitou, Spire. *The Paris Opéra: An Encyclopedia of Operas, Ballets, Composers, and Performers.* 4 vols. Westport, Conn.: Greenwood Press, 1983.

Poorman, Susan. *The Neal-Schuman Index to Performing and Creative Artists in Collective Biographies.* New York: Neal-Schuman, 1991. A reference intended for children and young adults, this is an excellent source for elementary, high school, and some college students.

Reynolds, Flora Elizabeth. *The Jane Bourne Parton Collection of Books on the Dance: A Selected Bibliography.* Oakland, Calif.: Eucalyptus Press, 1977.

Roatcap, Adela Spindler. *The Book of the Dance in the 20th Century: Selections from The Jane Bourne Parton Collection of Books on the Dance.* Oakland, Calif.: Mills College Library, 1984.

Robertson, Allen, and Donald Hutera. *The Dance Handbook.* Introduction by Merce Cunningham. Essex, England: Longman, 1988; reprint Boston: G.K. Hall & Co., 1990.

Robinson, Doris. *Music and Dance Periodicals: An International Directory and Guidebook.* Voorheesville, N.Y.: Peri, 1989.

Simmonds, Harvey, Louis H. Silverstein, and Nancy Lassalle. *Lincoln Kirstein: The Published Writings 1922-1977.* A First Bibliography. New Haven, Conn.: Yale University Library, 1978.

Stievater, Susan M., comp. *Biographies of Creative Artists: An Annotated Bibliography.* New York & London: Garland Publishing, 1991.

Uchitelle, Daniel. "Dance and the *New York Times Index.*" *Dance Research Journal* 17, no. 2 & 18, no. 1 (Fall 1985/Spring 1986): 31-33. An informative article about the scope, merits, and shortcomings of the index to "the paper of record" in the dance capital of the world.

Wearing, J.P. *The London Stage: A Calendar of Plays and Players.* Vol. 1- , 1890- . Metuchen, N.J.: Scarecrow Press, 1976- . Incorporates ballet and opera performances. Current issue, Vol. 16 (published 1993), takes this study through 1959. Includes indexes.

Works Progress Administration. "Dance Index: An Annotated Index in Bibliographical Form of Dance References, Composed of Source Material Extracted from Various Works on Anthropology, Ethnology, Comparative Religion, Travel, and the Arts, Contained in the Libraries of Greater New York," 1936. An unpublished card file of 45 drawers housed in the Dance Collection of The New York Public Library.

## BALLET GUIDES

Balanchine, George. *Balanchine's Complete Stories of the Great Ballets.* Edited by Francis Mason. Garden City, N.Y.: Doubleday, 1954.

——. *Balanchine's New Complete Stories of the Great Ballets.* Edited by Francis Mason. Garden City, N.Y.: Doubleday, 1968.

——, and Francis Mason. *Balanchine's Complete Stories of the Great Ballets.* rev. and enl. ed. Garden City, N.Y.: Doubleday, 1977.

——. *101 Stories of the Great Ballets.* Garden City, N.Y.: Doubleday, 1975.

Beaumont, Cyril. *Ballets Past & Present: Being a Third Supplement to the "Complete Book of Ballets."* London: Putnam, 1955.

———. *Ballets of Today: Being a Second Supplement to the "Complete Book of Ballets."* London: Putnam, 1954.

———. *Complete Book of Ballets: A Guide to the Principal Ballets of the Nineteenth and Twentieth Centuries.* New York: Grosset & Dunlap, 1938.

———. *The Sadler's Wells Ballet: A Detailed Account of the Works in the Permanent Repertory with Critical Notes.* rev. and enl. ed. London: C.W. Beaumont, 1947.

———. *Supplement to "Complete Book of Ballets."* London: Putnam, 1952.

Brinson, Peter, and Clement Crisp. *Ballet and Dance: A Guide to the Repertory.* rev. and enl. Newton Abbot, Devon & London: David & Charles, 1980. First published as *Ballet For All: A Guide to One Hundred Ballets* by Pan Books, London, 1970.

———. *The International Book of Ballet.* [With contributions by Don McDonagh and John Percival]. New York: Stein and Day Publishers, 1971. First published in England as *Ballet For All: A Guide to One Hundred Ballets* by Pan Books, London, 1970.

Crosland, Margaret. *Ballet Carnival: A Companion to Ballet.* London: Arco Publishers, 1955.

Davidson, Gladys. *More Ballet Stories for Young People.* London: Cassell, 1961.

———. *Stories of the Ballets.* London: T. Werner Laurie, 1949.

Drew, David. *The Decca Book of Ballet.* With an Introduction by Ernest Ansermet and a short History of Ballet by Arnold L. Haskell. London: Frederick Muller, 1958.

Goode, Gerald, ed. *The Book of Ballets: Classic and Modern.* Introduction by Leonide Massine. New York: Crown Publishers, 1939.

Gruen, John. *The World's Great Ballets: "La Fille Mal Gardée" to "Davidsbündlertänze."* New York: Abrams, 1981.

Heath, Charles. *Beauties of the Opera and Ballet.* Illustrated with ten highly-finished portraits, engraved on steel, and numerous engravings on wood, under the superintendence of Mr. Charles Heath. London: D. Bogue, [1845]. Taken from Théophile Gautier's *Les beautés de l'Opéra,* using the same plates, engraved illustrations and ornamental borders. The translation into English is not literal throughout. Reprint New York: Da Capo Press, 1977.

Kirstein, Lincoln. *Four Centuries of Ballet: Fifty Masterworks.* New York: Dover Publications, c. 1984. This is an unabridged, corrected republication of the work originally published in 1970 by Praeger Publishers, Inc., New York, under the title *Movement & Metaphor: Four Centuries of Ballet.*

Krokover, Rosalyn. *The New Borzoi Book of Ballets.* New York: Knopf, 1956.

Lawrence, Robert. *The Victor Book of Ballets and Ballet Music.* New York: Simon & Schuster, 1950.

McDonagh, Don. *The Complete Guide to Modern Dance.* Garden City, N.Y.: Doubleday, 1976.

Reynolds, Nancy. *Repertory in Review: 40 Years of the New York City Ballet.* Introduction by Lincoln Kirstein. New York: Dial Press, 1977.

———, and Susan Reimer-Torn. *Dance Classics: A Viewer's Guide to the Best-Loved Ballets and Modern Dances.* Pennington, N.J.: A Cappella Books, 1991. Originally published in different form as *In Performance: A Companion to the Classics of Dance,* Harmony Books, New York, 1980.

Robert, Grace. *The Borzoi Book of Ballets.* New York: Knopf, 1947.

Stokes, Adrian. *Russian Ballets.* London: Faber & Faber, 1935; reprint New York: Da Capo Press, 1982.

Terry, Walter. *Ballet Guide.* Background, Listings, Credits, and Descriptions of more than five hundred of the World's Major Ballets. New York: Dodd, Mead & Company, [1976].

——. *Ballet: A New Guide to the Liveliest Art.* New York: Dell Publishing, 1959.

Verwer, Hans. *Guide to the Ballet.* Translated from the Dutch by Henry Mins. [New York]: Barnes & Noble, 1963.

## COLLECTIONS OF CRITICISM

Anderson, Jack. *Choreography Observed.* Iowa City: University of Iowa Press, 1987.

Beaumont, Cyril W. *Dancers Under My Lens: Essays in Ballet Criticism.* London: C.W. Beaumont, 1949.

Bland, Alexander. *Observer of the Dance 1958-1982.* London: Dance Books, 1985.

Buckle, Richard. *Buckle at the Ballet.* New York: Atheneum, 1980.

Coton, A.V. *Writings on Dance 1938-68.* Selected and edited by Kathrine Sorley Walker and Lilian Haddakin. London: Dance Books, 1975.

Croce, Arlene. *Afterimages.* New York: Knopf, 1977.

——. *Going to the Dance.* New York: Knopf, 1982.

——. *Sight Lines.* New York: Knopf, 1987.

Denby, Edwin. *Dancers, Buildings and People in the Streets.* With an Introduction by Frank O'Hara. New York: Horizon Press, 1965.

——. *Dance Writings.* Edited by Robert Cornfield and William MacKay. New York: Knopf, 1986. Includes a biographical essay, "Edwin Denby, 1903-1983," by William MacKay (pp. 11-34).

——. *Looking at the Dance.* New York: Pellegrini & Cudahy, 1949; reprint, with an Introduction by B.H. Haggin, New York: Horizon Press, 1968.

Gautier, Théophile. *Gautier on Dance.* Selected, translated, and annotated by Ivor Guest. London: Dance Books, 1986.

———. *The Romantic Ballet as Seen by Théophile Gautier.* Being his Notices of all the Principal Performances of Ballet Given at Paris During the Years 1837-1848. Translated from the French by Cyril W. Beaumont. London: C.W. Beaumont, 1932; rev. ed. 1947; reprint of 1947 ed. Brooklyn, N.Y.: Dance Horizons, 1973.

———. "Théophile Gautier on Spanish Dancing." Selected, translated, and annotated by Ivor Guest. *Dance Chronicle* 10, no. 1 (1987): 1-104.

Haggin, B.H. *Ballet Chronicle.* New York: Horizon Press, 1970.

Jackson, Graham. *Dance As Dance: Selected Reviews and Essays.* Scarborough, Ontario: Catalyst, 1978.

Johnston, Jill. *Marmalade Me.* New York: Dutton, 1971.

Jowitt, Deborah. *Dance Beat: Selected Views and Reviews 1967-1976.* New York & Basel: Marcel Dekker, 1977.

———. *The Dance in Mind: Profiles and Reviews 1976-83.* Boston: David R. Godine, Publisher, 1985.

Levinson, André. *André Levinson on Dance: Writings from Paris in the Twenties.* Edited and with an Introduction by Joan Acocella and Lynn Garafola. Hanover, N.H. & London: University Press of New England/Wesleyan University Press, 1991.

———. *Ballet Old and New.* Translated from the Russian by Susan Cook Summer. New York: Dance Horizons, 1982. A survey and analysis of gradually accumulated theatrical impressions gathered together as a group of descriptive essays.

Macaulay, Alastair. *Some Views and Reviews of Ashton's Choreography.* Collected Writings, No. 1. Guildford, Surrey: National Resource Centre for Dance, 1987.

Macdonald, Nesta. *Diaghilev Observed: By Critics in England and the United States, 1911-1929.* New York: Dance Horizons; London: Dance Books, 1975.

Parker, H.T. *Motion Arrested: Dance Reviews of H.T. Parker.* Edited by Olive Holmes. Middletown, Conn.: Wesleyan University Press, 1982.

Reynolds, Nancy. *Repertory in Review: 40 Years of the New York City Ballet.* Introduction by Lincoln Kirstein. New York: Dial Press, 1977. Includes excerpts of reviews from many sources.

Siegel, Marcia B. *At the Vanishing Point: A Critic Looks at Dance.* New York: Saturday Review Press, 1972.

———. *The Shapes of Change: Images of American Dance.* Boston: Houghton Mifflin, 1979; reprint Berkeley, Los Angeles, London: University of California Press, 1985.

———. *The Tail of the Dragon: New Dance, 1976-1982.* Durham, N.C. & London: Duke University Press, 1991.

———. *Watching the Dance Go By.* Boston: Houghton Mifflin, 1977.

Swinson, Cyril, ed. *Dancers and Critics.* London: Adam & Charles Black, 1950. Contributions by Cyril Beaumont, Caryl Brahms, Anatole Chujoy, A.V. Coton, A.H. Franks, Arnold L. Haskell, Joan Lawson, Irène Lidova, P.W. Manchester, Pierre Michaut, Walter Terry, Léandre Vaillat, and Audrey Williamson.

Terry, Walter. *I Was There: Selected Dance Reviews and Articles, 1936-1976.* Compiled and edited by Andrew Mark Wentink. Foreword by Anna Kisselgoff. New York & Basel: Marcel Dekker, 1978.

## READINGS IN DANCE HISTORY, THEORY & CRITICISM

Cohen, Selma Jeanne, ed. *Dance as a Theatre Art: Source Readings in Dance History from 1518 to the Present.* Commentary by the Editor. New York: Dodd, Mead, 1974; 2d ed., with a New Section by Katy Matheson, Princeton, N.J.: Princeton Book Company, Publishers, 1992.

Copeland, Roger, and Marshall Cohen, eds. *What Is Dance? Readings in Theory and Criticism.* New York: Oxford University Press, 1983.

Steinberg, Cobbett, ed. *The Dance Anthology.* New York & London: New American Library, c. 1980.

## GENERAL, PERIOD, COUNTRY & COMPANY HISTORIES

## GENERAL HISTORIES:

Anderson, Jack. *Ballet & Modern Dance: A Concise History.* Princeton, N.J.: Princeton Book Company, Publishers, c. 1986; 2d ed., rev. and enl., 1992.

———. *Dance.* New York: Newsweek Books, c. 1974.

Au, Susan. *Ballet & Modern Dance.* Introduction by Selma Jeanne Cohen. World of Art. London & New York: Thames and Hudson, 1988.

Beaumont, Cyril W. *A Short History of Ballet.* Essays on Dancing and Dancers, No. 4. London: C.W. Beaumont, 1944.

Clarke, Mary, and Clement Crisp. *Ballet: An Illustrated History.* London: Adam and Charles Black, 1973; 2d ed., rev. and enl., London: Hamish Hamilton, 1992.

Conyn, Cornelius. *Three Centuries of Ballet.* Houston & New York: Elsevier Press, 1953.

de Mille, Agnes. *The Book of the Dance.* New York: Golden Press; London: Paul Hamlyn, 1963.

Fonteyn, Margot. *The Magic of Dance.* New York: Knopf; Toronto: Random House of Canada, 1979.

Garfunkel, Trudy. *On Wings of Joy: The Story of Ballet from the 16th Century to Today.* Boston & New York: Little, Brown and Company, 1994. A history of ballet for young readers, age 12 and up.

Guest, Ivor. *A Dancer's Heritage: A Short History of Ballet.* Foreword by Dame Margot Fonteyn. London: Adam and Charles Black, 1960; 6th ed., fully updated by Kathrine Sorley Walker, London: Dancing Times, 1988.

Haskell, Arnold L. *Ballet Panorama: An Illustrated Chronicle of Three Centuries.* 3d rev. ed. London & New York: B.T. Batsford, 1948.

———. *Ballet Retrospect.* London: B.T. Batsford, 1964.

———. *A Picture History of Ballet.* Hulton's Picture Histories. rev. ed. London: Hulton Press, 1957.

Kirstein, Lincoln. *The Book of the Dance.* New York: Garden City Publishing, 1942. A reissue, with an additional chapter, of *Dance: A Short History of Classic Theatrical Dancing.*

———. *Dance: A Short History of Classic Theatrical Dancing.* New York: G.P. Putnam's Sons, 1935; reprint Brooklyn, N.Y.: Dance Horizons, 1969; and reprint Princeton, N.J.: Princeton Book Company, Publishers, 1986.

———. *Four Centuries of Ballet: Fifty Masterworks.* New York: Dover Publications, c. 1984. This is an unabridged, corrected republication of the work originally published in 1970 by Praeger Publishers, Inc., New York, under the title *Movement & Metaphor: Four Centuries of Ballet.*

Lawson, Joan. *A History of Ballet and its Makers.* New York & London: Pitman Publishing, 1964.

Lynham, Deryck. *Ballet Then and Now: A History of the Ballet in Europe.* London: Sylvan Press, 1947.

Mackrell, Judith. *Out of Line: The Story of British New Dance.* London: Dance Books, 1992.

Magriel, Paul. *Ballet: An Illustrated Outline.* New York: Kamin Publishers, c. 1938.

McDonagh, Don. *The Complete Guide to Modern Dance.* Garden City, New York: Doubleday, c. 1976.

Reyna, Ferdinando. *A Concise History of Ballet.* Translated from the French by Pat Wardroper. London: Thames and Hudson, c. 1965.

Ryan, June. *Ballet History.* New York: Roy Publishers, 1960.

Sorell, Walter. *Dance in Its Time.* Garden City, N.Y.: Anchor Press/ Doubleday, 1981. [On cover: Dance in Its Time: The Emergence of an Art Form].

Terry, Walter. *Ballet: A Pictorial History.* New York: Van Nostrand Reinhold, 1970.

## PERIOD HISTORIES:

Banes, Sally. *Terpsichore in Sneakers: Post-Modern Dance.* Boston: Houghton Mifflin, 1980; reprint, with a new introduction and an updated chronology, Middletown, Conn.: Wesleyan University Press, 1987.

Beaumont, Cyril W., and Sacheverell Sitwell. *The Romantic Ballet in Lithographs of the Time.* London: Faber and Faber, 1938. Includes a significant amount of text on the ballet of the Romantic era and its dancers.

Binney, Edwin, 3rd, Introduction and Notes. *Royal Festivals and Romantic Ballerinas 1600–1850.* From the Collection of Edwin Binney, 3rd. Washington, D.C.: Smithsonian Institution, 1971. Exhibition catalogue of a show circulated by the Smithsonian Institution 1971-1973. Contains a wealth of information on productions of the period.

Chaffee, George. "The Romantic Ballet in London: 1821-1858, Some Hitherto Unremarked Aspects." *Dance Index* 2, nos. 9-12 (September-December 1943).

Chazin-Bennahum, Judith. *Dance in the Shadow of the Guillotine.* Carbondale & Edwardsville, Ill.: Southern Illinois University Press, 1988.

Chumbley, Joyce Arlene. "The World of Molière's Comedy-Ballets." Unpublished dissertation, University of Hawaii, 1972. Ann Arbor, Mich.: University Microfilms International, 1973. Order No. 73-05,260. DAI 33-09A, p. 5337.

Garafola, Lynn, ed. "Of, By, and For the People: Dancing on the Left in the 1930s." *Studies in Dance History* 5, no. 1 (Spring 1994).

Guest, Ivor. "The Alhambra Ballet." *Dance Perspectives* 4 (Autumn 1959).

———. *Ballet in Leicester Square: The Alhambra and the Empire 1860-1915.* London: Dance Books, 1992.

———. *The Ballet of the Second Empire.* London: Pitman Publishing; Middletown, Conn.: Wesleyan University Press, 1974. First published as two volumes in 1953 and 1955.

——. *The Ballet of the Second Empire 1847-1858*. London: Adam and Charles Black, 1955.

——. *The Ballet of the Second Empire 1858-1870*. Preface by Serge Lifar. London: Adam and Charles Black, 1953.

——. *The Empire Ballet*. London: Society for Theatre Research, 1962.

——. *The Romantic Ballet in England: Its Development, Fulfilment and Decline*. London: Phoenix House, 1954; reprint Middletown, Conn.: Wesleyan University Press, 1972.

——. *The Romantic Ballet in Paris*. Foreword by Dame Ninette de Valois. London: Sir Isaac Pitman and Sons, 1966; 2d rev. ed., with an additional Foreword by Lillian Moore, London: Dance Books, 1980.

Johnston, Elizabeth Carrington. "The English Masque and the French Court Ballet." Unpublished dissertation, Harvard University, Cambridge, Massachusetts, 1964. On file, but not available from UMI. Order No. 02-57,330. ADD X1964, p. 0129.

Johnston, Jill. *Marmalade Me*. New York: Dutton, 1971. A mix of critical commentary and autobiography from the 1960s, with a particular emphasis on Judson Dance Theater.

Kassing, Gayle Irma. "Dance on the St. Louis Stage: 1850-1870." Unpublished dissertation, Texas Woman's University, 1978. Ann Arbor, Mich.: University Microfilms International, 1979. Order No. 791,5873. DAI 40-02A, p. 0546.

Kriegsman, Sali Ann. *Modern Dance in America: The Bennington Years*. Boston: G.K. Hall & Co., 1981.

Lally, Kathleen Ann. "A History of the Federal Dance Theatre of the Works Progress Administration, 1935-1939." Unpublished dissertation, Texas Woman's University, 1978. Ann Arbor, Mich.: University Microfilms International, 1979. Order No. 791,5877. DAI 40-01A, p. 0006.

Lehman, Rhea H. "Virtue and Virtuosity: America's Vision of the Romantic Ballet, 1827-1840." Unpublished dissertation, University of Wisconsin-Madison, 1986. Ann Arbor, Mich.: University Microfilms International, 1986. Order No. 861,4380. DAI 47-09A, p. 3245.

Lloyd, Margaret. *The Borzoi Book of Modern Dance.* New York: Knopf, 1949; reprint Brooklyn, N.Y.: Dance Horizons, 1974; and reprint Princeton, N.J.: Princeton Book Company, Publishers, 1987.

McDonagh, Don. *The Rise and Fall and Rise of Modern Dance.* New York: Outerbridge & Dienstfrey, 1970; paperback reprint New York & Scarborough, Ontario: New American Library, 1971; and rev. ed. with new photographs, but without the choreochronicles, Pennington, N.J.: A Cappella Books, 1990.

Moss, Susan F. "Spinning Through the Weltanschauung: The Effects of the Nazi Regime on the German Modern Dance." Unpublished dissertation, New York University, 1988. Ann Arbor, Mich.: University Microfilms International, 1989. Order No. 891,0641. DAI 50-01A, p. 0007.

Ruyter, Nancy Lee Chalfa. *Reformers and Visionaries: The Americanization of the Art of Dance.* New York: Dance Horizons, 1979.

Skeaping, Mary. "Ballet Under the Three Crowns." *Dance Perspectives* 32 (Winter 1967). A study of ballet in Sweden, 1648-1792.

Souritz, Elizabeth. *Soviet Choreographers in the 1920s.* Translated from the Russian by Lynn Visson. Edited, with additional translation, by Sally Banes. Durham, N.C. & London: Duke University Press, 1990.

Winter, Marian Hannah. *The Pre-Romantic Ballet.* London: Sir Isaac Pitman and Sons, 1974; Brooklyn, N.Y.: Dance Horizons, 1975.

**COUNTRY HISTORIES**:

Amberg, George. *Ballet in America: The Emergence of an American Art.* New York: Duell, Sloan and Pearce, 1949. This is a joint publication with The New American Library of World Literature, Inc., whose paperback edition is entitled *Ballet: The Emergence of an American Art.*

"Ballet in Canada Today." *Dance Magazine* 45, no. 4 (April 1971). A special issue surveying the Canadian dance scene. William Como. From the Editor (p. 31). Olga Maynard. "Idea, Image, and Purpose: Ballet in Canada Today" (pp. 32-37, 74). Olga Maynard. "Idea: Arnold Spohr and the Royal Winnipeg Ballet" (pp. 38, 40, 44). Olga Maynard. "Image: Celia Franca and the National Ballet of Canada" (pp. 46, 48, 50, 52, 54). Olga Maynard. "Purpose: Ludmilla Chiriaeff and Les Grands Ballets Canadiens" (pp. 56, 58, 60, 62, 64). Olga Maynard's study is augmented by four articles on dance in Canada: Greg Thomson. "Dance with a Liberal Education" (pp. 66-67) [dance studies at York University]. "Canadian Carousel: A Pictorial Statement About Dance's Moods Today" (pp. 68-69). Barbara Gail Rowes. "Toronto Dance Theatre" (pp. 70,72). Doris Hering. "Neither Floods Nor . . ." (pp. 74-75). A look at the accomplishments of Gweneth Lloyd, Diana Jablokova-Vorps, and Nesta Toumine, three pioneers in the Canadian regional ballet movement.

Barnes, Clive. *Ballet in Britain Since the War*. Thrift Book, No. 21. London: C.A. Watts & Co., 1953.

Beaumont, Cyril W. *A History of Ballet in Russia (1613-1881)*. Preface by André Levinson. London: C.W. Beaumont, 1930.

Christopher, Luella Sue. "Pirouettes with Bayonets: Classical Ballet Metamorphosed as Dance-Drama and Its Usage in the People's Republic of China as a Tool of Political Socialization." Unpublished dissertation, The American University, Washington, D.C., 1979. Ann Arbor, Mich.: University Microfilms International, 1979. Order No. 791,8507. DAI 40-02A, p. 1063.

de Mille, Agnes. *America Dances*. New York: Macmillan; London: Collier Macmillan, 1980.

Grut, Marina. *The History of Ballet in South Africa*. Capetown, Pretoria, Johannesburg: Human & Rousseau, 1981.

Haskell, Arnold. "Ballet in Britain 1934-1944." *Dance Index* 4, no. 10 (October 1945).

———. *Ballet Since 1939*. The Arts in Britain, No. 2. London, New York, Toronto: Longmans, Green & Co., 1946.

Jordan, Stephanie. *Striding Out: Aspects of Contemporary and New Dance in Britain*. London: Dance Books, 1992.

Kane, Angela, and Jane Pritchard. "The Camargo Society, Part I." *DR* 12, no. 2 (Autumn 1994): 21-65. Part II will appear in *DR* 13, no. 2 (Autumn 1995).

Kane, Angela, and Jane Pritchard. "The Camargo Society, Part I." *DR* 12, no. 2 (Autumn 1994): 21-65. Part II will appear in *DR* 13, no. 2 (Autumn 1995).

Koegler, Horst. "In the Shadow of the Swastika: Dance in Germany, 1927-1936." *Dance Perspectives* 57 (Spring 1974).

Lawson, Joan. "The Soviet Ballet, 1917-1943." *Dance Index* 2, nos. 6-7 (June-July 1943).

Lifar, Serge. *A History of Russian Ballet from its Origins to the Present Day*. Translated by Arnold Haskell. London: Hutchinson, 1954.

Partsch-Bergsohn, Isa. *Modern Dance in Germany and the United States: Crosscurrents and Influences*. Choreography and Dance Studies, Vol. 5. Chur, Switzerland: Harwood Academic Publishers, 1994.

Pask, Edward H. *Ballet in Australia: The Second Act, 1940-1980*. Melbourne & New York: Oxford University Press, 1982.

———. *Enter the Colonies Dancing: A History of Dance in Australia*. Melbourne & New York: Oxford University Press, 1979.

Roslavleva, Natalia. *Era of the Russian Ballet*. Foreword by Dame Ninette de Valois. London: Victor Gollancz, 1966; reprint New York: Da Capo Press, 1979.

Sorley Walker, Kathrine. "The Camargo Society." *DC* 18, no. 1 (1995): 1-114.

Swift, Mary Grace. *The Art of the Dance in the U.S.S.R.* Notre Dame, Ind.: University of Notre Dame Press, 1968.

Tembeck, Iro. "Dancing in Montreal: Seeds of a Choreographic History." *Studies in Dance History* 5, no. 2 (Fall 1994).

van Praagh, Peggy. *Ballet in Australia*. The Arts in Australia. Victoria, Australia: Longmans, 1965.

Wyman, Max. *Dance Canada: An Illustrated History*. Vancouver & Toronto: Douglas & McIntyre, 1989.

**COMPANY HISTORIES**:

Acocella, Joan. *Mark Morris*. New York: Farrar, Straus & Giroux, 1993.

Albig, Pegeen Horth. "A History of the Robert Joffrey Ballet." (Vols. I and II). Unpublished dissertation, Florida State University, 1979. Ann Arbor, Mich.: University Microfilms International, 1979. Order No. 792,6708. DAI 40-06A, p. 2987.

Anderson, Jack. *The One and Only: The Ballet Russe de Monte Carlo*. New York: Dance Horizons, 1981.

Baer, Nancy Van Norman, ed. *Paris Modern: The Swedish Ballet, 1920-1925*. San Francisco: The Fine Arts Museums of San Francisco, 1995. The catalogue of the eponymous exhibition held at The Museum at the Fashion Institute of Technology, New York City, October 10, 1995-January 13, 1996; NcNay Art Museum, San Antonio, Texas, February 12, 1996-May 19, 1996; and California Palace of the Legion of Honor, San Francisco, June 15, 1996-September 9, 1996.

Banes, Sally. *Democracy's Body: Judson Dance Theater 1962-1964*. Studies in the Fine Arts: The Avant-Garde, No. 43. Ann Arbor, Mich.: UMI Research Press, 1983.

———. "An Introduction to the Ballets Suédois." *Ballet Review* 7, nos. 2&3 (1978-1979): 28-59.

Beaumont, Cyril. *Bookseller at the Ballet: Memoirs 1891 to 1929*. A Record of Bookselling, Ballet Going, Publishing, and Writing. London: C.W. Beaumont, 1975. Incorporates *The Diaghilev Ballet in London*. 3d rev. ed. London: Adam and Charles Black, 1951.

———. *The Diaghilev Ballet in London*. 3d rev. ed. London: Adam and Charles Black, 1951. Incorporated in Beaumont's *Bookseller at the Ballet: Memoirs 1891 to 1929*.

———. *The Monte Carlo Russian Ballet* (Les Ballets Russes du Col. W. de Basil). Essays on Dancing and Dancers, No. 5. London: C.W. Beaumont, 1934.

———. *The Vic-Wells Ballet*. Essays on Dancing and Dancers, No. 7. London: C.W. Beaumont, 1935.

Bell, Ken, photography, and a memoir by Celia Franca. *The National Ballet of Canada: A Celebration*. Toronto & London: University of Toronto Press, c. 1978.

Bland, Alexander. *The Royal Ballet: The First 50 Years*. Foreword by Dame Ninette de Valois. London: Threshold Books; Garden City, N.Y.: Doubleday, 1981.

Bradley, Lionel. *Sixteen Years of Ballet Rambert*. London: Hinrichsen Edition, 1946.

Brown, Ian F., ed. *The Australian Ballet 1962-1965: A Record of the Company, its Dancers, and its Ballets*. Victoria, Australia: Longmans, c. 1967.

Chujoy, Anatole. *The New York City Ballet*. New York: Knopf, 1953; reprint, with a new Preface by Edward Villella, New York: Da Capo Press, 1981.

Clarke, Mary. *Dancers of Mercury: The Story of Ballet Rambert*. London: Adam and Charles Black, 1962.

———. *The Sadler's Wells Ballet: A History and an Appreciation*. London: Adam and Charles Black, 1955; reprint, with a new Foreword by the author, New York: Da Capo Press, 1977.

———, and Clement Crisp. *London Contemporary Dance Theatre: The First 21 Years*. London: Dance Books, 1989.

Cohen, Selma Jeanne, and A.J. Pischl. "The American Ballet Theatre: 1940-1960." *Dance Perspectives* 6 (1960).

Cook, Susan, photography, with commentary by Joseph H. Mazo. *The Alvin Ailey American Dance Theater*. New York: Morrow, 1978.

Crisp, Clement, Anya Sainsbury, and Peter Williams. *Ballet Rambert: 50 Years and On*. rev. and enl. ed. N.p., 1981.

[de Marigny, Chris]. *Transitions Dance Company: 10th Anniversary Year, 1983-1993*. Introduction by Marion North. London: Laban Centre for Movement and Dance, 1993.

Dafoe, Christopher. *Dancing Through Time: The First Fifty Years of Canada's Royal Winnipeg Ballet*. Winnipeg: Portage & Main Press, 1990.

Fisher, Hugh. *The Sadler's Wells Theatre Ballet*. London: Adam and Charles Black, 1956.

———. *The Story of the Sadler's Wells Ballet*. London: Adam and Charles Black, 1954.

Garafola, Lynn. *Diaghilev's Ballets Russes*. New York & Oxford: Oxford University Press, 1989.

García-Márquez, Vicente. *The Ballets Russes: Colonel de Basil's Ballets Russes de Monte Carlo 1932-1952*. New York: Knopf, 1990.

Goodwin, Noël. *A Ballet for Scotland: The First Ten Years of The Scottish Ballet*. Edinburgh: Canongate Publishing, 1979.

Grigoriev, S.L. *The Diaghilev Ballet 1909-1929*. Translated and edited by Vera Bowen. London: Constable, 1953.

Häger, Bengt. *Ballets Suédois (The Swedish Ballet)*. New York: Abrams, 1990.

Haskell, Arnold L. *The National Ballet: A History and a Manifesto*. Overture by Ninette de Valois. London: Adam and Charles Black, 1943.

Kane, Angela. [Rambert Dance Company]. Part 1: "Rambert Doubling Back to the Sixties"; Part 2: "Rambert: Moving Forward to the Seventies"; Part 3: "Rambert Dance Company: Side Steps or Giant Strides?" *Dance Theatre Journal* 8, no. 3 (Autumn 1990):

34-37; *Dance Theatre Journal* 8, no. 4 (Spring 1991): 36-39; and *Dance Theatre Journal* 10, no. 1 (Autumn 1992): 36-39.

Kirstein, Lincoln, text, with photography by Martha Swope and George Platt Lynes. *New York City Ballet.* New York: Knopf, 1973.

———. *Thirty Years: Lincoln Kirstein's "The New York City Ballet."* New York: Knopf, 1978. Expanded to include the years 1973-1978, in celebration of the company's thirtieth anniversary.

Kochno, Boris. *Diaghilev and the Ballets Russes.* Translated from the French by Adrienne Foulke. New York & Evanston, Ill.: Harper & Row, 1970.

Kragh-Jacobsen, Svend. *The Royal Danish Ballet: An Old Tradition and a Living Present.* Copenhagen: Det Danske Selskab; London: Adam and Charles Black, 1955.

Lieven, Prince Peter. *The Birth of Ballets-Russes.* Translated from the Russian by L. Zarine. London: George Allen & Unwin, 1936.

Manchester, P.W. *Vic-Wells: A Ballet Progress.* London: Victor Gollancz, 1942.

Matson, Tim. *Pilobolus.* New York: Random House, 1978.

Mitchell, Jack, photography. *Alvin Ailey American Dance Theater.* Foreword by Judith Jamison. Introduction by Richard Philp. Kansas City: Andrews and McMeel, 1993.

Palmiotto, Carol Elaine and Kristine Lee Wilson. "An Historical Account of the United States Tours of the Royal Ballet of Great Britain from 1949-1970." Unpublished dissertation, United States International University/School of Performing Arts, Los Angeles, California, 1984. Ann Arbor, Mich.: University Micro-films International, 1984. Order No. 841,7510. DAI 45-05A, p. 1241.

Payne, Charles. *American Ballet Theatre.* With essays by Alicia Alonso, Erik Bruhn, Lucia Chase, and Nora Kaye. New York: Knopf, 1978.

Propert, W.A. *The Russian Ballet in Western Europe, 1909-1920.* With a chapter on the music by Eugene Goossens. London: John Lane The Bodley Head; New York: John Lane Company, 1921; reprint New York: Benjamin Blom, 1972.

———. *The Russian Ballet 1921-1929.* Preface by Jacques Emile Blanche. London: John Lane The Bodley Head, 1931.

Ramsay, Margaret Hupp. *The Grand Union (1970-1976): An Improvisational Performance Group.* Artists and Issues in the Theatre, Vol. 2. New York: Peter Lang, 1991.

Reynolds, Nancy. *Repertory in Review: 40 Years of the New York City Ballet.* Introduction by Lincoln Kirstein. New York: Dial Press, 1977.

Sexton, Jean Deitz. *San Jose/Cleveland Ballet: A Legacy for the Future.* San Francisco: Henry Holth & Company, 1993.

Shead, Richard. *Ballets Russes.* Secaucus, N.J.: Wellfleet Press, 1989.

Sorley Walker, Kathrine. *De Basil's Ballets Russes.* London: Hutchinson, 1982.

———, and Sarah C. Woodcock. *The Royal Ballet: A Picture History.* London: Threshold Books, 1981.

Steinberg, Cobbett. *San Francisco Ballet: The First Fifty Years.* Edited by Laura Leivick. Researched by Russell Hartley. Introduction by Lew Christensen and Michael Smuin. Forewords by Lincoln Kirstein, Oliver Smith, and Lucia Chase. San Francisco: San Francisco Ballet Association & Chronicle Books, c. 1983.

Whittaker, Herbert. *Canada's National Ballet.* Toronto & Montreal: McClelland and Stewart, 1967.

Wilms, Anno, photography. *Lindsay Kemp and Company.* Introduction by David Haughton. Preface by Derek Jarman. London: GMP Publishers, 1987.

Wilson, Kristine Lee. See Palmiotto, Carole Elaine.

Woodcock, Sarah C. *The Sadler's Wells Royal Ballet: Now the Birmingham Royal Ballet.* London: Sinclair-Stevenson, c. 1991.

Wyman, Max. *The Royal Winnipeg Ballet: The First Forty Years.* Toronto: Doubleday Canada; Garden City, N.Y.: Doubleday, 1978.

## THE ART OF CHOREOGRAPHY

Cunningham, Merce. *Changes: Notes on Choreography.* Edited by Frances Starr. New York: Something Else Press, 1968.

Graham, Martha. *The Notebooks of Martha Graham.* New York: Harcourt Brace Jovanovich, 1973.

Humphrey, Doris. *The Art of Making Dances.* Edited by Barbara Pollack. New York and Toronto: Rinehart & Company, 1959.

Kaplan, Peggy Jarrell. *Portraits of Choreographers.* New York: Ronald Feldman Fine Arts; Paris: Éditions Bougé, 1988. Bilingual: English/French. A collection of photographic portraits, accompanied by brief artistic statements by the choreographers.

Kirstein, Lincoln. *Four Centuries of Ballet: Fifty Masterworks.* New York: Dover Publications, c. 1984. This is an unabridged, corrected republication of the work originally published in 1970 by Praeger Publishers, Inc., New York, under the title *Movement & Metaphor: Four Centuries of Ballet.*

Lawson, Joan. *A History of Ballet and its Makers.* London: Sir Isaac Pitman & Sons, 1964.

Noverre, Jean Georges. *Letters on Dancing and Ballets [1760].* Translated by Cyril W. Beaumont from the rev. and enl. ed. published at St. Petersburg, 1803. London: C.W. Beaumont, 1951.

Rowe, Patricia Ann. "Identification of the Domain of Modern Dance Choreography as an Aesthetic Discipline." Unpublished dissertation, Stanford University, Stanford, California, 1967. Ann Arbor, Mich.: University Microfilms International, 1967. Order No. 670,4313. DAI 27-11A, p. 3791.

Sorley Walker, Kathrine. *Dance and Its Creators: Choreographers at Work.* New York: John Day Company, 1972.

van Praagh, Peggy, and Peter Brinson. *The Choreographic Art: An Outline of its Principles and Craft.* London: Adam & Charles Black, 1963.

Wigman, Mary. *The Language of Dance*. Translated by Walter Sorell. Middletown, Conn.: Wesleyan University Press, 1966.

## THE ART OF THE DANCER

Bland, Alexander, and John Percival. *Men Dancing: Performers and Performances*. New York: Macmillan, 1984.

Clarke, Mary, and Clement Crisp. *Ballerina: The Art of Women in Classical Ballet*. London: BBC Books, 1987; reprint Princeton, N.J.: Princeton Book Company, Publishers, 1988.

——. *Dancer: Men in Dance*. London: British Broadcasting Corp., 1984.

Cohen, Selma Jeanne, ed. "The Male Image." *Dance Perspectives* 40 (Winter 1969).

Earl, William L. *A Dancer Takes Flight: Psychological Concerns in the Development of the American Male Dancer*. Lanham, Md.: University Press of America, 1988.

Johnston, Gordon. *Dancing . . . A Man's Career*. New York & London: Cornwall Books, 1985.

Montague, Sarah. *The Ballerina: Famous Dancers and Rising Stars of Our Time*. New York: Universe Books, 1980.

——. *Pas de Deux: Great Partnerships in Dance*. New York: Universe Books, 1981.

Philp, Richard, and Mary Whitney. *Danseur: The Male in Ballet*. New York: McGraw-Hill, 1977.

Swinson, Cyril. *Great Male Dancers*. Dancers of To-Day, No. 16. London: Adam & Charles Black, 1964. Volume completed by Ivor Guest after the author's death.

Terry, Walter. *Great Male Dancers of the Ballet*. New York: Anchor Books, 1978.

——. *On Pointe: The Story of Dancing and Dancers on Toe*. New York: Dodd, Mead & Co., 1962.

# INDEX

The index contains names of contributors to a publication—author, joint author, editor, compiler, translator, photographer, illustrator, notator—whether separately listed or itemized within an entry. Other than personal names, such contributors may be organizational name (e.g., National Diet Library). In cases of no specified author, the listing is by title: book (e.g., *Choreography by George Balanchine*); article (e.g., "Alonso, Alicia"); collective (e.g., "Homage to Ashton"); or publication (e.g., *Ballet Review*). Key books are appended to the author listing (e.g., Guest, Ivor; GUE) or, in the case of no other entries by the author, alphabetically by the abbreviation.

Asterisk with a page number indicates that the name appears within an entry; numbers in parentheses, the number of times the name appears printed on the page in discrete entries.

## COLOPHON

The text was set in Bodoni Book, a typeface designed by Giovanni Battista Bodoni, ( 1740-1813 ). Born in Turin, he worked for Propaganda Fide in Rome, for the Duke of Parma, and later for Napoleon Bonaparte. The alphabet letters for the chapter openings and tabs are Parisian.

The book was typeset by Alabama Book Composition, Deatsville, Alabama.

Leslie Getz is the founder/editor of *Attitudes & Arabesques* (1980-  ). Her two-part translation of *The Diaries of Antoine Bournonville from 1792* appeared in *Ballet Review*. She has contributed a number of annual book lists and specialized bibliographies for conference proceedings to the Dance Critics Association. Leslie Getz lives in the San Francisco Bay area and New York City.

Dance Research Foundation is a not-for-profit group whose purpose is to publish material of serious critical or historical interest about the field of dance. This includes ballet, modern dance, ethnic dance, and popular and show dance. They have for the past twenty-seven years published the quarterly, *Ballet Review*.